Signs of Hope
in the City

Signs of Hope in the City

Ministries of Community Renewal

Revised Edition

Edited by
Robert D. Carle and
Louis A. DeCaro Jr.

Judson Press
Valley Forge

Signs of Hope in the City: Ministries of Community Renewal,
Revised Edition
© 1999 Judson Press, Valley Forge, PA 19482-0851

Bible quotations in this volume marked NAB are from the NEW AMERICAN BIBLE, copyright © 1970 by the Confraternity of Christian Doctrine, Washington, D.C. (Books I Samuel to 2 Maccabees, 1969). All rights reserved.

Bible quotations in this volume marked NKJV are from The New King James Version. Copyright © 1972, 1984 by Thomas Nelson Inc.

Bible quotations in this volume marked NIV are from HOLY BIBLE: *New International Version*, copyright © 1973, 1978, 1984. Used by permission of Zondervan Bible Publishers.

Signs of hope in the city : ministries of community renewal / edited by Robert D. Carle and Louis A. DeCaro, Jr. — Rev. ed.
  p. cm.
Includes bibliographical references.
ISBN 0-8170-1324-5 (pbk. : alk. paper)
1. City missions—New York (State)—New York Case studies. I. Carle, Robert D. II. DeCaro, Louis A., 1957-
BV2805.N5S54 1999
253'.09173'2—dc21   99-29086

Printed in the U.S.A.
04 03 02 01 00 99
5 4 3 2 1

Contents

Foreword

In her brilliant book, *The Global City: New York, London, Tokyo* (Princeton University Press, 1991), Saskia Sassen of Princeton University describes the rewiring of the world since the 1960s, which has been led by the rapid internationalization of the financial industry and the dispersion of manufacturing. The three emerging global cities named in the title of that book now manage this new agglomeration of worldwide business.

I have long ago concluded that New York City is the information capital of the world and functions as a world-class R & D unit for the church of Jesus Christ in a world now overwhelmingly urban. We in Chicago and other cities study New York not because it's so unique or different from every other city but for the opposite reason: New York is the way all of our cities are moving. This city points the way to the future, like it or not. That is why I teach a doctoral seminar in New York each year for church leaders from around the world. They need to know New York to better understand their own places of ministry.

In the mid 1720s Dutch pastor Theodore Frelinghuysen inaugurated parish visitation, and a spiritual revival we know as the Great Awakening began in the City and spread to Connecticut where Jonathan Edwards fanned those flames in the 1730s. An alliance of energy, intelligence, wealth, and American Victorianism known as the Evangelical United Front launched a "Plan of Union" to win the West between 1790 and 1830 under the slogan "Errand of Mercy." Concerts of Prayer, Anniversary Weeks, and many other "new measures" joined with revivalism, and social reform spread from New York along the Erie Canal in 1825 and into the West to energize the second Great Awakening. In the nineteenth century both rescue missions and social gospel movements came from New York as a result of the massive influx of foreigners and the growth of slums and ghettos.

"Most of our great cities have been in the hands of mobs at one time or another," wrote Josiah Strong in 1907, and that includes New York, where saloons surpassed churches in public influence. Nonetheless, Protestant institutional churches flourished. Dorothy Day and the *Catholic Worker* in New York influenced the world and led the way for millions of marginalized workers. Since World War II, the East Harlem Protestant Parish and the Urban Action Training Movement have profoundly affected New York and cities around the world. Since 1900 in New York, if you were white, you were likely Catholic (or Jewish), and if Protestant, you were black.

So we are still reinventing the church in New York City. Indeed we must, for the nineteenth-century words of Lyman Abbot still ring true:

> On the one hand, the city stands for all that is evil—a city full of devils, foul and corrupting; and on the other hand, the city stands for all that is noble, full of the glory of God, and shining with a clear and brilliant light. . . . Every city has been a Babylon, and every city has been a New Jerusalem; and it has always been a question whether the Babylon would extirpate the New Jerusalem. . . . The greatest corruption, . . . vice, . . . crime, the greatest philanthropy, . . . purity, . . . and aggressive courage are to be found in the great city. [Cities] are full of devils and also full of the glory of God.

In 1911 the American Baptist Publication Society and the Baptist Movement for Missionary Education persuaded Charles H. Sears, general secretary of the Baptist City Mission Society, to write up his marvelous research on New York churches in the book entitled *The Redemption of the City*. He in turn went to other great Baptists like Walter Rauschenbusch and Edward Judson for some of his material. We American Baptists have been part of this history for a long time. First Baptist Church celebrated its 250th anniversary in 1996. Out of that church came Abyssinian Baptist Church, now in Harlem, and out of the Abyssinian congregation came Concord in Brooklyn over 150 years ago. Our historic roots are part of the story of this book called *Signs of Hope in the City: Ministries of Community Renewal*.

This book is not the complete story of all that God is doing in New York, but it is a marvelous diagonal cut across the denominations old and new, mainline Protestant, Catholic, and Pentecostal. Dr. Bob Carle has special interpretative sensitivities for this project by virtue of his many years of theological study and ministry service in Asia. Clearly New York is moving in Asian and Latin directions demographically and ecclesiastically.

Millions of Americans would like to build a wall around the United States to keep the foreigners out. I'm afraid many Christians also would be counted in that number. That was true in 1911 when Charles Sears wrote, at which time Rev. Edward Judson responded: "Instead of regarding the advent of the foreigner as the last straw that breaks the camel's back, we are coming to see he may prove the very salvation of our churches" (Sears, p. xi). The authors of this volume follow Judson by reminding us that the God we worship was both an Asian-born baby and an African refugee (Matthew 2:1, 14-15). Half of the babies in the world today are Asian; half of the refugees are African.

The new reality in the twenty-first century is that the frontiers of mission have shifted to the cities and that the local church must also be the global church; mission is less geographically distant than culturally distant. Our challenge is to learn how to be the church reaching out in mission within this new reality, and New York ministries are showing us the way.

RAY BAKKE, Executive Director
International Urban Associates

Acknowledgments

We want to thank the many articulate, talented, and committed people who have made this volume possible. First of all, we thank the writers, who challenged us as we challenged them to produce a book that we can all be proud of. We want to thank Katie Sweeting, McKenzie Pier, and Beverly Cook of Concerts of Prayer for preparing the manuscript and keeping lines of communication open between the writers and the editors. We are very grateful to Ray Bakke, whose book *The Urban Christian* taught us how to love the city. He suggested this project and has been a constant source of inspiration for those of us involved in it.

We want to thank the staff and the board of directors of the Henry Luce Foundation, whose generous financial support made this project possible. We also want to thank the staff of Trinity Church, Wall Street, from whom we have learned a wealth of information about the ministries in this volume.

Signs of Hope in the City, put together by New Yorkers of different cultures, races, and denominations, is a vivid sign of Christian unity. This book stands as a witness that New Yorkers can overcome their divisions and can work together to address the public good. In a sense, then, the project itself has in a modest way inspired the Christians of New York to become a community that is united in service to the shalom of our city.

The writers and editors of *Signs of Hope in the City* donate the profits from the sale of this book to the New York City Rescue Mission, which has been serving the poor of our city since 1872.

To the pastors of New York

New York City

Manhattan
1.7 million people
  327,000 black
  387,000 Hispanic
    155,000 Puerto Rican
    137,000 Dominican
  867,000 white
  72,000 Chinese
  11,000 Japanese

Staten Island
380,000 people
  31,000 black
  30,000 Hispanic
  322,000 white

Brooklyn
2.5 million people
  900,000 black
  465,000 Hispanic
  1.0 million white
  100,000 Asian

The Bronx
1.5 million people
  450,000 black
  523,000 Hispanic
  430,000 white
  36,000 Asians

Queens
2.0 million people
  425,000 black
  380,000 Hispanic
  1.1 million white
  87,000 Chinese
  57,000 Asian Indian
  50,000 Korean

1

Introduction

Salt in the City

Robert D. Carle

New York is, in the words of political scientist John Mollenkopf, a "dual city." It is a "capital for capital," resplendent with luxury consumption and high society, yet it also symbolizes urban decay, the scourges of crack, AIDS, and homelessness. New York is an educational center with seventy colleges and universities, yet New York has a high school dropout rate of 33 percent, and 40 percent of the adult workforce lacks a high school diploma. New York leads the nation in biomedical research, graduate medical training, and new operative procedures, yet 1.6 million of the city's residents are on Medicaid, and the infant mortality rate is 26 percent higher than the national average. Some New York hospitals report that as many as half of the babies they deliver are born cocaine-addicted, HIV-positive, or with fetal alcohol syndrome. AIDS is the leading cause of death among New Yorkers under forty; homicide is next.[1]

Robert D. Carle holds a Ph.D. in theology from Emory University. He has worked for six years in Asia with the United Board for Christian Higher Education and currently works in church-based community development programs for Trinity Church, Wall Street.

In 1990, the top one-fifth of Manhattan's households had thirty-three times the income of Manhattan's bottom fifth. In the United States, only a former leper colony in Hawaii has a sharper differentiation between rich and poor. New York City's Commission on the Year 2000 describes the effect of this gulf between rich and poor: "Today's poor live in neighborhoods segregated by class with few connections to jobs. . . . A city that was accustomed to viewing poverty as a phase in assimilation to the larger society now sees a seemingly rigid cycle of poverty and a permanent underclass divorced from the rest of society."[2] In spite of the largest social service force in the nation, 23 percent of New York residents and 40 percent of New York's children live below the poverty line.[3]

Even more distressing than the physical poverty afflicting young New Yorkers is the acute *moral* poverty affecting our children. John DiIulio defines moral poverty as "being without loving, capable, responsible adults" who "habituate you to feel joy at others' joy, pain at others' pain, happiness when you do right, remorse when you do wrong."[4] Most predatory street criminals—white, black, adult, juvenile—have grown up in abject moral poverty, and today's Bloods and Crips are much more violent than their 1950s counterparts. "The next class of juvenile offenders will be even worse," DiIulio predicts. "On the horizon are tens of thousands of severely morally impoverished juvenile super-predators. They are perfectly capable of committing the most heinous acts of physical violence for the most trivial reasons."[5]

In the midst of this, churches are among the few remaining institutions of trust in many of New York City's neighborhoods. This is increasingly true as people lose faith in the systems that were supposed to cure the city's problems: school districts, public housing, Medicaid, and welfare. A study funded by the Lilly Endowment found that

> the physical presence of churches . . . represent community stability and continuity. They are places of beauty, peace, and serenity . . . ; they are equally linked in the minds of community residents as the place where physical and emotional needs are met. The houses of faith are, indeed, vessels for service and identifiable, stable institutions to community residents.[6]

DiIulio's research supports the Lilly findings. In a recent speech in New York, he discussed mounting scientific evidence that religious congregations not only save souls but also save lives: "Active religious congregations," he said, "are the principal factor in reducing violence and increasing neighborhood stability in truly disadvantaged inner-city neighborhoods. Based strictly on empirical data," he went on, "even an atheist would have to admit that religious institutions have a significant positive role to play in reducing the frequency of crime, delinquency, substance abuse and other social ills . . . in America's poor urban neighborhoods."[7]

Since the founding of the city, the church has been a bulwark against violence, poverty, and urban decay. This role became especially prominent in the nineteenth century as massive immigration and burgeoning slums overwhelmed the city's infrastructure. Businessmen's prayer movements and "salvation in the slum" enterprises brought the gospel to New Yorkers at both economic extremes. Every major denomination developed strong urban programs that sought to feed the hungry and offer skills education to the poor. The Salvation Army opened ministries to prisoners, vagrants, unwed mothers, and prostitutes. By 1906 St. Bartholomew's Episcopal Church had 8,496 societies, classes, or clubs. Nineteen worship meetings were conducted every Sunday, including services in German, Armenian, Chinese, and English.

Today, churches remain the most effective proponents of urban renewal and community development. A community leader writes, "If it weren't for the churches, nothing would be happening. This is the only really hopeful group in terms of development. The rest are fragmented, kept quiet, coopted."[8] The East Brooklyn Congregations, the South Bronx Churches, and the Harlem Congregations for Community Improvement have built homes and rehabilitated thousands of units of housing in the poorest neighborhoods of New York. The 180 American Baptist Churches of metropolitan New York are working in partnership with the city to open residences and day treatment centers for homeless AIDS patients. New York's 1,600 Korean congregations serve as virtual clearinghouses for the newly arrived, helping them with housing, employment, and English language instruction. Bethel Gospel Assembly in Harlem provides programs in drug rehabilitation, prison ministry, and adolescent leadership development that provide a hedge against the social forces destroying that community. "When you look at the gutbucket stuff," John DiIulio says, "the everyday, in-your-face work . . . almost all of it is being done by people who are churched."[9]

Signs of Hope in the City seeks to show how churches with vision and tenacity in America's largest city are reversing the trend toward urban decay and social disintegration. This book recommends ways in which the church can offer leadership toward rebuilding the social life of urban America. As the only integrating centers of community life in many neighborhoods, churches alone have the credibility and the resources to preserve and revitalize their communities. This project challenges its audiences to see the church as vital to the future of urban America.

THE NEED

Signs of Hope in the City had its inception at a Gatekeepers Consultation organized by Raymond Bakke in New York City in March 1995. The consultation brought together the leading practitioners of urban ministry in New York to promote cooperation among city churches so that we may evangelize more effectively and minister more appropriately. During the consultation, it was determined that member churches should launch a book project to tell the stories of representative ministries in New York City. Such a book and video project would draw upon the talents of the most articulate urban ministers from African American, Latino, Asian, and Anglo congregations to fill four pressing needs: the project would (1) energize and inspire the Christian community, (2) recommend ways in which the church can offer leadership toward rebuilding the spiritual, economic, and social life of the city, (3) be a handbook for new pastors in New York, and (4) inform people in government and in the foundation world about the church as a resource for reconciliation, peacemaking, and community development.

This project fills vital gaps in the resources available for urban ministry, and it corrects current misconceptions about the viability of churches in secular cities. Since World War II, there has been a withdrawal of the Protestant mainline from center-city settings. As suburbia captured the heart of the Protestant mainline, thousands of center-city churches closed, merged, or left for the suburbs.[10] This book shows that despite these shifts, the city provides fertile ground for evangelism and for creative, holistic expressions of the gospel. Today, New York has hundreds of dynamic new and established congregations, and this book will highlight a representative sample of these.

Resources exist that address the challenges of urban ministry, but there is currently no resource that deals with the special challenge of ministering in New York. This book offers an integrated vision that will educate and inform people from a variety of backgrounds. The stories highlighted by the project dramatize ways in which the church is rebuilding New York's most devastated neighborhoods. They correct current misconceptions about the viability of churches in secular cities, and they address and inspire Christian laypeople in urban congregations who are wondering what the relevance of the church is in the face of the crisis that surrounds them.

The narratives in this volume provide a theology of urban ministry by dramatizing the ways in which Scripture shapes the lives of urban Christians. The word *city* occurs 1,090 times in the Old Testament and 160 times in the New, and the Bible lists at least 133 different cities by name. The Scriptures also contain dozens of references to urban characters who put flesh and bones and life on biblical ministry models. Thirteen chapters of Genesis, for example, focus on an economic developer named Joseph, who developed, for a pagan pharaoh, two seven-year plans, one for budget deficits and one for budget surpluses. Moses led a flock the size of a megacity, and his congregation consisted of unemployed refugees, living for forty years on food stamps called "manna," with no city to call home. Daniel grappled with faith and culture in the urban context, graduating at the top of his class in the palace school while rejecting the value systems of Babylon. Nehemiah, general contractor and two-term governor of Jerusalem, made many deals with state officials to rebuild the walls of his ruined city.[11]

The New Testament presents a strategy for evangelism that "followed the contours of the urbanized Roman Empire."[12] The Gospels tell the story of Jesus' journey to Jerusalem—the center of religious, economic, and political power. It was in Jerusalem that, at Pentecost "Parthians, Medes, Elamites, and residents of Mesopotamia, Judea, and Cappadocia, Pontus and Asia, Phrygia and Pamphylia, Egypt and the parts of Libya belonging to Cyrene, and visitors to Rome, both Jews and proselytes, Cretans and Arabs" heard about God's deeds and power. The Book of Acts takes us from Jerusalem through Antioch, Ephesus, and Corinth to Rome. Through Paul's missionary journeys, the gospel spread to every corner of the known world. Paul did not have to travel to every village in the Mediterranean to achieve this. He rather preached in cities that were the transportation and information hubs of his day. Whatever happened in the cities radiated throughout the ancient world, and as Paul preached and taught in cities, the gospel spread to Asia, Africa, and Europe.

The men and women whom you encounter in this volume are people who mold their lives and ministries around the examples of faith set forth in Scripture. As community developers, city planners, relief workers, and evangelists, their lives are built upon the foundations established by Joseph, Moses, Daniel, Nehemiah, and Paul. They are, with all their faults, fresh exemplars that teach us about the relevance of Scripture in the modern world and about God's love for the city.

Beyond the Christian world, this project will be directly useful for professionals in the worlds of business, government, and foundations who are seeking to support new and more effective models of community development. As evidence mounts that secular programs alone cannot effect social transformation, policy makers and academics are reevaluating the role of religious commitment in the renewal of communities. David Larson of the National Institute of Health shows that teenage students who attend religious services at least once a month are about half as likely as other teenagers to participate in socially destructive behaviors. Richard Freeman of Harvard University shows that among black males, church attendance is a better predictor of who will escape the destructive cycle of poverty, drugs, and crime than any other variable—including income, sports, and family structure. Catherine Hess, director of New York's first methadone program for drug addicts, concluded that Christian drug rehabilitation programs that emphasize prayer, conversion, and the Holy Spirit are much more effective than secular programs. Teen Challenge, for example, has a 95-percent success rate for heroin users and an 83-percent success rate for alcoholics. Compare this with a federal study's finding that only 1 percent of drug addicts and alcoholics receiving disability benefits ever recover from their addictions or find work.[13]

DiIulio's research shows that high concentrations of liquor outlets create "negative externalities" in poor communities and high concentrations of churches create "positive externalities": "Other things being equal, poor run-down neighborhoods where churches outnumber bars have fewer problems than poor, depressed neighborhoods where bars outnumber churches." DiIulio sees the present challenge for corporate leaders and government officials as enlisting "religious institutions in the battle to solve urban problems": "I don't know precisely what bundle of religion-centered spiritual enhancing policies to embrace," he writes, "but I think it's clear that we need to invest more funds, both public and private, to empower local churches to serve [their neighborhoods]." He admits that such a proposal raises constitutional concerns, but "most Americans believe in God (90 percent) and pray each day (80 percent). It is time to capitalize on our religiosity as a people in matters of public policy." The alternative to such a strategy is accelerated moral and physical deterioration. DiIulio concludes, "So let our guiding principle be, 'Fill churches, not jails; or let us be prepared to reap the whirlwind of our own moral bankruptcy.'"[14]

The use of churches to enhance community well-being is a major theme in current literature in the field of community development. Community developer Van Johnson believes that there is no substitute for the resources of energy, enthusiasm, political clout, and economic pull that churches offer to community developers: "I [will] never again attempt to help people with economic revitalization," Johnson said, "unless it is under the umbrella of a church, and the church helped. It makes no sense, especially in the black community, to leave the church out. The church is the most important institution we have. It holds most of the resources that our community needs."[15] Carol Steinbach describes how community development can enhance the spiritual mission of religious institutions: "Community development provides an antidote to the disorder and negative attitudes brought about by profound and rapid change. Its central tenet carries a powerful spiritual message. When community development groups join forces with churches and synagogues, the impact of that message is almost always magnified."[16] Calvin Butts of Abyssinian Baptist Church in Harlem calls his own church's role in community development "an extension of the role that the black church has played since its inception." "The Church," he said, "is the first place of social cohesion. It was where economic empowerment began in the black community. People pooled their nickels and dimes to bury the dead and help widows. It is also where we started our first schools and where we began our political development."[17]

Signs of Hope in the City will build on these observations by dramatizing the ways in which spiritual transformation is an essential component of effective community renewal. Until recently, such a statement would have appeared ludicrous to policy elites and government planners. But the depth of the current crisis is permitting new questions to be asked and new models to be explored, making this a propitious time to launch this project.

Signs of Hope in the City begins with a historical review of the "cloud of witnesses" who have gone before contemporary New Yorkers and who continue to inspire us. The first two chapters dramatize the ways in which men and women like Bishop Hobart, Walter Rauschenbusch, Dorothy Day, and Gardner Taylor addressed issues of evangelization, prayer, race relations, and poverty relief. Contemporary ministries are set on the foundations built by these foreparents and by the institutions that they shepherded. The chapters that follow feature New York City churches, church-based coalitions, and ministries that represent a diversity of characteristics: black, white, Latino, Asian, and integrated; denominational, independent, and parachurch; mainline Protestant, Pentecostal, baptistic, and Roman Catholic. Several of the ministries have been serving New York since the nineteenth century; others were established in the last decade. This survey does not presume to be comprehensive or exhaustive. There are hundreds of effective ministries in New York City that could have been included in this book in place of the ones chosen. This book is merely a first step in telling the countless stories that practitioners of ministry in New York City need to tell. It is our hope that our work will inspire more publications of this kind.

2

Seeking the Shalom of the City

New York City Missions in Historical Perspective

Robert D. Carle

When the British inherited New York from the Dutch in 1664, the city was already an ethnic and religious melting pot. There were eighteen nationalities represented in the city, including Dutch burghers and patroons, English aristocrats and commoners, French restaurateurs and glove makers, Irish farmers, German and Swedish workmen, and Chinese, African, and Native American laborers. Trinity Church (Anglican), built in 1697, was colonial New York's quasi-official church. Successive governors maintained their pew and insignia at Trinity. Royal grants and taxes as well as private contributions supported the parish. Trinity's wardens and vestry were political leaders in the colony, and its clergy often addressed matters of public policy. By 1766 Trinity Church had authorized the construction of two new parishes—St. George's and St. Paul's—to accommodate the city's growing population. The first commencement of King's College (Columbia University) was held in St. George's chapel, and St. Paul's hosted a service of thanksgiving and blessing in honor of George Washington following his inauguration on April 30, 1789.

Despite Trinity's privileged position in the city, Anglicanism was always a minority faith in New York's pluralistic religious setting. In 1711 a Presbyterian minister reported that New York had "two ministers of the established church of England, two Dutch ministers, one French minister, a Lutheran minister, an Anabaptist, and also a Quaker meeting."[1] By the time of the Revolution, New York had twenty-two churches, but the city was in need of moral reform and social concern. Four hundred alehouses and five hundred "ladies of pleasure" served the small town, and New Yorkers left a bad impression on visitors. One visitor sardonically complained that "they all drink here from the moment they are able to lick a spoon." In his diary, John Adams called New Yorkers people of "little breeding" who "talk loud, very fast, and all together."[2] New York was divided into an old section that extended from the Battery to the city hall and a "new town," a jungle of cheap, small wooden houses huddled solidly together without yards. In these hovels people hived two or three families to a room, four to twelve families to a house without running water or sewage disposal.[3]

THE NINETEENTH CENTURY:
REVIVALISM AND SOCIAL OUTREACH

The Great Awakening revitalized churches in New York and made Bible reading, church going, sobriety, sabbath observance, and social work fashionable. In the latter part of the eighteenth century, the Great Awakening swept across frontier America, and by 1800 the new religious enthusiasm found converts in every major eastern town and city, reshaping the religious life of entire areas of New England and New York State. This revival converted ministers, prominent merchants, lawyers, college presidents, faculty, and students. This was an age of religious activism, Bibles, tracts, and missions. The Evangelical United Front launched the American Bible Society, the American Board of Foreign Missions, and a "Plan of Union" to win the West under the slogan "Errand of Mercy." Church membership grew rapidly. Church historians estimate that in 1800 one in fifteen Americans belonged to a Protestant church.

By 1835 one out of every eight did. Church membership, given the tremendous rise in population during these years, far more than doubled.[4] New converts flooded new Methodist and Baptist churches and revitalized established parishes. Church members raised the prestige of Christianity to the point where belief, or at least the pretense of belief, was the norm of American behavior.

John Henry Hobart, who joined the staff of Trinity Church in 1800 and was promoted to bishop in 1813, was one of New York's great turn-of-the-century luminaries. When Hobart joined the staff of Trinity, the Episcopal Church was at a low ebb, both nationally and in New York. The Episcopal denomination had suffered a loss of vitality following American independence and religious disestablishment. Methodists had separated from Episcopal congregations to form their own churches, and the evangelization of the frontier was being conducted by Methodist, Presbyterian, and independent churches. Hobart's campaign to promote "Evangelical Truth and Apostolic Order" succeeded in bringing new life to American Episcopalianism. As bishop, Hobart traveled tirelessly from Long Island to the Canadian border, establishing new parishes and missions, raising funds, and reinvigorating congregations. Hobart continued to serve as rector of Trinity during his tenure as bishop, and between 1800 and 1830 he presided over Trinity's establishment of seventy-five mission parishes at a cost of more than $1 million.

One consequence of the Great Awakening was reconciliation—at least temporarily—between African, European, and Native Americans and between various Protestant denominations. Prior to this time, after riots precipitated by a slave uprising in 1712, the governor issued ordinances that prohibited blacks from worshiping together and severely limited religious education. The city's most effective catechetical school for blacks (located at Trinity Church on Wall Street) was closed. Its founder, Elias Neau, who had prepared hundreds of African Americans for baptism, was "abused so shrilly that for a while he hardly dared appear in public."[5] In the early decades of the eighteenth century, a historian noted that African Americans were much discouraged from embracing the Christian religion, upon account of the very little regard showed them. . . . Their marriages were performed by mutual consent only, without the blessing of the Church; they were buried by those of their own country or complexion in the common field, without any Christian office. . . . No notice was given of their being sick that they might be visited; on the contrary frequent discourses were made in conversation that they had no souls.[6]

The Great Awakening challenged many Americans' perceptions of race. During these eruptions of religious fervor, fiery ministers offered salvation to all, regardless of social and economic position. During tent meetings, Americans of all races and backgrounds had rebirth experiences accompanied by trances, visions, shouting, dancing, "fits," and other ecstatic acts. Native and African Americans attended evangelical revivals and took part in these conversion experiences alongside European Americans. There was, in the tent meetings, a complete and unself-conscious integration of races, prompting religious enthusiasts to proclaim that the color line had been washed away in the blood of the Lamb. The Great Awakening crossed denominational lines and created new religious communities, many of them biracial in membership. African Americans were ordained and given charge of mixed congregations. The Baptists and Methodists drew the largest number of African Americans for several reasons. These groups worked extremely hard at gaining converts from all races. Some of their leaders were antislavery in sentiment. Both groups deemphasized an educated clergy, enabling new converts to become exhorters and preachers. Racial harmony, however, was short lived. As predominantly white congregations instituted segregationist policies, African Americans gradually withdrew from these congregations to form their own independent churches.

A more enduring form of reconciliation took place between the various Protestant denominations. The goal of churches affected by the Great Awakening was the conversion of every nonevangelical person in the world. Protestant denominations set up an Evangelical United Front to achieve this purpose. In the 1820s only four of America's fourteen leading benevolent societies were under denominational control, and none of these were among the leaders.[7] Protestant unity and goodwill were evident throughout city missions. In 1819, for example, a society for promoting the gospel among seamen opened a mariners' church on Roosevelt Street near the East River docks. A Presbyterian minister presided at the dedication, which treated its audience to three sermons, delivered in turn by Protestant Episcopal, Reformed Dutch, and Methodist Episcopal clergymen.

The New York City Tract Society[8] was one of New York's most significant and long-lived united front societies. The society was formed in 1812 by Episcopalians, Methodists, Baptists, Congregationalists, and Presbyterians to print religious pamphlets "consistent with the Reformation." The tract society sought, through the efforts of individual members, to reach all classes and sections of the city. Members circulated tracts among their friends, left them on steamships and stagecoaches, gave them to strangers on the street and to inmates of the city's charitable institutions. The object was not to meet any specific temporal needs, but to convert the city to Christ.[9]

Gradually, however, the society's contact with the poor became intimate and direct. As members visited the slums in hopes of converting particular households, volunteers reacted with horror at the poverty they found. Visitors found dilapidated buildings housing dozens of families, streets crowded with children who neither worked nor attended school, and women seeking to raise families in unheated and unfurnished hovels. The Tract Society's annual reports began to publish descriptions of slum conditions by concerned visitors. A tract visitor wrote in the 1836 report, "In visiting the abodes of the sick and afflicted this past month, I have witnessed an increased amount of wretchedness. Almost every day brings me in contact with cases so appalling and distressing that it requires a nerve of steel to prevent the mind and body from sinking under personal excitement."[10]

Because existing Protestant parishes could not (or would not) accommodate the city's poor, tract visitors began to offer special services in the slums. They organized Sunday schools, weekly Bible classes, and prayer meetings in the city's worst tenements. As the tract volunteers became involved in the lives of slum dwellers, they began delivering food, money, and clothing to the poor along with tracts and prayers. By the 1840s the minutes of the society's executive committee were filled almost completely with discussions of the needs of the poor, with debates as to the most efficient and economical means of distributing charity. In 1846 the Tract Society's board of directors voted to emphasize the society's work in the slums even at the expense of missionary labors with other classes of society. Poverty-stricken immigrants, it seemed apparent, would never attend one of the city's established churches, and the society became the bearer of New York Protestantism to the poor. By 1870 the society had constructed large church buildings in slum neighborhoods that housed schools, libraries, meeting rooms, even coffee lounges. Missions stations were opened at night to provide a bed and meal to homeless men.[11]

Along with this commitment to the poor came major structural changes in the Tract Society itself. The executive committee began to hire salaried, full-time workers to labor exclusively in the slums. These protoprofessional workers not only prayed and exhorted; they became expert in such matters as job placement, wage scales, public health, and coordination of the city's charities.[12] To facilitate this work, the Tract Society, now called the Missions Society, divided Manhattan into seventeen districts corresponding to its political wards. The districts were then subdivided into smaller districts, each containing some twenty-five poor families. Missions Society personnel were taught to put into practice principles of detection, discernment, and visitation.[13]

With the institutional commitment to the poor came an activist stance against the environmental conditions of slum life. In 1854 the society published a detailed ward-by-ward description of slum housing conditions in New York. It reported in depth the horrific conditions of the largest and worst of the city's tenements. This report remained for decades a specific guide for American housing reformers and public health workers. In 1856 and 1858 the society lobbied successfully in Albany to secure the appointment of special legislative committees to investigate health and housing in New York City.[14] In the 1860s and 1870s the society worked for the passage in the New York legislature of a model tenement house code and a law to regulate the production and sale of milk. The society also spearheaded movements to improve the city's sewer system, regulate slaughterhouses, and prohibit farm animals from being stabled in tenement apartments.

While the Missions Society was bringing the gospel to the poorest New Yorkers, on July 1, 1857, Jeremiah Lanphier began holding daily prayer meetings in New York's downtown business district. Within six months, ten thousand businessmen were gathering daily for prayer, and within two years, a million converts were added to the American church. The number of conversions was so great that New York papers ran daily columns of those who made commitments on the previous evening. During the 1860s this spiritual awakening helped solidify antislavery sentiment in the North.

In the latter part of the 1800s the Salvation Army and other community ministries joined the Missions Society as one of New York's most distinguished social service agencies. In 1889 Mrs. Ballington Booth organized the first Slum Brigade—a Salvation Army outreach—in New York City. The Slum Brigade was best known for its program of visitation and relief. As Adjutant Ida Turpin said, "The daily work in the homes of people, watching over the sick and dying, and loving service in trying hours have given to the Salvation Army a weight of influence that no amount of charitable gifts of food and money would ever have done."[15] Visitation prepared the way for formal religious meetings, run by "doughty lasses" who were often subject to insult. Through sheer persistence, these young women won their way into saloons and beer halls. When they were ordered out of saloons, they would invariably return the next night to "see whether [the owner] had changed his mind."[16]

The experience of the Slum Brigade prompted the formation of a series of relief agencies. In 1891 Ballington Booth established a food and shelter depot at Downing and Bedford Streets. In 1892 the brigade opened a rescue house for prostitutes, and in 1893 the brigade established a day nursery for children whose parents were unable to care for them. In 1897 the Cherry Tree Home for orphans opened in Fordham, New York, and in the following year a school for training nurses in "poverty medicine" was established in Fordham. Prominent doctors of New York not only offered courses at the school but also aided in the Salvation Army's work among the poor. In extremely cold periods of winter, the Salvation Army opened its well-heated halls to people living in hovels and tenements. On Thanksgiving and Christmas, the army offered free meals to the poor in Madison Square Garden. During the sweltering summer months, the army was on hand with fresh-air crops, steamboat excursions, and cheap ice.

In the late 1800s denominational agencies were busy setting up mercy missions and social services. In the early 1900s the Episcopalian House of Mercy, Home for the Homeless, Sheltering Arms, Infant Asylum, and St. Barnabas House organized into the New York Protestant Episcopal City Mission. Closely associated with the City Mission were a series of brotherhoods and guilds and workingmen's associations. These organizations provided relief to the poor as well as instruction and recreation for members. There were no religious qualifications for membership; any eighteen-year-old of good moral character was privileged to join.[17] The workingmen's clubs helped to counteract the "virus of aristocracy" that plagued the Episcopal Church and provided a model of solving social problems through association.[18]

Lutherans and Roman Catholics devoted special attention to immigrant populations. In 1873 the synods of the General Council of the Lutheran Church established a home, which in the following twelve years cared for over eighty-five thousand people. This home provided spiritual instruction, handled finances, reunited immigrants with friends and relatives, and provided an employment agency. By 1900 the Catholic Church had twelve mission communants, of whom five-sixths were urban immigrants. Isaac Hecker established the central parish of the Paulist Fathers in the midst of Irish shanties.[19] "Thus a movement designed to convert Mr. Emerson and his friends, and the educated people of America," wrote James Parton, "was made, first of all, to minister to the spiritual wants of the poorest and most ignorant people living in the Northern States."[20]

In addition to the work of parachurch organizations, individual parishes started creative programs of urban evangelization

and poverty relief. During his fifteen years as rector of Holy
Trinity Church, Stephen Tyng perfected one of the great mission churches in America. In 1864 Tyng started the Pastoral Aid
Society and two additional organizations, one each for men and
women. Tyng enlisted the help of parish members in these aid
societies by assigning people to tasks in accord with their
secular callings—for example, doctors to care for the sick and
lawyers to protect the rights of the poor. Holy Trinity became
valued throughout the city for its ability to influence the
indifferent, the destitute, and the outcast. When the church
encountered financial trouble in 1878, New York philanthro-
pists endowed it with an annual income for the support of
"undenominational, evangelistic, and humanitarian work
among the poor of New York City."[21]

The Reverend William M. Muhlenberg of the Church of the
Holy Communion was one of New York's most effective cru-
saders against poverty. His church, located at Sixth Avenue and
Twentieth Street, was surrounded by groups of low, wooden
"airless and unsanitary" tenements. From these hovels, the
poor showed up at Holy Communion to worship alongside New
York's elite. "Never had there been such a mingling of rich and
poor in an Episcopal Church," the Millers write. "The atmosphere was unaffectedly friendly and so appealing that many
coming first from curiosity, could never be satisfied elsewhere."[22]

The Church of the Holy Communion was constantly experi-
menting with new ideas. Muhlenberg considered rented pews
a sacrilege, and he offered free seating to all who came to Holy
Communion. He defied Protestant opinion by establishing an
order of deaconesses, the first in the English-speaking world.
Muhlenberg was instrumental in starting St. Luke's Hospital,
which opened in 1859. As superintendent and chaplain of St.
Luke's, Muhlenberg was "all gentleness and democracy":

> It was a church hospital, but ministers of other faiths were
> welcomed. Roman Catholic priests administered their rites,
> the while warning their parishioners against the faith of the
> hospital. . . . Once when a sister came to [Muhlenberg] all
> excited, to say that a Methodist minister was praying aloud
> in the middle of the ward, he said "Indeed! Make haste to
> stop the prayer before it reaches heaven."[23]

Muhlenberg called himself an "Evangelical Catholic." "If there would have been a New York City Council of Churches," the Millers write, "then surely he would have been the president."[24]

The draft riots of 1863 brought to New York "the foulest stain that ever marked the history of the city." It was, the Missions Society reported, "an unprovoked attack upon the Colored race. There were many houses destroyed, innocent Negroes attacked and hung to a tree." The North Presbyterian Church, whose pastor, Dr. Edwin Hatfield, was an abolitionist, was threatened by rioters. The church was saved only when a neighboring Catholic priest, Father Donnely, mounted the church steps and shouted to the mob that the church would be burned only over his dead body. The rioters set fire to the Colored Orphan Asylum, and "the two hundred twenty children of the orphanage escaped [the fire] as by a miracle." St. Luke's Hospital was on the list for burning. For two days and nights the rioters milled around the hospital cursing and yelling. The mob was not appeased until Muhlenberg brought one of the rioters (who had been injured in the melee) into the hospital for treatment.[25]

Toward the end of the nineteenth century, St. Bartholomew's Episcopal Church inaugurated the largest program of social reform of any church in the United States. In 1891 the Vanderbilt brothers supported the building of a three-and-a-half-acre parish house "devoted to humanitarian as well as religious objects."[26] During the following ten years, nearly $11 million was expended, an average annual outlay exceeding that of "many American colleges and universities." St. Bartholomew's became distinguished for its excellent medical and surgical clinic, which held over twenty thousand consultations and wrote over ten thousand prescriptions each year. An employment bureau secured positions at a rate of about fifteen hundred a year. The church's loan association provided money in sums from fifty cents to one hundred dollars at low rates of interest to people in temporary difficulty. Activity at the parish house was supplemented by a girls' club, a boarding house, a working girls' summer home, and a children's home. In its spiritual mission, the church specialized in caring for Asian immigrants, being equipped to minister in Armenian, Syriac, Turkish, and Chinese.[27]

THE SOCIAL GOSPEL

At the turn of the century, Walter Rauschenbusch developed a theology of urban mission that made a profound impact on American Protestantism. Rauschenbusch began his pilgrimage among poor New Yorkers in 1886, when he assumed his duties as pastor of Second German Baptist Church in Hell's Kitchen, one of the city's notorious slums. Out of this experience came a prophetic passion for social reform. "It came through personal contact with poverty," Rauschenbusch wrote. "When I saw how men toiled all their life long, hard, toilsome lives, and at the end had almost nothing to show for it; how strong men begged for work and could not get it in hard times; how little children died—oh, the children's funerals! They gripped my heart."[28]

Nothing in Rauschenbusch's training or seminary education had equipped him to understand the powerful social, economic, and intellectual currents sweeping American life. Rauschenbusch had been reared in pietistic traditions that had no concern for relating the gospel to social problems and struggles. As Harry Fosdick wrote, "The churches' attention was centered not on seeing to it that the Will of God was done on Earth as it is in Heaven but on seeing to it that individuals were prepared to escape from earth to the joys of heaven."[29] During his eleven years in Hell's Kitchen, Rauschenbusch undertook an intense schedule of reading, discussion, and writing.[30] At the same time he teamed up with Jacob Riis to attack corrupt politics and to secure playgrounds, fresh-air centers, and decent housing. In 1897 Rauschenbusch received a call from Rochester Theological Seminary, where for twenty-one years he made a profound influence as a teacher and a writer. Rauschenbusch challenged the individualistic otherworldliness of American Protestantism by showing that the kingdom of God was a predominant factor in Jesus' message and that devotion to the coming kingdom is the church's all-inclusive mission. Rauschenbusch taught that the reign of God in a redeemed society is something so big that absolutely nothing that interested him was excluded from it.

Personal religion, worldwide evangelism, justice for workers, the cleansing of politics, and the reformation of the economic order were all included. For Rauschenbusch, "the Kingdom was here and now, as well as in the future, and to have faith in its possibility, and to further it with dedicated lives, until in justice and goodwill God reigns in all human affairs, was the very heart of Christianity."[31]

Unlike many of his twentieth-century followers, Rauschenbusch never promoted social Christianity at the expense of personal reformation and individual rebirth. He deplored the exclusive blaming of environment for all human evil, which attitude, he said, "instead of stiffening and awakening the sense of responsibility in the individual, teaches him to unload it on society." "Most of the social reformers," he wrote, "claim that if only poverty and fear of poverty could be abolished, men would cease to be grasping, selfish, overbearing and sensual. . . . We do not see it so. . . . We can conceive of a state of society in which plenty would reign, but where universal opulence would only breed universal pride and wantonness." Personal rebirth and social rebirth are inseparably necessary. "The social order cannot be saved," he said, "without regenerate men."

During the 1930s and 1940s several developments in society and in churches created a movement in Roman Catholicism analogous to the social gospel movement within Protestantism. The poverty and want of the depression era, the struggle of labor to gain recognition, and the blatant racial discrimination following the northern migration of southern blacks all conspired to prick the consciences and fire the imaginations of Catholic New Yorkers.[32] In 1933 Dorothy Day founded the Catholic Worker to forge a new American style of Catholic social action. Within a few years, Day had formed lecture groups, houses of hospitality, and halfway homes and founded a newspaper with a circulation of two hundred thousand. Day became, according to David O'Brian, "the most significant, interesting, and influential person in the history of American Catholicism."[33]

Dorothy Day converted to Catholicism in 1927 after a tempestuous adolescence that included an affair, an abortion, and the birth of a daughter from a common-law marriage. Day spent the five years following her conversion practicing the rituals of her faith and searching for a vocation within her church. By 1932 the massive suffering of depression years had brought Day to the brink of losing her faith. "During the early years of the Depression," she said, "people walked the streets, hundreds and hundreds of them, looking dazed and bewildered. They had no work. They had no place to go. Groups tried to help them, but neither state nor church seemed alarmed." Day prayed that "some way would open for me to use what talents I possessed for my fellow workers, for the poor."[34]

In 1933 Day teamed up with French peasant-author Peter Maurin to publish the *Catholic Worker*. On May Day, Dorothy and Peter began selling the paper to people in New York's Union Square for a penny a copy. Committed to racial equality, the *Worker* had a masthead depicting a black worker and a white worker, and it featured articles attacking lynching and denouncing racism and anti-Semitism. Although anti-Communist, the *Worker* commiserated with Communist dedication to social and working-class objectives. The *Worker* reported all major labor disputes of the 1930s, beseeching readers to exercise moral responsibility by supporting strikers and boycotting products of oppressive managements. In 1938 the *Worker* began championing the plight of migrant workers, a cause for which Day was jailed for eleven days in 1973 at age seventy-seven.[35]

Shortly after the publication of the *Worker*, Day and Maurin started the Catholic Worker movement to implement the ideas defended in the paper. The purpose of the movement was to make the Catholic Church "a dominant social force." Houses of hospitality, where the poor, homeless, and unemployed could find hot food, warm conversation, and a place to sleep, were at the heart of the Catholic Worker movement. Hundreds of New York's young intellectuals moved into houses of hospitality to experience voluntary poverty and learn about corporal works of mercy. The houses became centers for regular discussions about everything from steel strikes to new developments in Catholic theology. Another, less successful, phase of the movement was the rural commune or farm. As social experiments, the farms failed, but they served as rural retreat centers, halfway houses, and suppliers of produce to urban houses.[36]

Jay Dolan writes that "the Catholic Worker was a radical move-ment. . . . [It] put no hope in the modern state; it put faith in the community of the sacred."[37]

In 1939 Day teamed up with Russian immigrant Baroness Catherine de Heuck to establish the Committee of Catholics to Fight Anti-Semitism. De Hueck's commitments to social jus-tice, voluntary poverty, and minority rights mirrored those of Day. After a failed marriage, de Heuck resolved to devote herself to the lay apostolate and live among the poor. In 1938 she opened a Friendship House in Harlem where staff persons and volunteers lived in voluntary poverty. The Friendship House engaged in three areas of work: direct assistance to the needy by providing food and clothing and helping people find housing; the combating of racism through lectures, workshops, and publications; and social action to combat discrimination at the local, state, and national levels. The success of the Harlem Friendship House spurred the opening of Friendship Houses in cities across the nation. Thousands of recruits were attracted to de Hueck's program of "holy poverty." The people who joined Friendship Houses were "for the most part young, well educated, idealistic, outraged at injustice, and determined to change the world."[38] One of the most famous volunteers was Thomas Merton, who served at the Harlem House before enter-ing the Trappists.[39]

CONTEMPORARY COMMUNITY MINISTRY

As the drug problem spread across the nation in the 1960s, David Wilkerson's Brooklyn-based program for the recovery of drug addicts (called Teen Challenge) became recognized as the most effective effort of its kind in North America. Wilkerson's vision began in 1958 when he started weeping over a *Life* magazine picture of young New York City street kids on trial for murder. Feeling a call from God to minister to such kids, Wilkerson left his Pennsylvania country-church pastorate to preach the gospel on inner-city street corners. Wilkerson's message challenged the toughest gangs on their own turf.

In the early 1960s Wilkerson founded a biblically based residential treatment center in Brooklyn (the Teen Challenge Center) to minister to addicts. Since then Teen Challenge has grown into a worldwide ministry with 120 centers in the United States and 60 centers overseas. The published story of Wilkerson's ministry, *The Cross and the Switchblade,* has sold in excess of fifteen million copies in thirty languages, and in 1969 it was made into a major motion picture.

In 1986 after an absence of over ten years, Wilkerson returned to New York City to establish the Times Square Church, which he described in his book *The Cross and the Switchblade* as "a church of repentance and holiness in the heart of Manhattan." Today, Times Square Church is one of New York's largest congregations. Its five thousand members are a "mirror of the city." They include both affluent and needy, and they represent at least fifty-six nationalities. "God has established a church," Wilkerson says, "where hundreds of repentant believers from many nationalities are reaching out to the poorest and neediest in this crumbling city." Times Square Church is located in a former opera house—the Mark Hellinger Theater. It has six services every week and an extraordinary array of community ministries.

Times Square Church staffs and operates the Upper Room, a center for feeding and clothing people. The church conducts weekly ministry to inmates in fourteen New York City prisons and provides food, clothing, and toys to children and families of hundreds of inmates. The church owns and operates a mobile food truck from which hot food and beverages as well as gloves, blankets, and sweaters are distributed on a daily basis to the poor and needy. The church runs residential rehabilitation facilities for homeless men and women. Recently the church purchased an eight-story warehouse on West Forty-first Street at Eighth Avenue that will be known as the Isaiah House, a center for multiple charity outreaches.

Redeemer Presbyterian Church is located a couple of miles uptown from Times Square Church. Like Times Square Church, Redeemer was started in the late 1980s and is today one of New York City's fastest-growing churches. Although the congregation at Redeemer reflects the diversity of the city, the Reverend Tim Keller is especially concerned to meet the spiritual and intellectual needs of Manhattan's educated elite. He describes the services as "warm but dignified and continuous with historical and liturgical forms." He describes the preaching as "intelligent, bordering on the intellectual, but showing familiarity with urban life issues." Today, Redeemer meets in Hunter College auditorium and has a weekly attendance of 2,100, 99 percent of whom are professionals.[40] Eighty-five percent of the members are single, and the average age is early thirties. "At least twelve percent of the members of this theologically conservative and evangelical congregation are known to the pastors to [have been] homosexual," Keller writes, "The actual proportion, of course, is probably much higher."

The phenomenal growth of Redeemer Presbyterian Church among Manhattan's cultural elite has surprised even the founders of the church. How has a small, southern, theologically conservative denomination achieved such phenomenal success among New York's sophisticates?[41] Tim Keller identifies a variety of factors that he sees as key to Redeemer's success.

First, Redeemer presents the evangelical message in an educated mode. Many newcomers exclaim, Keller writes, "This is the first church I ever saw that really believes there are some answers to life questions, and yet doesn't tell people 'Don't question, just believe.'" Second, Redeemer's worship is "in the vernacular," avoiding both the coldness of traditional worship and the emotional hype of some charismatic churches. Third, Redeemer offers choices: three services on Sundays with different liturgical and worship styles. Fourth, Redeemer encourages lay-led programs that address personal problems among congregants (divorce recovery, job transition, AIDS outreach, etc.). This gives people the impression that Redeemer is a church where people can receive help if they need it. Fifth, through house churches and small groups, Redeemer builds connections among New Yorkers, for whom "loneliness is the greatest single need to address." Sixth, Redeemer provides a wide variety of volunteer possibilities, ranging from an HIV outreach to a mentoring program to work with Habitat for Humanity. Seventh, prayer is one of Redeemer's "irreplaceable foundations." Since its inception, Redeemer has "received dozens of letters from big and little churches telling us that we were being prayed for," Keller said. "I know of no single mission work that has ever had such visible prayer support—

certainly in our church circles it was unprecedented. So why should we be surprised at the result?"[42]

The two "new" churches that conclude this history of Christianity in New York dramatize a significant shift that has taken place in the nature of Christianity in New York since the 1960s. For three hundred years, a limited cluster of mainline Protestant denominations wielded enormous cultural and social authority in the city. Today, the Roman Catholic Church is broadening its influence in the city, and a whole host of new evangelicalisms have formed a new center in Protestant life. The most dramatic of these advances are taking place in predominantly black, Latino, and Asian neighborhoods. Yet, most of the old established churches are managing to keep their doors open and are serving their neighborhoods in small but important ways. Local mainline churches are developing hospices for AIDS sufferers, welcoming refugees, and caring for the homeless. Endowed parishes are using their resources to renew neighborhoods and serve the poor.[43] Through the Industrial Areas Foundation, mainline churches are organizing politically to improve public safety, sanitation, and public schools.

Perhaps most significantly, the mainline is tending to "go home."[44] After decades of neglecting their traditions to work for social justice, mainline churches are selectively retrieving elements of meditative and devotional traditions, and they are devoting more attention to prayer and spirituality. Luminaries of the past like Martin Luther, John Calvin, the Puritans, and Bishop Hobart are given more of a hearing than they were previously, and established churches are celebrating their centenaries with greater zeal and pride than would have previously been thought appropriate.

Martin Marty compares the established churches to the Greeks who were eclipsed by the energetic and efficient Romans: "The Greeks thought of themselves as having the longer traditions, the more profound cultural achievements, a better way of life. The Greeks lost energy to shape a new empire, however, and left the task to the aggressive, improvising, and, in their eyes, more superficial Romans."[45] In New York the established denominations continue to contribute to the spiritual and social life of the city in profound ways. Meanwhile, they watch their bustling evangelical and Pentecostal brethren sometimes with gratitude, sometimes with anger, often with bewilderment.

3

Shelter in the Time of Storm

The Black Church in New York City

Robert D. Carle

Although African Americans were intimately involved in mainline Protestant and Roman Catholic efforts to address issues of poverty and race relations, it was primarily through the black church that black Christians expressed their social concerns. In response to conditions of racial and economic oppression and of discrimination within white churches, black congregations emerged as places where an "alternative culture" was nurtured, prophetic language and action were shaped, and liberating visions were celebrated.[1] Black churches sheltered runaway slaves; they furnished meeting places and platforms for the abolitionist movement; they cared for the sick and gave food and shelter to the destitute. Above all, they developed strong and intelligent leaders through whom African Americans of New York "learned to stand with confidence, united in a common understanding of their rights."[2] Black leaders not

only equipped their congregations to survive the dehumaniza-
tion of racism; they also made claims upon the nation's identity
and conscience. "The public mission of the black church,"
Robert Franklin writes, "was to compel America to become
America for everyone."[3] As such, African American churches
challenged Christians of every stripe to offer hope to their
members and to fight for a more just and loving society.

Peter Williams of John Street Methodist Church was the
founder of the first black church in New York City. Williams
became the sexton of John Street Methodist Church in 1778,
and in 1783 he presented the trustees of John Street with a very
unusual proposition. He asked the church to purchase him
from his master and then allow him to repay the church. The
church reacted favorably to his request, and within three years
Williams had repaid the church in full. As black membership
at John Street increased, blacks came to resent the various
restrictions that white leaders placed upon them. The color line
was drawn at the Communion table and baptismal font, and
blacks were excluded from sitting in certain pews. An open rift
came in 1795 when a number of black members of the John
Street Methodist Church, led by Williams, decided to hold
separate meetings. The final break came three years later when a
lot was purchased on the corner of Church and Leonard Streets,
where in 1800 a building that became known as the African
Methodist Episcopal (A.M.E.) Zion Church was erected.[4]

Within a few years splits occurred in other churches. First
Baptist Church's black members split from the fold in 1808 to
form the Abyssinian Baptist Church in a building on Anthony
Street. Led by Peter Williams's son, Peter Jr., African American
members withdrew from Trinity Church in 1809 to form St.
Philip's Episcopal Church. St. Philip's was formally received
into the Episcopal Diocese of New York in 1818, and in 1820
Peter Williams Jr. was the first African American to be ordained
in the Episcopal Church. Under the leadership of Peter Williams Jr., St. Philip's opened a day school, an evening school,
and a music school. Williams was one of the founders of the
African Association of Mutual Relief in 1808 and the African
Dorcas Association in 1828. He was also a spokesman in
movements against slavery and colonization.[5]

Brooklyn was one of the earliest centers for New York's black churches. In 1814 the first steam ferry began transporting passengers between Manhattan and Brooklyn, making Brooklyn an attractive and accessible city for free blacks. In the early nineteenth century, house churches sprang up to address the spiritual needs of Brooklyn's black population. Many of these house churches evolved into New York's most thriving black congregations: Concord Baptist Church, Siloam Presbyterian Church, and Bridge Street African Wesleyan Methodist Episcopal (A.W.M.E.) Church.

During the antebellum period, black congregations were active agents in the struggle against slavery. Both Bridge Street A.W.M.E. and Concord Baptist became sanctuaries for runaway slaves, while Siloam Presbyterian Church created a fund for the Underground Railroad. Sampson White of Concord and L. C. Speaks of Bridge Street A.W.M.E. were organizing ministers of the Christian Union Convention, formed in 1861, to support the abolitionist cause through fasting, prayer, and political activism.[6] The A.M.E. Zion church was the spiritual home of such abolitionist luminaries as Sojourner Truth, Harriet Tubman, Jermain Louguen, Catherine Harris, Thomas James, and Frederick Douglass. A.M.E. Zion was a center for the Underground Railroad and came to be known as the "Freedom Church."

As African Americans moved into Harlem at the turn of the century, the large "institutional" black churches followed their flocks northward. The Abyssinian Baptist Church and St. Philip's Episcopal Church became two of Harlem's best-known centers of financial stability and social service. After selling its site on West Fortieth to the *New York Times* for $190,000, Abyssinian Baptist moved into a large Gothic structure on West 138th Street in Harlem in 1916. By 1965 Abyssinian Baptist Church, with a membership of fourteen thousand, was the largest Protestant church in the United States. Abyssinian's outreach programs—the Benevolent Daughters of Esther, the Highways and Hedges Society, and its Vocational Training School—became models of urban evangelism and social concern.

By the time St. Philip's Episcopal Church moved to Harlem in 1911, St. Philip's was reputed to be the most exclusive black church in New York City and the wealthiest black church in the country. The move to Harlem boosted St. Philip's resources considerably. In 1909 the church sold its building on West Twenty-fifth Street for $140,000; the adjoining cemetery was sold two years later for $450,000. The pastor of St. Philip's, the Reverend Dr. Hutchens C. Bishop, bought dozens of houses and land in Harlem in his name from 1906 to 1910, including a site for a new church. Because landlords were committed to keeping the neighborhood white, Bishop, who was light in complexion, bought the property by subterfuge, that is, by passing as a white man during the transactions. It came as no surprise to Bishop when some of the sellers assured him that they would "never sell property to a Negro."[7] In 1910 Bishop turned all the property over to St. Philip's and prepared to move his congregation to Harlem. In 1911 St. Philip's opened a newly constructed church, designed entirely by African American architects, on 134th Street.

In 1911 the vestry of St. Philip's decided to take advantage of the depressed condition of Harlem real estate and invest the church's capital in Harlem apartment houses. In 1911 St. Philip's bought a row of ten new apartment houses on West 135th Street between Seventh and Lenox Avenues for $640,000. This was the largest single real estate transaction involving African Americans in the history of New York. Before the sale, signs that hung in renting offices of the white realtors on 135th Street read: "The agents promise their tenants that these houses will be rented only to WHITE people." Shortly after the transfer of property to St. Philip's, a new sign was displayed, telling prospective tenants to contact black real estate agents: "For Rent, Apply to Nail and Parker."[8] In addition to being a major player in the development of middle-class housing in Harlem, St. Philip's set the pace in the areas of social and political concern. Bishop was an active member of both the NAACP and the Urban League. Under his leadership, St. Philip's became a center through which programs of these organizations were administered. Men of St. Philip's participated in the Urban League's Big Brother program, and the women of the church gave clothing to the poor through the Dorcas Society. The church also operated a home for the aged and the infirm in the Bronx.[9]

Through the nineteenth and early twentieth centuries, churches were the cultural centers of black New York. Churches offered concerts, lectures, discussions, reading rooms, and literary societies. In Manhattan, the Abyssinian Baptist Church and the African Methodist Episcopal Zion Church took great pride in their musical and literary jubilees, and St. Mark's Methodist Episcopal Church opened a lyceum for African Americans. But the early centers of black cultural life were the churches of Brooklyn rather than Manhattan. By 1860 Bridge Street African Wesleyan Methodist Episcopal Church, Concord Baptist Church, and Siloam Presbyterian Church established the Brooklyn Sabbath School Union whose purpose was to teach literacy as well as religion. In 1859 these three churches together had 36 teachers and 263 students, most of whom were adults. Both Concord and Siloam had libraries, reporting fifty-five and one hundred books, respectively. Toward the end of the century, Siloam, Concord, and St. Augustine's Episcopal had thriving literary societies that sponsored debates, lectures, elocution contests, recitations, musical recitals, and discussion of pertinent issues facing black America.[10] These cultural pursuits were well publicized, and in 1892 the Brooklyn *Eagle* reported that no class of its city's citizens is "fonder of literary pursuits than the Afro-American."[11]

In the twentieth century, dozens of New York's black clergy have been involved in political efforts to address crucial issues facing their parishioners. In 1925 Rev. Thomas Harten of Holy Trinity Baptist Church in Brooklyn became head of the Brooklyn chapter of the National Equal Rights League, and he later organized the Afro-Protective League. Both groups protested lynchings in South Carolina and combated police brutality and racial discrimination in New York City. For twenty years Holy Trinity was a hotbed of political activity. The church hosted numerous protests against police brutality and was a forum where "labor problems, lynching, discrimination, Jim Crowism, and other evils of the present day social system" were discussed and opposed.

Another activist-pastor was Theopholis Joseph Alcantara of the African Orthodox Church. Alcantara was the cochair of the Brooklyn Federation of Better Housing, a community group that fought for the abolition of slums in Bedford-Stuyvesant. When $25 million was set aside by the federal government for slum clearance in New York City, Alcantara lobbied to have some of those funds go to Brooklyn. In the 1940s these efforts resulted in the construction of the Kingsboro Project. In 1959 Rev. Milton Galamison, pastor of Siloam Presbyterian Church, formed the Parents' Workshop for Equality in New York City Schools to fight for school integration. Through the 1960s this group organized citywide boycotts of schools. Throughout New York, black churches opened "freedom schools" to instruct children in math, reading, and black history during the boycotts.

During the 1950s and 1960s Concord Baptist Church in Brooklyn and Abyssinian Baptist Church in Harlem emerged as New York's largest and most influential black churches. In 1948 Gardner Taylor came to New York from Louisiana to pastor the five-thousand-member Concord Baptist Church. In New York, Taylor joined an elite fellowship of ministers. "I don't think ever in the history of these two millennia," Taylor said, "have so many pulpit geniuses come together in one setting as I found in New York in the early 1950s."[12] Michael Dyson describes how Taylor's unique blend of gifts quickly placed him at the forefront of even this great cadre of preachers:

> His mastery of the technical aspects of preaching is remarkable. He brilliantly uses metaphor and has an uncanny sense of rhythmic timing put to dramatic but not crassly theatrical effect. He condenses profound biblical truths into elegantly memorable phrases. . . . His stunning control of narrative flow seamlessly weaves his sermons together. . . . He superbly uses stories to illustrate profound intellectual truths and subtle repetition to unify sermons. . . . What was once alleged of southern Baptist preacher Carlyle Marney may be equally said of Taylor: he has a voice like God's—only deeper.[13]

In 1993 Wyatt Tee Walker introduced Taylor as "the greatest preacher living, dead, or unborn."[14]

During Taylor's forty-two years of service, the membership of Concord Baptist tripled, and Concord built a home for the aged, organized a fully accredited grade school, and developed the Christ Fund, a million-dollar endowment for investing in the Brooklyn community. In addition to his role as pastor and preacher, Taylor entered the political fray in the 1960s. For years, Taylor lobbied to align the National Baptist Convention (N.B.C.) with the political activist movement headed by Martin Luther King. When these efforts failed, Taylor and his supporters left the N.B.C. to form the Progressive National Baptist Convention, which currently has a membership of more than two million.[15]

Adam Clayton Powell Jr. of the Abyssinian Baptist Church in Harlem was a close associate of Gardner Taylor, and he is remembered today as among New York's most influential activist-clergymen. In 1944 Powell was elected to the House of Representatives, and he eventually became the chairman of the House Committee on Education and Labor, making him the most powerful black politician since Reconstruction. In Congress, Powell's legislative contributions paved the way for the rise of the civil rights movement.[16] "Adam . . . with his angry oratory . . . was withering, blazing," Taylor says of Powell. "He was bon vivant."[17]

In addition to the heroes of the civil rights movement, black churches produced countless parishioners who had the energy and faith to take courageous stands against racism and segregation. During the civil rights era, black churches were the major points of mobilization for mass meetings, and black church members housed civil rights workers from SNCC, CORE, and other religious and secular groups. Most of the civil rights demonstrators were members of black churches and were acting out of convictions that were religiously inspired. Black church culture permeated the movement for racial integration and civil rights, "from oratory to music, from the rituals and symbols of protest to the ethic of non-violence."[18]

For about fifty years, Pentecostal churches have played a significant, albeit apolitical, role in the lives of black New Yorkers. By the 1930s dozens of storefront Pentecostal churches had sprung up in Brooklyn and Harlem to serve as alternatives to "mainline" black churches. According to Allen Spear, these churches were especially attractive to black migrants from the South: "The migration brought into the city thousands of Negroes accustomed to the informal, demonstrative, preacher-oriented churches of the rural South. Alienated by the formality of the middle-class churches, many of the newcomers organized small congregations that met in stores and houses and that maintained the old-time shouting religion."[19]

In *Black Churches of Brooklyn*, Clarence Taylor describes how the intimate fellowships that Pentecostal churches offered met the social and psychological needs of the working poor. Nettie Kennedy, for example, worked as a domestic servant after moving to Brooklyn from North Carolina. Her Pentecostal church was "like a family," Kennedy said, where newcomers to New York from the South "banded together for worship and social events." Members met on Sunday for services and during the week for prayer meetings, choral rehearsal, and club meetings.[20] The storefront Pentecostal church became the most important institution in the lives of many of New York's marginalized southern blacks. Melvin Williams writes that the Pentecostal church "serves as a place where members take refuge from the world among familiar faces. It is a source of identity and matrix of interaction for the members it recruits. It is a subculture that creates and transmits symbols and enforces standards of belief and behavior."[21] Clarence Taylor describes the process in which Pentecostal churches have been agents of social mobility among poor New Yorkers:

> Holiness-Pentecostals developed an appreciation for hard work, a desire for economic independence, and a respect for ownership. This in turn created a culture that helped black Holiness-Pentecostals to adjust to the demands of larger society and to avoid becoming members of a socioeconomic underclass increasingly identified by its involvement in violent crime and a cycle of unwed pregnancies and welfare dependency.[22]

Unlike their mainline counterparts, Pentecostal churches have generally focused on individual salvation rather than on political activism. For members of Pentecostal congregations, social mobility was to be secured through moral living and hard work rather than through challenges to the dominant system. Clarence Taylor explains:

> With the exception of a few Church of God in Christ institutions, black Holiness-Pentecostal ministers were not politically active or involved in the social issues of the community. They usually did not back candidates for political office, use

their churches for political rallies, participate in demonstra-
tions . . . or run for public office.[23]

During the 1950s membership in many Pentecostal churches
increased dramatically, making them among the largest
churches in New York. Congregations that had begun meeting
in storefronts or tents grew to the point that they needed to
purchase schools and theaters to accommodate new members.
Today, churches like Bethel Gospel Assembly in Harlem, Elim
International Fellowship in Bedford-Stuyvesant, the Christian
Life Center in Brownsville, and Bethel Gospel Tabernacle in
Queens have thousands of members and dozens of programs
that serve their neighborhoods. And the influence of black
Pentecostalism has spread far beyond the confines of black
Pentecostal churches. Lawrence Mamiya describes how contact with Pentecostalism has enriched the black mainline:
"Among black denominations, it was the [Pentecostal] Church
of God in Christ that upheld the banner of the Holy Spirit, while
others had let it slip." Church of God in Christ members believe
that accepting Jesus as one's personal Savior is not enough; a
person needs "the baptism of the Holy Spirit," which is evi-
denced by such gifts of the Spirit as speaking in tongues.[24]

While the theology of a second blessing is debated among
African American clergy, many black pastors are grateful to the
Pentecostal movement for bringing to their attention deficien-
cies in their theology and worship. Rev. John Bryant of the
A.M.E. Church, for example, admits that his own denomination
had emphasized the Father and the Son of the Trinity and had
largely neglected the Holy Spirit. "I also maintain," Bryant said,
"that the A.M.E. Church made its greatest strides when it was
not ashamed of its feelings. In trying to be accepted by the white
world and trying to be sophisticated, [we] threw them out."
Bryant attributes the remarkable growth in his own A.M.E.
congregations to balance between "worship praise and the Holy
Spirit" and active involvement in the transformation of his
community. This combination, says Bryant, is biblical because
"Jesus fed the fold. He delivered folk. And he led them in
prayer."[25]

Despite the enormous variety in African American
congregations, black churches share a common core culture

that has enabled African Americans to feel affirmed and safe in a dangerous and discriminatory world. Energized and imaginative worship and preaching are the marks of this core culture. Robert Franklin describes black worship as "a full sensory experience":

> The sacred drama and motion of call-response preaching and colorful choir robes are seen; the rhythmic power of choirs, drums, tambourines, horns, and electric keyboards is heard, the wafting aromas of Sunday dinner being prepared in the church kitchen are often taken in; touching, hugs, and holy kisses are exchanged; and one's inner core is deeply satisfied to know that in this crowd of loving people, one is in the safest place on earth.[26]

The black church has also set high standards for excellence in preaching. Franklin describes the strength of black preaching in terms of the "anointing of the Holy Spirit," the "virtuosity of imaginative, lyrical and poetic language," and "co-creativity with a responsive congregation":

> Black people expect the sermon, as a word inspired by God and located within the community, to be spiritually profound, politically relevant, socially prophetic, artistically polished and reverentially delivered.... Many white preachers express some envy, and not a little intimidation, at the prospect of such congregational investment in, and quality control over, their weekly proclamations.[27]

Melvin Williams has said that the black church "allocates social status, differentiates roles, resolves conflicts, gives meaning, order, and style to its members' lives, and provides for social mobility and social rewards within its confines."[28]

4

Booming Churches in Burned-out Districts

Christians in New York

Tony Carnes

In 1957 Billy Graham warily approached New York for his Madison Square Garden crusade. "We face the city," he said, "with fear and trembling. I'm prepared to go to New York to be crucified by my critics, if necessary."[1] Twenty-five years later, in 1991, a turning point in the church's visibility and role in New York City was reached in another Billy Graham crusade, this time in Central Park, with the largest religious gathering in New York City history, according to the *Daily News*. This highly symbolic punctuation mark in New York City's religious history was followed in 1993 by the ousting of public schools chancellor Jose Fernandez by a coalition of Catholics, Jews, and

Tony Carnes is the director of Seminar on Contents and Methods in the Social Sciences, Columbia University, and president of International Research Institute on Values Changes (IRIVC).

ethnic evangelicals who were upset over his pro-gay "I Have Two Daddies, I Have Two Mommies" curriculum.

In 1957, looking out over the city with Calvary Baptist pastor Stephen Olford from the top floor of the New Yorker Hotel, Graham broke down in convulsive weeping over the city's apparent hardness to the gospel message. Today God's good news is echoing in ghetto, barrio, and boardroom.

New York City is a big, brawling city divided into turfs, ethnic and class strongholds, and myriad networks, all saturated with an anonymity of the mass of individuals. The church received a severe battering from migrations, fiscal poverty, social problems, scandals, mistakes, and secularization.

However, starting in the 1980s New York City and its church started to change. Fiscal bankruptcy, unemployment, and demographic flights were replaced with budget surpluses, job growth, and one of the most massive immigrations in New York City's history. Most important, the Spirit has raised up an increasing number of believers who are founding churches and institutions at a rapid pace.

Walking down Church Street in Brooklyn, one may run into four African American churches per block! In Chinatown there is one street on which there is a church on every block. Every six weeks a new church is founded in the Hunts Point–Morris Park area of the Bronx. Young professional churches like Redeemer Presbyterian in Manhattan have grown as the number of financial service jobs has increased.

As one of the two major *entrepôts* for immigration (the other is Los Angeles), New York was the only major northern industrial city to actually gain population and jobs between 1980 and 1990. In 1995 New York City's estimated population was 7,312,076. The New York metropolitan area is still the largest in the United States (19.7 million versus 15 million for the Los Angeles metropolitan area).[2] The ethnic diversity in the city has become the highest in the world (with people from more than 150 countries with hundreds of subgroups, according to the U.S. Census).

"More and more, what happens to this city is hooked into the foreign born," says Joseph J. Salvo, director of population studies at the city's Department of City Planning. City schools

Religious New Yorkers

- 82% say religion is very or fairly important to their lives (Dec. 1991 Gallup Survey for *N.Y. Newsday*).
- 90% identify with a religious group and believe in God (Dec. 1991 Gallup Survey for *N.Y. Newsday*).
- 46% attend church once per month or more (*New York Times*/CBS TV-2 Survey, May 10–14, 1994).
- 66% believe that New Yorkers are paying less attention to moral and religious questions than 10 years ago (The Empire State Survey, May 16–June 8, 1992).
- 26% Manhattanites regularly attend religious services compared to 37–43% for people of other boroughs (1995 *New Yorker* New York Poll).

---

are receiving about 20,000 additional students per year. In 1994, 141,235 foreign-born immigrants to New York City applied for citizenship, almost 12,000 per month.

A cultural consequence for the church is that there is a wider-than-ever divide between a New York City international urban core and the suburbs, which continue to be mostly white and native born. From the Pahwah parade of the Guyanese community of Richmond Hill, Queens, to the liturgical beat of the Royal Order of Seraphim and Cherubim Church's Nigerian drums, the Christians of New York City display a renewed international style that may seem foreign to outsiders.

Other cultural impacts of the new immigrants are also surprising to some people. For example, with the immigrants the city is becoming more Christian and law-abiding. Also, many immigrants have conservative inclinations. Politically, West Indian evangelicals are conservative on many issues though often voting Democratic. Dominican Christians vote Democratic, but 10 to 20 percent swing Republican. More than half of the Christian voters of Colombian and Ecuadorian background supported Republican mayoral candidate Rudolph Giuliani.[3]

Part of the dramatic 50 percent drop in serious crime in New York City could plausibly be related to the growth of the ethnically diverse church. Many new immigrants practice a strong brand of law and order in their homes and lament the loss of "biblical" discipline in the schools. In fact, new immigrants believe that Americans spoil their children and are too quick to spare the biblical rod. Emma Henderson, who grew up in Dominica and is now the mother of three, complains, "The first thing a child learns here is, 'If you spank me, I'll call 911.' There's something wrong about that."

Mary C. Waters, a Harvard sociologist who interviewed immigrants and their children in New York City from 1991 to 1993, said corporal punishment was the central issue for them. "When I asked what's different about the United States, they said: 'The state comes between you and your children. Americans don't discipline their children well, and when you do it the *right way*, there's the danger your kids can call social services on you" (my emphasis). George Mathelier, a Haitian immigrant and social worker at Prospect Heights High School in Crown Heights, Brooklyn, observed that Caribbean children "quickly realize the system here is lax and loose and they can get away with murder."[4]

Massive immigration along with a popular multicultural ethic also means that New York City Christian ethnic identification is extremely diverse and only solidifies into the standard "white, black/African American, Hispanic, and Asian" during conflict.[5] Some elites still demand that the church operate with a "political" presumption of racial identities that don't take into account the new fragmentation of identities and a rise of "racelessness" as a social norm among many Christians. Of course, sometimes the political identities need to be activated when the needs and desires of one group are ignored. Indeed, in the Book of Acts we are told that the diaconate originated as a way of dealing with the touchy political issue of ethnic discrimination within the church.

New York City Christians also face divisions within the church between rich and poor and between youth and adults. How they handle those divisions will determine how well they live up to the standards of Christ and grow as vibrant, unified churches. The various housing and community development programs like Concord Baptist Church's Federal Credit Union, the Allen A.M.E. Neighborhood Preservation and Development Corporation, and South Bronx Churches' Nehemiah Homes

**Degree of Interaction Between Evangelical Pastors
(IRIVC surveys)**

	NYC–N.J. (1996)	Syracuse, N.Y.
(May 1995) **Within the last year I have more than 10 times:**		
Visited a church other than my own.	41%	15%
Visited a church with an ethnicity that is mostly different from my own.	32%	2%
Had a personal meal with a pastor of an ethnicity that is different from my own.	27%	4%

help bridge the gap between rich and poor. Many churches are also wrestling with how to bridge the gap between youth and adults.

Though the church is divided by ethnicity, class, age, and location, New York City churches interact with one another at a far higher level than churches in suburban areas. A comparison of two surveys of evangelical pastors indicates that New York City churches are forging a unity that could become the standard for the American church as a whole. New York City area pastors are six times more likely than suburban pastors to sit at their dining room table with pastors of different ethnicities. Diverse and conflictual, New York City seems to be a crucible for forging unity in the church. The four largest groups of New York City Christians are Catholics, evangelicals, African Americans, and Hispanics.

NEW YORK CITY CATHOLICS

Hardly a week goes by without a news story about life in New York using the words or actions of John Cardinal O'Connor as a punctuation mark. Since the mid-nineteenth century, Roman Catholicism has been the largest denomination in the city.

According to the 1990 National Survey of Religious Identification (1990 NSRI), 43 percent of New Yorkers identified themselves as Roman Catholics. Parochial schools educate over 170,000 children in the city and adjoining counties of New York State.[6]

Although the Catholic Church in New York seems to be ineradicably identified with Irish and Italians, the majority of the church in the New York archdiocese, which covers Manhattan, Staten Island, and the Bronx (the diocese of Brooklyn includes Queens) is Latin American. Seven percent of Catholics in New York State are black.

Every Good Friday the people of the Church of the Incarnation in Queens Village pilgrimage around the neighborhood with leaders proclaiming the gospel in Spanish, English, and French. Once primarily an Irish parish, the people there have learned to live with one another other. Parishioner Hermina Jaramilo observes that Catholic parish life has changed both in diversity and tolerance: "The faces and the language have changed but not the Word."

Over 70 percent of New Yorkers of Irish, Italian, and Polish backgrounds identified themselves as Catholic in the 1990 National Survey of Religious Identification. Historically, New Yorkers of German background have also been heavily Catholic.

An Irish priest in the church working hand in hand with an Irish cop on the beat is a staple of New York mythology. Indeed, the hierarchies are still heavily Irish. Since the 1870s, every bishop of New York has been Irish. And the St. Patrick's Day parade every March 17 remains a powerful symbol of Irish Catholic cultural and organizational presence in the city (although the parade was actually led by Irish Protestants in its beginning years).

Italian Catholics have succeeded the Irish in government (for example, Mayor Giuliani and Senator D'Amato) but have had lower attendance and organizational loyalty to the Catholic Church. Italian immigrants felt distant from the Irish-American dominated church and stayed away in droves. In 1917 an Irish priest reciprocated the feeling, claiming "the Italians are not a sensitive people like our own. When they are told that they are about the worst Catholics that ever came to this country, they

Profile of New York City Christians

- The churches are growing.
- About 75% of New Yorkers say they are Christians.
    - 43% say they are Catholic.
    - 31% say they are Protestant (11% Baptist, 3% Methodist, 2% Episcopal, 1% Presbyterian).
- 19–25% of New Yorkers are evangelicals.
    - 12–17% Protestant evangelicals
    - 7–8% Catholic evangelicals
- Half of Asian immigrants to NYC are Christians.
- The most rapidly growing institution among NYC Hispanics— the church!
- African American evangelical churches are ready for leadership.
- Several key churches have attracted young urban professionals.
- A critical need for the churches to unite and to enter the public square.
- Other religions: 11% Jewish, 1.9% Eastern, alternative, or Unitarian religions, 1.5% Muslim, 1% Jehovah's Witness, .2% Mormon, 7.4% no religion/agnostic.

Source: CUNY 1990 National Survey of Religious Identification (NRSI) and IRIVC.

---

don't resent it or deny it."[7] Quite a few evangelical leaders (Daniel Mercaldo of Gateway Cathedral and radio executive Joseph Battaglia and others) have come out of Catholic heritages.

Although Catholic white ethnics have been moving out of the city, causing the closing of many churches and schools, the vast immigration to New York has revitalized many congregations. Ruth Doyle, director of research for the archdiocese of New York, says, "One of the great untold stories of the Catholic Church in New York City is the filling up of the parishes with new immigrant liveliness." Every week Mass is now celebrated in more than two dozen languages. Recently, new nationality parishes were opened for Arabs, Portuguese, Koreans, and Albanians, to name a few.

By the 1940s a number of African Americans in New York were converting to Roman Catholicism. Using a then-current baseball allusion, priests and nuns called their conversion campaign working in "the Negro league." Black New Yorkers have been most impressed with Catholic education. In Harlem, for example, 75 percent of the students in Catholic schools are black Protestants. In Brooklyn and Queens the number of Haitians and Trinidadians has significantly expanded the ranks of black Catholics.

In the United States and probably in New York as well, 66 percent of Hispanics are Catholics. However, there is a changing preference of Hispanics for evangelical and Pentecostal/charismatic Protestantism.[8] In 1990 Puerto Rican and Latin American high school students had a significantly lower preference (52 to 54 percent) for Catholicism than their parents' generation and proportionally more preference for Protestantism.[9]

The defections are set up by low religious practice rates by Hispanic Catholics (23 percent nationally) and a scarcity of Hispanic priests (4 percent nationally).[10] The "explosion of Protestantism" in Latin America also pre-evangelizes many Hispanics before they arrive in New York City, and immigration leaves them looking for new attachments. David Martin says that the evangelical stress on intimacy, running their own churches, and having a good work ethic appeals to upwardly mobile Hispanics.[11] One doesn't have to be in a Spanish-speaking evangelical church long before being approached to be involved in the spiritual life of the church by its leader—who is often soon followed by earnest Amway distributors telling how to better one's income.

EVANGELICALS

One of the most significant changes in New York City life is the rise of evangelicals. In the late 1970s and early 1980s the predominately white evangelical churches that had been providing leadership for city evangelicals were weak and shrinking. The growth of Hispanic and Asian churches was relatively unnoticed. The changes in the national immigration laws in the 1970s were just beginning to impact the churches.

Like any categorization, *evangelical* is a term that has fuzzy boundaries in real life and may not be used as a self-identifier by some theologically conservative churches. The term *evangelical* does, however, capture the reality of a common doctrinal and social unity between New York City churches that in practice has significant impact on church cooperation and identities. Also, American evangelicals have created several religious movements that have become crucial "change agents" in society. The most well-known of these movements alive today are fundamentalism, holiness-Pentecostalism, the charismatic movement, and evangelicalism.

Historically, sociologists James Guth and Corwin Smidt say, four doctrines have defined evangelicals: (1) belief that salvation comes only through faith in Jesus Christ; (2) experience of conversion, or being "born again"; (3) belief that it is necessary to spread the gospel through missions and evangelism; and (4) belief in the truth, or inerrancy, of Scripture.[12]

In the absence of a detailed religious census, the number of evangelicals in New York City can be only indirectly inferred from various surveys. First, we should note that about 7 percent of New Yorkers (over 488,000 people) may be classified as Roman Catholic evangelicals according to belief in the four essential evangelical doctrines listed by Guth and Smidt.[13] Additionally, recent Catholic immigrants from Asia, Africa, and the Caribbean (particularly Trinidad and Haiti) are even more likely to be evangelical, increasing the percent of evangelical Catholics in the city.

Second, national surveys have found that about 40 percent of U.S. Protestants have evangelical beliefs. Since 31 percent of New Yorkers say that they are Protestant (1990 NSRI), this might mean that about 12 percent of New Yorkers are evangelical Protestants.

This figure is certainly too low, however, because New York Protestants are more likely to belong to ethnic groups like African Americans, Asians, and Hispanics that are significantly more evangelical than white Americans. For example, most surveys find that African American Protestants are much more likely to affirm evangelical beliefs. African Americans are more than twice as likely as white Americans to believe in a literal reading of the Bible and to believe that the only hope for salvation is through personal faith in Jesus Christ.[14]

Adjusting for other ethnic effects,[15] we estimate that as many

Percent of Evangelicals in NYC Adjusted for Ethnicity

	1996 U.S. Census Population	New York Times/ CBS-TV 2 survey May 10-14, 1993 Ethnicity of Protestants	Percent Protestant of NYC population	Percent Evangelical of NYC population
White	39	10	3.9	1.6
Black	26	59	15	9
Hispanic	27	15	4	2.9
Asian	9	— [50%]	4.5	3
Total			27	16.5

as 18 percent of New Yorkers are evangelical Protestants and that 25 percent of New Yorkers are evangelicals of all types (Protestant and Catholic). With these numbers, evangelical community action to battle corruption and to help the needy can have real impact. Already politicians like Mayor Giuliani have begun to notice, appointing evangelicals like Baptist pastor Michel Faulkner to the commission planning the city government's reorganization. The mayor observes, "Evangelicals are playing a greater and greater role in New York City and its politics."[16]

Evangelicals are united by their high commitment to biblical doctrines. Between 1994 and 1998 New York City evangelicals consistently have rated doctrinal integrity as one of their highest concerns.[17] In contrast James Hunter reported in his *Evangelicalism: The Coming Generation,* that Christian colleges and seminaries are turning out a new generation of leaders who are significantly more liberal in theology and lifestyle than previous generations of evangelical leaders. These leaders may not be theologically compatible with contemporary urban evangelicals.

However, New York City evangelicals are also as ethnically and denominationally diverse as one could possibly imagine. As a local TV program says, they are "in the mix." In recent surveys New York City evangelicals offered 86 ethnic identifications and 55 denominational ones. This diversity often extends all the way down to the family, which can be like a patchwork quilt in the making. Take Caroline Miranda, who directs the daily work of Operation Exodus, an educational ministry for Hispanics. Her parents are from El Salvador and Colombia, her church is mainly Puerto Rican, her mentor a Cuban, and her ministry mainly to Dominicans. In the mix!

Churches also have to cope with the mix. Redeemer Presbyterian Church pastor Tim Keller doesn't push denominationalism. He believes that today younger people are not as denominationally orientated, and his members come out of many different types of churches. Redeemer itself has pastors originally from three different denominational backgrounds.

The overall trend among New York City evangelicals has been toward the charismatic/Pentecostal denominations. About 27 percent of New York City evangelicals identify their denomination as charismatic/Pentecostal, 25 percent Baptist, 5 percent Presbyterian/Reformed, 5 percent nondenominational, 4 percent Methodist, and 3 percent Christian Missionary Alliance.[18]

New York City evangelicals' household income averages $29,000. This is pretty low and emphasizes the financial challenges of living in the city. Probably 8 to 12 percent of the evangelicals are below the poverty line. The low average income level is also an ominous figure because the lower one's income is in New York City the more discontented one usually is with living in the city.[19] Faced with lower incomes, crime, high taxes, and poor schools, many younger evangelicals dream of leaving the city for the suburbs. Carmen, a young evangelical Hispanic recently graduated from college, is all too typical. "Why do I want to stay in the city?" she says. "My neighborhood is ugly, and you are scared for your life." A large youthful exodus from the city would damage the future of the churches. Thus, building financially viable communities in New York City is also a church concern.

AFRICAN AMERICAN CHRISTIANS

African American Christians are one of the most important groups in New York City. Even in the poorest, most chaotic neighborhoods, church leaders and lay members man their outposts of faith, hope, and charity. Sometimes they are beaten, robbed, or killed. In his examination of the social sinews of trust, Francis Fukuyama reminded his readers that it "would be a mistake to portray poor African Americans as uniformly isolated and atomized individuals. . . . Black churches and religious groups . . . have provided an important counterweight to the atomizing forces to which the community was subject."[20]

The leaders of New York City African American Christians are the best educated and most committed to community building that their churches have ever had. In the 1930s only a small minority of New York City African American church leaders had even some college training.[21] By 1996, 44 percent had completed at least four years of college. Their community involvements range from running church-based lending institutions to labor unions to prolife counseling centers.

Rev. Richard Lewis's combination of gospel presentation with community involvement is not untypical of African American church leaders. When "on the job" as New York City's most decorated police officer, Rev. Lewis preached the gospel. Now, as a pastor of Freedom House Church of God, he is bringing the church back into the community to work with youth gangs. When the drug dealers in Red Hook district of Brooklyn see Rev. Lewis coming, they shout, "Preacher Cop is coming!" WNBC News's Ben Farnsworth says, "While Lewis opposed godlessness in the streets, he witnessed the gospel. An ordained minister, . . . Richard is the brightest, bluest and bravest of those who carry the badge."[22]

As a whole, however, African Americans in northern central cities like New York have the lowest "churched" rates (28.4 percent) of African Americans in different regions of the country.[23] In comparison the national average in 1987 for the "churched" African American population was 78 percent.[24] Perhaps rough times for the African American churches burned out the nominal Christians, leaving only the deeply committed. Indeed, William Turner, director of Black Church Affairs at Duke University Divinity School, observes the high national "churched" rate covers "a meaningless religiosity" in many churches.[25] There is some anecdotal evidence that since the 1980s the New York City African American Christian community has been recovering its strength due to deeper community and spiritual commitments.

Key Findings on African American Church Leaders
- the rise of a new, more evangelical church leadership
- a deepening split between liberals and evangelicals
- rising educational achievement
- a new politically moderate to conservative majority
- a holistic perspective on ministry
- civil rights minded within a racially neutral framework
- deep lingering distrust of others

The African American church has deep roots, going back to the Puritan movement and the founding the United States. The earliest recorded account of African Americans organizing for religious purposes was Cotton Mather's effort to draw up "Rules for the Society of Negroes" in 1693.[26] The first independent African American denominations arose primarily out of northeastern cities of Philadelphia, New York City, and Baltimore. A group of African American members of New York City's John Street Methodist Episcopal Church started an African chapel in 1796 amid rising tensions with and discrimination from the white members. The African Methodist Episcopal Church began in 1816 in Philadelphia, while the African Methodist Episcopal Zion Church began in 1822 in New York City.[27]

New York City churches now include some of the most well-known African American churches in the United States. With 10,000 members, Concord Baptist Church of Brooklyn, pastored by Rev. Gary Simpson, is one of the largest African American churches in the United States. In 1994 Church of God in Christ (COGIC) bishop Ithiel Clemmons of New York became the first head of the new united interracial Pentecostal/charismatic fellowship, the Pentecostal Churches of North America.

Two Types of Churches

New York City African American churches are divided over whether their theology is institutionally centered or biblically centered. This is not an easy concept for outsiders to grasp, for the doctrinal words are often the same. The difference is that some African American churches affirm their doctrines because to do so is to affirm loyalty to their church and its traditional role in the African American community. They are "churchcentric" institutions. Other African American churches are more bibliocentric in that their primary identity is to be Bible-centered. In the first type of church the church is the downtown of life while the Bible is in the suburbs. In the second type the Bible is the downtown of life. In the first type of church traditional stories enchant while in the second type a God-given History rules and instructs.

For a long time African Americans had no other choice but to make the church their primary social institution. It became the place where everyone in the African American community could gather, talk, educate, and govern themselves. The preacher role was the most important and accessible leadership role available for African Americans. This was both a blessing and curse for the church. The blessing was the forced involvement of the church in all aspects of life. An early twentieth-century African American sociologist concluded that the church "embraces all the complex functions of Negro life."[28] The curse was that the church was an unholy conglomerate of the faithful and the merely social, of both Mosés-like leaders and institution builders.

For many African Americans, their childhood churches were more like neighborhoods or friendships that one loved but left behind as one moved away geographically, educationally, and socially. Journalist Beverly Hall Lawrence observes about her leaving the church, "It is not unlike what happens to some friendships that fade when one moves away."[29] As a child she had never thought about not being baptized—"To have not done so showed either orneriness or—something I didn't even think about—an *opinion* about religious expression."[30]

Ironically, African American church-centered institutions may find it easier to cooperate, overlooking theological, stylistic, or cultural differences, because the salient factor is whether the church is the honored part of the cooperation. Bibliocentric African American churches are much more cautious—overcautious, some say—to avoid worldly contamination and giving out an endorsement to what they consider as "too social" or "too political" churches. However, bibliocentric

NYC African American Church Leaders'
Views of the Bible, 1997

An ancient book of legends, history and moral precepts	3%
A useful resource for teaching about the meaning of life and morality	11%
Authoritative in its teachings about the meaning of life and morality	26%
Without error in its teachings about the meaning of life and morality but makes some mistakes in its historical and scientific reporting	3%
Without error in its teachings about the meaning of life and morality but culturally accommodates in its historical and scientific reporting	4%
Without error in its teachings about the meaning of life and morality and in its historical and scientific reporting	45%

churches are pressured by their beliefs to cooperate to some extent with other bibliocentric peoples.

According to a 1997 International Research Institute on Values Changes/New York Theological Seminary survey, African American church leaders in New York City almost equally bifurcate in their views of the Bible between conservative and liberal views.[31] This is a breathtaking divide and totally unexpected. In the future we will see mainline and evangelical–charismatic/Pentecostal churches headed by African Americans. What will this bifurcation mean for the African American community and the various denominations?

New York City church leaders prefer the label "Pentecostal-charismatic" (30 percent) over "evangelical-fundamentalist" (26 percent). Nationally, African American church leaders are more likely to prefer "evangelical-fundamentalist" (33 percent) over "Pentecostal-charismatic" (29 percent). In New York City even fewer (2 percent) identify themselves as liberal or neo-orthodox than do their counterparts nationwide (4 percent).

A breakdown of theological preference by age reveals a strong preference on the part of younger church leaders for the "charismatic-Pentecostal" label; almost half of the leaders in their twenties and thirties identify themselves as such. Much of this appeal comes at the expense of the "evangelical-fundamentalist" label,

**Denominational Profile of NYC African American
Church Leaders, 1997**

Church Denomination	Percent
Baptist	35
Pentecostal denominations	17
Presbyterian	6
Methodist	4
Episcopalian	1
Lutheran	.4
Other Protestants	14
Catholic	<1
Other Religion	1

to which nearly 40 percent of leaders in their fifties adhere while a minuscule 3 percent in their twenties do. The clear implication is that the charismatic message has been much more successful in reaching younger generations of African Americans.

Heterogeneity of denominational affiliation significantly marks New York City African American church leaders, who listed 42 different denominational affiliations for their home churches. Thirty-five percent of New York City African American church leaders in the 1997 IRIVC/New York Theological Seminary survey made some sort of Baptist affiliation.

Community Interests

New York City African American church leaders have a strikingly large interest in helping the poor. The church has always been a community and economic center, providing the help and values that keep one's soul together and a roof over the head. The great turn-of-the-century African American leader Booker T. Washington taught that one cannot go "up from slavery" without developing the inner resources of Christian discipline and character. Without the inner values, he warned, the black race would fall from slavery into poverty and, worse, into degradation of character and dependency. The African American community, he said, needed to move from an ethic of survival to an ethic of development.

The church leaders also have a very high interest in protecting

**NYC African American Church Leaders Rate the
Importance of Christian Active Involvement in
Social Problems, 1997**

	Most/very	Some	Little
Helping the poor in America's cities and towns	82%	5%	0%
Helping the poor around the world	74	12	1
Protecting the rights of minorities	73	12	2
Abortion issues	65	16	6
Environmental issues	56	26	7
Work for lower taxes	39	28	19

the rights of minorities. The high interest in helping the poor probably goes along with this historically founded emphasis on protecting the rights of minorities. New York City voters in general favor (71 percent) "the government helping minorities" at a higher rate than any other area of the country.[32]

New Yorkers of other ethnicities sometimes cannot fathom an African American clergyman like Rev. Al Sharpton. In fact, New York City African American church leaders are divided about Rev. Sharpton, an activist pastor known for his angry confrontational style. Rather, they are much more inclined to a moderate interracial approach.

Tolerance of racialist community activists in the black church as its roots in the racial anxiety that African Americans could become a target of racial prejudice and discrimination. Trust has been a casualty of racial discriminations, prejudices, and memories of such. The African American churches were founded, in the words of the legendary AME Zion bishop James W. Wood, as the product of "a grand united Negro movement. It was a race oppressed, it was a race that moved . . . to find its own organization, that religious liberty which was denied it in the white church."[33] As New York Theological Seminary Dean Trulear observed, "Thus, the Black church was important not only as a religious institution but also as a race institution." Black preaching resonates with a "response to the underlying Black experience in America, past and present."[34]

Yet without trust a society cannot endure or grow deep and rich in its culture. While power or economics may bind a society together like wires twisted around staves, trust acts as an inner glue that gives a deep inner bonding that mere coercion or economic reward and punishment can seldom give. This poses a challenge to the African American church. Surveys indicate that the New York City African American pastor is more likely to trust a drug addict than an owner of a big corporation. Although 20 percent of African American mayoral voters cast their lot with Rudolph Giuliani and African American church leaders are trending toward moderate politics, only 5 percent of African American pastors in New York would trust the mayor's word. An astounding 56 percent have little or no trust in the word of their mayor.[35] The high level of distrust among African American Christians and their leaders can undermine community trust. In the past this distrust has hampered united evangelistic and community building efforts.

The Christian commitment of many African American church leaders spurs them on to bridge the gaps in New York City. As one pastor observed, "Skin color is no great difference in relating the messages of Jesus. There is no black church but God's church." Most African Americans in New York seem to have followed the healers' examples. In *The Closest of Strangers,* Jim Sleeper has observed that black New Yorkers favor candidates who promise to promote racial harmony, not division. Black racialist candidates can't win even in black voting districts against white candidates.

It is absolutely crucial to New York City that its peoples reciprocate this example on the road of forgiveness and renewed trust. Francis Fukuyama has observed that a society's "well-being, as well as its ability to compete, is conditioned by a single, pervasive cultural characteristic: the level of trust inherent in the society."[36]

HISPANIC CHRISTIANS

Hispanic Christians are taking serious strides to expand their leadership role in the greater New York City church and community. Their churches have grown so rapidly that their leaders have been running just to keep up with caring for the local congregations. Lately New York City Hispanic Christians have been working with leaders from other ethnic communities to promote education and community development.

A great wave of Hispanics into New York City is currently taking place. A 1994 Census survey revealed that about 27 percent of New Yorkers are Hispanic.[37] In 1970 barely one in five Hispanics in the United States was foreign-born. Today more than one in three is foreign-born; among adult Hispanics one in two was born outside the United States. In New York City the most important sources of immigration were, historically, Puerto Rico, Dominican Republic, Cuba, and Mexico. Increasingly, Central and South Americans have also become important sources of Hispanic immigration.

Despite romantic notoriety in *West Side Story* and *The Cross and the Switchblade,* New York City Hispanics have been called the invisible minority, largely because of language and social barriers, low participation in elections, and an orientation, particularly for Puerto Ricans, back to the home country. Often the older generations have had the mentality of "birds of passage," earning money today for the dream of the nice house and farm in Puerto Rico.

Younger Hispanic Christians also often have dreams of moving out of the city to American suburbs. In fact, Hispanics are buying homes and moving away from New York.[38] Also, a survey of Dominican garment factory owners found that most of them want to move their factories out of New York City, mostly preferring New Jersey. And about one-third of all U.S.-born Hispanics under age thirty-five are marrying non-Hispanics.[39]

The desire to move could siphon leaders and members away from the city's Hispanic churches. As George Barna puts it, a "lack of longevity touches the Church as well. . . . Building a community of faith is by nature a long-term proposition. Without stability it is difficult to invest in future-orientated outcomes and partnerships."[40]

Thirty years ago in the heavily Hispanic Williamsburg section of Brooklyn, there was one Presbyterian, one Pentecostal, and one Catholic church. Now, within a ten-minute walk of one another, there are over thirty churches. Latinos, says Anthony Stevens-Arroyo, "are really looking for the faith experience."

About 66 percent of New York City Hispanics are Catholic, 25 percent Protestant. The trend for over a decade has been toward Protestant and Catholic evangelicalism. "One of the reasons many people are leaving to join evangelical churches," writes Olga Scarpetta, a sociologist at John Jay College of Criminal Justice, "is the lack of community in the Catholic Church. The evangelical churches offer much more community feeling."

Rev. Julio (age forty-three) and Mrs. Leonor (age forty-one) Rodriguez are typical examples of what is happening in this new wave of immigrants to New York City. They came for the American dream and left Catholicism for evangelicalism. Unsettled by immigration, the Rodriguezes looked for a warm, spiritual community for their family. "In 1990 we came from Santiago, Dominican Republic, to make money. That's the American dream," Rev. Rodriguez recalls. Shortly after their arrival, Mrs. Rodriguez met evangelists from the nondenominational charismatic New Life Fellowship. She says, "I was looking for something different from the Catholic Church. The people from New Life had songs and drama for the children."

The immigrant's struggle had also been hard on their marriage. Mrs. Rodriguez thought, "This could be a new beginning for us." It was, and now the Rodriguezes work together to help other new immigrants. Three years ago, Rev. Rodriguez became senior pastor at New Life Fellowship's Latino congregation, *Iglesia Nueva Vida.*

New York City Hispanic Christians have preferred churches with intimacy, opportunity, and intense expression. As a result, they have migrated to Hispanic Protestant churches, which are much more likely than Catholic churches to have a high intensity about their faith. For example, according to a 1991 Gallup/*New York Newsday* survey, 79 percent of "non-Catholic" Hispanics said that religion is "very important" in their lives compared to only 60 percent of Hispanic Catholics. In particular, charismatic/Pentecostal and Baptist congregations have been growing fastest. In 1995 the majority of Hispanic Protestant Bible institute students in New York City identified themselves as charismatic/Pentecostal, part of *la iglesia caliente* (the hot, spicy church). (It would appear that the Baptists have fallen behind the charismatic/Pentecostals in New York City.)

Although two-thirds of Protestant Hispanics have leadership positions in their churches, their leadership potential is not yet fully developed. Hispanic pastors still find that their lay leaders depend too much on pastoral direction. One prominent Hispanic pastor recounts the blank response of his elders when he asked them for their strategic policy ideas for the church. One elder responded, "Pastor, just tell us what to do. We support you!"

A serious issue for Hispanic churches in New York City is the dropout rate of younger, more educated members. Part of the solution may be to decrease the amount of time lay leaders spend in church-wide meetings while continuing and deepening their involvement in separate fellowship or cell groups. Increased emphasis on fellowship groups and the like would encourage Hispanic lay leader initiative and creativity. Some churches have successfully used less legalism and empowered English-speaking congregations. "Yet, there is still a lack of understanding of how to reach out to second-generation Hispanics," cautions Manny Ortiz, New York City–born Puerto Rican professor at Westminster Theological Seminary.

Over 40 percent of Hispanics in New York are of Puerto Rican background. After the passage of the Jones Act in 1917, all Puerto Ricans became U.S. citizens. However, citizenship for many Puerto Ricans didn't take on real meaning until World War II, in which many served with great valor. Hispanics as a whole earned more Congressional Medals of Honor per capita than any other group. This generation thought they should be fully integrated into American society and fought for it through groups like the American G.I. Forum.

In 1949 Puerto Rico elected its first governor, Luis Muñoz Martin. However, a militant independence movement also arose, which in 1950 attempted to assassinate President Harry Truman and in 1954 gunned down and wounded five members of the U.S. Congress. The independence fervor also affected the New York City Puerto Rican churches and Bible institutes. In 1957 a substantial part of the Assembly of God Puerto Rican churches declared their independence, taking the Hispanic

Disturbing Trends in the Puerto Rican Community*
- 39% female-headed family
- 53% out-of-wedlock children
- % of men in workforce lowest of all groups
- % of welfare highest in NYC
- 12 years of education average

*Bureau of the Census, *The Hispanic Population in the U.S.: March 1988,* Current Population Reports, p. 20, no. 438 (Washington: GPO, 1989).

---

mother church in New York City and its Bible institute with them to form a new denomination.

The first large wave of Puerto Rican immigrants, sometimes called the "Pioneers," arrived in New York City in the 1920s. The great migration of Puerto Ricans, the legendary "La Migracín," came in the 1940s and 1950s. In the 1950s Puerto Ricans bought homes and established churches. Some blocks were totally bought up and remain even today as oases of order and family, a village life transported to the city. Many of the significant New York City Hispanic churches like Bay Ridge Christian Center emerged from storefront churches into settled congregations.

Unfortunately, Puerto Ricans, particularly women, also came into the economic niche of the garment industry just as it was shrinking. Overall, in the 1950s and '60s the city lost nearly 40 percent of its manufacturing jobs. But fatefully, Puerto Rican families chose to stay in the city and many ended up on welfare. By the 1960s 50 percent of all Puerto Rican families were already receiving some form of public assistance.[41]

As L. H. Gann and Peter Duignan observed in their *The Hispanics in the U.S.,* Puerto Ricans were "the first immigrant group who unwittingly moved into what became . . . a welfare economy with a powerful and intrusive bureaucracy, a high level of public expenditure, and a strong commitment to social planning."[42]

The state of the Puerto Rican family has immense impact on the churches. Among Puerto Ricans, where the family is strong and intact, achievement is high. Intact families provide the

Impact of Family on Puerto Rican Vocational/Educational Achievements

	Puerto Rican Children of Intact Families	Puerto Ricans in General
Completed college	20%	4%
Professional or managerial occupations	40%	15%
Laborer, service or operation occupations	20%	50%

Sources: Lloyd H. Ragler and Rosemary Santana Cooley, *Puerto Rican Families in NYC: Intergenerational Processes* (New York: Maplewood Press, 1984). U.S. Bureau of the Census, *Persons of Spanish Origin . . .* (March 1975).

time, money, stability, and commitment to achieve. In the 1970s Fordham University ran a small but revealing study of 100 stable Puerto Rican families. The parents were typical Puerto Rican immigrants who were in their fifties when the study was done. They had kept their families intact, and their children excelled as a group in comparison to other Puerto Ricans. Almost all were church members.

Lugo's Barbershop on Lexington Avenue in New York City is a lively place where neighbors talk surrounded by family snapshots and maps of San Juan and Puerto Rico. Alejandro Lugo, a deacon at St. Cecilia Church, "the cathedral of the barrio," ministers during the day to his customers and visits shut-ins at night. "You find good and bad all over the world," he muses. "I always wanted to come to this country." Glancing to the street, Lugo then returns to ministering to his customer, his eyes briefly resting upon one of the little slogans he has written on his shop's walls: "Never become a victim of fear or envy; that will keep you from doing good." Day in and day out people like Deacon Lugo are putting God into the soul of the barrio and into the soul of the city.

PART ONE

---

*New York City Mission in the
African American Context*

Black Americans are, by many key indices, worse off today than they have been at any time since emancipation. A century ago, there were 240 African American banks; today, there are fewer than 30. In 1910 blacks owned twenty million acres of land; today, they own fewer than four million. In 1940, 90 percent of black households had a male head; today, fewer than 30 percent do. In 1970, 21 percent of black families earned less than $10,000 annually; today, 26 percent do. A young black man has a 1 in 20 chance of becoming a victim of homicide; a young white man's chances are 1 in 186. A generation ago African American church attendance was 80 percent; today, it is 40 percent, and 70 percent of the congregants are women.

There are many reasons for the problems that plague black neighborhoods, but it is clear that black churches are a key to the resolution of these problems. According to a Lilly study, "Churches have realized that if they don't act to save their neighborhoods, no one else will. It is a locally based bid for economic transformation—like the struggle for civil rights, educational opportunities and community services that galvanized African-American churches in earlier decades."[1]

This section of *Signs of Hope in the City* tells the stories of four black churches that are responding effectively to the social and spiritual challenges facing their communities. These churches stand in the four-hundred-year prophetic black church tradition while developing cutting-edge, sophisticated methods of ministry. Their work is energizing their neighborhoods through housing projects, microenterprise development, social service agencies, and schools. Concord Baptist Church has started nine community development corporations that have a combined annual income of $32 million. Concord's ministries include a credit union with $3 million in assets and a foundation, the Christ Fund, that has a $1 million endowment. In addition to being known as a "hospital in Harlem," Bethel Gospel Assembly in Harlem has a commitment to missions that rivals such a commitment of any church in New York City. Bethel supports missionaries in Zambia, Sierra Leone, Nigeria, Israel, Japan, India, and the Caribbean, and Bethel has adopted its own unreached people group (the Bakka) who live in the rain forest of southeast Cameroon. Allen A.M.E. Church in Queens, in addition to an extraordinary array of social ministries, has developed a unique public ministry—the congregation has sent its pastor, Floyd Flake, to Washington to serve as the congressman from its district.

5

Concord Baptist Church

Taking Care of Business in Bed-Stuy

Pamela Ann Toussaint

Pastor Gary V. Simpson smiled when I asked him what percentage of his ten-thousand-member Brooklyn congregation was involved in the church's community development efforts. He replied, "People are involved in our church *because* our church is involved in community development."[1] Simpson notes that both regular and not-so-regular members can be found in and around the church's buildings on weeknights and Saturdays, volunteering for one ministry or another: "A faithful member of my congregation may be here twice a month on Sunday, but will come through here several times during the week to serve. That's because we are a social outreach church, so ministry opportunities are themselves worship stations." About 40 percent of Concord's members commute from other boroughs and even other states to attend there. For them the church is more than just a place to worship; it is a place to use their gifts and

---

Pamela Ann Toussaint is a writer, editor, and author who resides in New York City.

skills to meet needs. For the members who reside in "Bed-Stuy" (the Bedford-Stuyvesant section of Brooklyn), being part of a church that cares about their community means there is hope that their own neighborhood will improve.

Historically, black churches have often been the rescuers of inner-city communities left to die by the larger society. It is important to note that while black churches like Concord were doing a valiant job of caring for their members and their community, they were still battling an overtly racist society. Sadly, that brand of racism was also very present in the church at large—a church that is still reticent about wholly embracing black Christians. As renowned teacher Tom Skinner recalls, "The Christian church in America was strangely silent. It did not speak out or take a stand as a whole against the lynchings, the murders, and the other forms of immorality that were heaped upon black people. It wanted black people saved but did not want to help them deal with their dilemma. In fact, they didn't even know what our dilemma *was*."[2] This is one reason why the burden of improving the quality of life for black people became an important mission of the black church. Concord Baptist was a pioneer in establishing institutions that have addressed the societal ills suffered by Bed-Stuy residents: unemployment, inadequate housing, elder concerns, youth violence, and an education crisis, to name a few. Folks in the neighborhood expect much more from a local black church than a rousing sermon and a firm handshake from the pastor on the way out.

But remedying the vast cadre of problems afflicting an inner-city neighborhood is no small task. The leaders of Concord Baptist decided early on that without established ministries that address these issues, the church would face what Simpson calls "pastoral concerns to the nth degree." He explains, "I think the challenge in doing ministry in urban contexts is to find a way to remedy situations without having a procession of people with the same types of problems coming in time and time again, and doing the same little things."

Concord decided to create ministries that were large enough to be set institutionally, like the church itself. This vision echoes that of Pastor Gardner C. Taylor, Simpson's renowned predecessor, who pastored Concord Baptist for forty-nine years. Taylor said, "Our churches are our IBMs, our General Motors; they are our corporations." Out of this philosophy came the nine not-for-profit corporations spawned by Concord Baptist over the past forty-five years. They are Concord Federal Credit Union (1951), Concord Clothing Exchange (1971), Concord Nursing Home (1975), Concord Home Services for the Elderly (1977), Concord Seniors Residence (1984), Concord Baptist Christ Fund (1988), Concord Family Services (1989), and the Concord Community Development Corporation (1994). Only the Concord Baptist Elementary School (1960) remains as a direct ministry of the church. The combined ministries of Concord Baptist Church represent one of the largest employers in Brooklyn, bringing hundreds of job opportunities to the community.

THE WAY THINGS WERE:
CONCORD'S HISTORY IN BRIEF

Scanning Concord's 149-year history of community involvement clarifies one thing: these folks did not sit around having theological discussions about whether the gospel was spiritual or social. What takes some churches years to accomplish—just getting people's hearts attuned to the idea of serving an underserved community—was a nonissue for Concord. Of course, its location in the middle of rough-and-tumble Bedford-Stuyvesant makes it difficult for churchgoers to ignore felt needs: once-stately brownstones riddled with boarded-up windows, mom-and-pop shops still closed at midday, older men and youth on the corners "just hangin'." Yet the area around Gardner C. Taylor Boulevard, where the church is located, seems vibrant. A newly renovated high school across the street is an encouraging presence, as are the pleasant older residents who bid good morning to any friendly passerby. There is work worth doing here—and Concord members have been doing it for decades.

From the start, Concord showed itself to be a church centered on an incarnational gospel. Many inner-city black churches have likewise found it almost impossible to "have church" without addressing the pressing social, economic, and political issues that bear on its members on a daily basis. "All of our efforts are undergirded by the idea of loving God with all our hearts, minds, souls, and strength and loving our neighbor as ourselves," says Simpson.

The idea of community was heavy on the minds of the six former members of Abyssinian Baptist Church who founded Concord Baptist almost 150 years ago. They were all Brooklyn residents who were tired of traveling to Manhattan to attend church at Abyssinian (the "home" church of Martin Luther King Jr. when he was visiting New York). These founding members desired to create a neighborhood church that could serve neighborhood folks and attend to neighborhood business. In 1847, in the living room of one of these pioneers' homes, the Concord Street Baptist Church of Christ was born.[3]

Concord grew steadily over the next few decades, even as other black churches that began during the same period remained small. Many enslaved blacks who fled north to find freedom from oppression arrived on Concord's doorstep. The black church was always seen as a place where folks of darker hue could find safety and acceptance. Thus, churches like Concord became important players in the struggle on many fronts for the liberation of black people.

Concord was a hostel for runaway slaves before the Emancipation Proclamation declared black people "free." William Dixon, Concord's pastor from 1863 until his death in 1923, fought for the worldwide abolition of slavery, and he opposed the government-proposed closings of "colored schools." Perhaps in reaction to this, Concord members established a sabbath school, which sought not only to provide religious instruction but also to combat illiteracy—one of the most pressing problems impeding black progress at that time. Sabbath, or Sunday, schools were open to children and adults and were vehicles for attracting the unchurched. In 1877 Concord also created the Dorcas Home Missionary Society, an outreach program that provided food, clothing, money, and other assistance to those who needed it.

By the 1930s juvenile delinquency became the major concern in the church community. Concord again responded by offering scouting programs, vacation Bible school, and sports programs for youth. Historians note that Concord's scouting program was one of the most active in Brooklyn, offering boys and girls what grateful parents described as "clean speech, clean sport, clean habits and . . . a clean crowd."[4] Concord mothers and fathers planned, supervised, and ran the scouting program, becoming valuable role models for the children of the church and community. In an effort to meet the needs of human beings as whole people, Concord and other black churches also became social centers for cultural events, concerts, lectures, and literary debates.

Despite Concord's many successful programs, Bed-Stuy was fast becoming a slum. Racism and gentrification were infecting the community with a lingering disease that could not be cured with even the most well-oiled programs. Sweeping reforms were needed for Bed-Stuy to thrive again. Enter the young pastor Gardner C. Taylor, a man who was convinced that fighting for civil rights was directly in line with Christian values, a man who was unafraid to mix church and state in order to effect change.

DR. GARDNER C. TAYLOR:
PASTOR, PREACHER, ACTIVIST

In 1948, at the age of thirty, Gardner C. Taylor began his pastorship at Concord. He proved to be a dynamic and ebullient preacher, clearly a man who knew the times. Taylor has since been honored with such titles as "pulpit king" by *Christianity Today* and "dean of the nation's black preachers" by *Time*.[5] But those who knew him during his pastorate note that his gifts were not limited to the pulpit. He was a pastor, a preacher, and an activist with a strong grasp of the holistic gospel. Taylor was ardent in his fight to see government take action against racial injustice, and he believed that the church can and must play an active part in holding government accountable to the people it governs. This view was often not shared by other black pastors who preferred to stay—and pray—on the sidelines rather than become politically outspoken.

Taylor's close friendship with civil rights leader Martin Luther King Jr. and his ties to King's Southern Christian Leadership Conference (SCLC) were applauded by some and criticized by others. In Taylor's words, "One must get out of life and into the Bible, but there are also times when one must get out of the Bible and into people's lives!"[6] In a letter he wrote to the Associated Negro Press in 1957, Taylor asserted, "The National Baptist Convention (NBC) must relate itself on a continuing, day-to-day basis to our Civil Rights struggle, both in fulfillment of our Christian witness and for the sake of our country and Negro Community."[7] Dissatisfied with the National Baptist Convention's lukewarm position on civil rights issues, Taylor and his supporters formed a new organization, the Progressive National Baptist Convention, which promised to be more outspoken on issues of justice and liberty.

Taylor stepped down from Concord's leadership in 1990, after a forty-two-year term as senior pastor. Today, he enjoys the legacy of leading a church that serves as a model of commitment to Christian community development in the inner city.

CONCORD TODAY

Pastor Gary V. Simpson

"They're making a pastor out of me," said Rev. Gary V. Simpson, referring to the members of his congregation at Concord, many of whom see him as a son, some even a grandson. Molded and shaped by seminary, a pastorship, and six years of apprenticeship under Gardner Taylor, Simpson took the helm as Concord Baptist's senior pastor in October 1990. Being a young, thirty-something pastor with the responsibility of leading a huge, historic congregation each week and overseeing nine large community development ministries, while walking in the shadow of a great and much-loved leader, is certainly enough to give most people high blood pressure. But Simpson was blessed with a smooth transition into his leadership role.

"Our church has a history of investing in and growing with a young pastor," says Simpson, with an air of gratitude. Simpson is only the tenth pastor in Concord's almost 150 years, making the average stay fifteen years: "If you read books on urban ministry and look at what makes a successful church, I think you'll find that having long pastorates is one key to it." Simpson also credits Gardner Taylor for making his transition easier—though he did not always understand his mentor's methodology. "Dr. Taylor was very gracious in that for a year he would not come near the church—even when I asked him to. I, of course, didn't think it was gracious at the time," he recalls, "but I certainly understand it now." Taylor still encourages Simpson weekly by phone. "Our relationship is a part of what makes it work," he said, adding, "I'm his number one fan and I think he's my number one fan too."

CHURCH DEMOGRAPHICS AND STRUCTURE

Since its modest beginning in the home of one of its six founders, Concord Baptist has blossomed into a church of ten thousand members, with about half attending regularly. The informal demographics show a pleasant mix of older, middle-aged, and younger folks, something Simpson feels very good about: "We're very blessed in that we are an intergenerational church. I believe it is essential to church stability." More than eight hundred members were recently honored by induction into the church's Golden Circle, which is reserved for those who have attended Concord for forty years or more. Simpson remarks, "The Lord calls the young because they're strong and the old because they're wise, and I think that we have a great combination of strength and wisdom here at Concord, which makes us quite a force to reckon with."

Though Concord could be described as a middle-class church, a profile of the "typical" Concord member is difficult to come by, as members' occupation, age, and economic status vary widely. When I visited, I saw many young, professional-looking women smartly dressed as well as older men and women in suits and felt hats. "You name it; they're in here," says Simpson, "and I think that's what makes the place exciting. Concord is a ripe place."

Structurally, Concord Baptist Church has a senior pastor, a pastor, an associate pastor, a youth minister, music ministers, and several administrative staff on its payroll. About one hundred laypeople assist in caring for church members through small groups. Each of the community development ministries is its own corporation with tax-exempt, nonprofit (501c3)

status, and each has a president or leader who reports regularly
to Simpson.

COMMUNITY DEVELOPMENT PROJECTS AT CONCORD

The Nitty Gritty

Very sophisticated methodology was employed by Concord
members as they embarked on community development. I
would describe it as seeing, praying, and doing. In 1951 a small
group of congregants shared their dismay and anger at being
turned down for loans at New York's commercial banks. Later
that year the eight-member group began the Concord Federal
Credit Union (CFCU) with forty dollars in share deposits.
Today, CFCU has almost one thousand members and assets of
close to $3 million.

In 1960 educator Laura Scott Taylor, wife of Pastor Gardner
Taylor, became upset about very poor reading scores for students in Bed-Stuy, as reported in a newspaper story. Later that
year she and other members opened Concord Elementary
School, which now has 150 students—many of whom go on to
programs for gifted and talented high schoolers.

In 1971 two elderly sisters, active Concord members, were
having difficulty caring for one another as they aged, so they
let their church family know their need. Four years later, the
group built the Concord Nursing Home, now a 123-bed facility
and one of the largest single-entity employers in all of Brooklyn. Similar stories could be told for each of Concord Baptist's
nine community development corporations—they saw the
need, prayed about the need, and began to fill the need.

Now, you might think that pulling all of this off required
highly skilled, experienced individuals and a great deal of
organization—not to mention some rich uncles. Not so. Simpson explains, "Inevitably there are people in the congregation
who have expertise but who have perhaps not been challenged
to use the God-given gifts that they use in their 'secular' lives
in the context of ministry. Much to my predecessor's credit, he
had the uncanny ability to inspire people to a vision and then
to put people in place who could pull it off."

INSIDE CONCORD BAPTIST ELEMENTARY SCHOOL

As an eight-year-old student at the Concord Baptist Elementary School in the early 1970s, Vicki McMillan was not dreaming of becoming a teacher, far less a school principal.[8] After completing a degree in political science at Spelman College, she set her sights on becoming a lawyer—that is, until God gave her a new vision for her old community.

"I came back home after college, intending to work for a year before I went to law school," explains McMillan. "I had taken some education courses as an undergrad, just as a backup, so I was about to apply for a teaching position at an elementary school here in Brooklyn." McMillan went to her former principal, Laura Scott Taylor, for a letter of recommendation, but instead got a job offer to teach at her alma mater. The one-year teaching stint she was hoping for became a seven-year stay. In 1990 McMillan was secretly nominated for the position of principal, and she accepted. "I was flattered and surprised, but I had never seen myself even teaching long-term, and never imagined myself as a principal." While teaching, McMillan attended law school part-time, still hoping to pursue a legal career, though feeling unsettled. She now realizes that God was intervening and showing her the divine plan for her life: "It's amazing to see how God works things out his way."

Concord Baptist Elementary school is intentional about serving neighborhood children. Its tuition is one of the lowest in Brooklyn, and most of the children come from families with no church background. McMillan emphasizes the fact that the children of Concord members and other "church kids" make up only a portion of the student body: "The goal has never been so small as to only serve the church; we've always had a goal to serve the larger community." Many of the students' parents cannot identify with a personal relationship with God. Yet they *can* identify with what Concord has to offer their children.

"Parents know that their children will be taken care of and properly educated here," says McMillan, who notes that each school day begins with a time of devotion. Bible instruction is also a regular part of the curriculum. "The Christian thrust with its high moral standards is what most parents want for their children," explains McMillan, "even if they don't have a personal relationship with God themselves." Concord capitalizes on this opportunity to involve the children in church activities such as Sunday school, special after-school programs, and performances to which parents are invited. School is often the only place where the children receive regular spiritual guidance and exposure to Christian principles: in the words of the principal, "What we're really doing is ministry work. And it makes all the difference."

At Concord Baptist Elementary School, the same high standards are applied to English and math classes as to spiritual development. Founder and former principal Laura Scott Taylor decided thirty-six years ago that she would challenge the popular notion that black children "can't learn." "You couldn't tell Mrs. Taylor that," recalls McMillan. Taylor served as the unsalaried principal of the school for thirty-two years, no small effort considering that her husband was pastor of an inner-city church that served black people in the 1960s.

"We had a few older kids who were *very* slow," McMillan recollects, "students who just could not read. Mrs.Taylor took them on and tutored them herself, using whatever materials were necessary to help them learn to read. And they all did. In fact, one of those former students still came back to visit her year after year, just out of gratitude." McMillan adds, "She just would not accept any defeat in terms of teaching."

Taylor's resolve today guides McMillan and the teaching staff at Concord Elementary, many of whom have been devoted and much-loved teachers there for decades. Vicki McMillan remembers the impression caring teachers at Concord made on her. "I never forgot the Bible stories I was taught in chapel," says McMillan, "and I remember going to my first-grade teacher's house. Very few people can say that they really spent *time* with their first-grade teacher," notes McMillan. "At school here, I saw how teaching was supposed to be done."

McMillan had the privilege of teaching alongside her first- and fourth-grade teachers when she returned to Concord: "It says something when you come back and see teachers who have taught at a place for thirty years. They always made themselves available to me. Most of my peers don't have that mentoring process in their schools." McMillan has also taught the children of several of her classmates, another testimony to the strength of the school.

Once distinguished as the district with the lowest reading scores in the borough, Bed-Stuy can now boast of its distinguished students. Many graduates of Concord Elementary go on to attend prestigious high schools and colleges. Though there is no active plan in place to encourage youngsters to return to the community after college, as McMillan did, it seems to happen anyway. And when it does not, Concord is not disappointed. Explains McMillan, "Our goal is to develop our students as thinkers, people who are able to deal with society's problems. We want to instill confidence in them to succeed in whatever career path they choose and in whichever community they choose to serve."

Enrollment and individual classes at Concord are kept small to ensure a quality environment for maximum learning. Only 150 to 160 students are enrolled at the school each year, and the student-teacher ratio is as low as fifteen to one in some classes, with the average class being about twenty-five to one. This is a marvel when you consider that the average New York City public school, where the majority of the city's black children attend, might easily have forty students per class.

The school was built in 1960, eight years after Concord suffered a major fire that left only one wall of their church standing. With the help of local banks, the congregation raised $1 million to rebuild their church. In keeping with their tradition of community development, they decided to build a school right onto their new church building at the same time. Concord Elementary is the only one of the church's nine community development programs that has not yet become its own 501C3 and thus is still subsidized by the church. This subsidy is a great help in keeping tuition fees so low, according to McMillan. "If it were not for the support of the church, it would be completely impossible to run the school," admits McMillan. Concord Elementary has made it through some turbulent times. It began during the "civil rights sixties" and is thriving in the midst of the "cut-back nineties." "Sadly, several long-standing Christian schools have closed around us," notes McMillan.

Fortunately, many children from those schools now attend Concord Elementary.

"I do think it's commendable that we saw a need and didn't just complain about it, but we said, 'Let's do something,'" adds McMillan. "As Christians, we need to be living what we're preaching. So the agencies we've created help do some of that 'living.'"

INSIDE CONCORD FEDERAL CREDIT UNION

A popular TV commercial begins, "Turned down by the banks? Don't know what to do?" Concord Baptist Church members would respond, "Create one." That is just what eight members did after experiencing racism at traditional lending institutions.

Staying true to the unwritten Concord pledge to not just complain but to do something about it, the eight pioneers applied to the National Credit Union Administration, who gave them their charter and provided them with the guidelines of how to run a credit union. In 1951 the group began the Concord Federal Credit Union (CFCU) with forty dollars in share deposits. In the fifties, a group as small as eight or ten could be approved to begin a credit union; today, you may need two hundred or more signatures to prove eligibility. At the time, shares were five dollars apiece; today, they are twenty-five dollars. Today, CFCU offers a number of services, from payroll deduction to auto loans, and boasts almost one thousand members and just under $3 million in assets.[9]

Structure. Aside from a paid, part-time manager who does general administration, the CFCU is a totally volunteer enterprise. There is a fourteen-member board of directors as well as several functioning committees. The credit committee reviews loan applications and authorizes all loans; the supervisory committee makes sure that the board runs in accordance with the Federal Credit Union Act; and the education and marketing committees keep current members of the credit union informed of CFCU's offerings and recruit new members.

Membership in the CFCU is open to members of Concord Baptist Church and all employees of Concord's nine community development subsidiaries and their families. CFCU's offices are on the second floor of the church building, and it is open two days per week: one weekday and, conveniently, on Sunday afternoons so members can stop in right after church.

Challenges. "There are just some people who will not *join* something," says Aleathia V. Boddie, CFCU's president and a Golden Circle member of Concord Baptist. Undaunted, she and her board and committee members developed ways to encourage nonjoiners to become depositors. "We offered a Christmas club, something most of our people were already familiar with and were participating in at various banks," recalls Boddie. Many people responded to the announcement and joined CFCU because of it. Introducing auto loans also gained the attention of potential members, many of whom never realized that CFCU made loans at all. "Though we are located right here in the church building, so many people don't know what we have to offer," remarks Boddie.

The CFCU recently made a payroll deduction service available to the employees of the Concord Nursing Home in order to promote a more painless way to save and to facilitate on-time repayment of loans. It has worked. "We noticed . . . that some people would come to get their money out almost before we received the deduction," observed Ms. Boddie, laughing. "They could have easily said, 'I need to stop this deduction so I can quit having to come over here to get the money out,' but no one did. They realize that it's a good thing, and we think *that's* a good thing."

Vision. "Both Gardner Taylor and Pastor Simpson have a vision for the credit union to offer mortgages, specifically for the rehabilitation of buildings for home ownership." Boddie's personal project is getting more children to become CFCU members. "We want more children to learn how to save on a regular basis," she explains. Even one-dollar deposits would be welcomed from youngsters, a few of whom are already depositors. Principal Vicki McMillan and Boddie are working out a plan to make the credit union accessible to students during the school day. Boddie says, "We want to impress upon them that someday it will become *their* credit union and they can have some say in how it runs."

Praise reports. "One of the things that excites me now is when I hear other people talking about starting a credit union,"

says Simpson, who notes that the CFCU was one of the only
such institutions in the neighborhood when it began. Boddie
and her team have been able to build relationships with the
leaders of other credit unions now established in Bed-Stuy,
who have often sought them out for counsel. The CFCU is seen
as a model for how to do economic development in a church
setting.

As churches in poor neighborhoods seek to serve their
members more effectively, reliable banking services are often a
top priority. Over the past fifteen years, New York has suffered
a severe erosion of bank branches in low-income areas. In
Brooklyn, the ratio of residents to bank branches in the poorest
zip codes is eighteen thousand to one—more than four times
the ratio in the most affluent zip codes. In place of banks, scores
of check-cashing outlets have emerged. Poor New Yorkers are
forced to cash their paychecks at local check cashers—for hefty
fees—and carry cash home through unsafe streets. They must
buy money orders to pay bills. In the meantime, they hide their
money at home and hope for the best in neighborhoods notorious for theft.

Challenges

With Concord's long history of social outreach ministry, one
can hardly believe that they are concerned about being focused
too inwardly or lacking adequate visibility in the community.
But, they are. Admittedly, serving the *church* community was
Concord's primary intent. The community at large was served,
in effect, by default. Simpson discussed the need for this
inward focus to evolve: "The church has to wrestle with itself
and ask, 'What do we really mean by *community*?' If we just
mean ourselves, then we're missing it. We ought to have a
broader sense of community that focuses on this vicinity." He says,
"I'm sad to say that some people in this community have no idea
what we do, even though they walk by this church every day."

Simpson recalls passing on the street in front of the church
an older woman who did not recognize him as Concord's
pastor. She studied the church marquee, which read, "Sermon:
'Soul Food,'" describing that coming Sunday's message. While
walking away, the woman mumbled, "'Soul Food'? What they

really need to be doing is providing clothing for the poor people of this neighborhood. . . . " Little did she know, the church had been doing exactly that at the Concord Christ House—just across the street from where she stood—for almost ten years.

Simpson has addressed neighborhood needs by focusing on leadership development and nurturing fresh ministry approaches—though he sometimes walks a tightrope to do so. He explains with the example of youth minister Mellissa Brathwaite: "We recently hired Mellissa, who is a Howard University Divinity School graduate and who came from a Catholic background. Traditionally, we thought youth ministry was what we do for our kids in the church. But she has the parish concept, which says youth ministry should be to the larger community. Under her leadership there are young people running all over this building, driving some people very crazy." Simpson says proudly, "Mellissa never asks them, 'Whose granddaughter are you or whose grandson are you?' She has brought us a very fresh idea of what community is." Under Brathwaite's leadership, the church now offers everything from basketball to crocheting classes as a way to attract and serve neighborhood youth—and it is working.

Simpson makes a point of giving the youth minister public support and coaching, explaining Concord's culture to her and to the youth and interpreting the youth culture to the older members of the church. He also mediates the inevitable clashes that take place between leaders from different generations, something he feels gifted to do: "I think the older folks, who are really the backbone of our congregation, see the transitional propensities in the younger generation and they get very nervous." He notes, "Growth is frustrating and painful for some people. But I'm a facilitator, and my job is to bridge the gap. I try to get people to see us ten years down the line." He adds, "It's a constant work."

Lack of effective public relations has also limited Concord's visibility and has fed the perception that Concord was church focused. Obtaining local media exposure for their significant community efforts has proved difficult. "When the Christ Fund was inaugurated in 1988, I remember personally stuffing mailboxes, sending out press releases—everything. Not

one newspaper, not one radio station, not one television station picked it up," Simpson recalls with dismay, adding, "I
guess it wasn't newsworthy that black people from the community had set aside a million dollars to give back to the black
community." In recent years, Concord Baptist's efforts have
gained some much-deserved press that is beginning to clarify
the church's purpose in the minds of community residents.

As the church's community development projects mature,
Simpson sees a clear need to bring in skilled managers and to
create a better administrative structure. He hopes to add a
lawyer and a finance manager to the staff over the next few
years: "In the early days, we were just blessed to have faithful
people in our congregation who had big hearts. That worked
out well for the first few years with many of these programs,
but now with regulations as tight as they are, we really need
some crackerjack people with expertise on board."

THE FUTURE

So, what is left to do when you have spawned nine ministries
that have become successful corporations serving the felt needs
of your community? You use your resources to enable others.
"In the mid-eighties, we began to think about community
development beyond ourselves. We wanted to give back to the
larger community in tangible ways," recalls Simpson. In 1988
the Concord Baptist Christ Fund was started with $1 million
raised by the congregation.

The Christ Fund gives one-year grants of between one thousand and thirty thousand dollars to qualified applicants who
are doing community work in Brooklyn. The grants are given
to Christian and secular organizations alike, but it is made clear
to recipients that Concord is a Christ-centered organization.
Each award letter begins with the words, "With all thanks to
God you have been selected. . . ." "I think we make a great
statement to the world that we are not embarrassed about who
we are, and we are not ashamed of having the resources to do
these kind of things," says Simpson. "We think it's important
to let people know that this money didn't just come from some
social agency; it came from a church." Simpson adds, "Those
letters are evangelism too! I have found people we have worked

with come to the knowledge of Christ through these opportunities."

The Fund has given almost a half-million dollars to worthy social causes, principally in the Bed-Stuy community, including boxing centers, after-school programs, and sponsorship of the award-winning television documentary *Eyes on the Prize,* which tells the civil rights story. "The Lord cannot continue to bless us if we just coffer money so we can swell up and show people what God has done for us," says Simpson. "We are challenged by Jesus to let our light so shine that others may see our good works and glorify our Father in heaven."

6

This Far by Faith

Allen African Methodist Episcopal Church

Catherine O. Sweeting

The African Methodist Episcopal (A.M.E.) denomination was born in 1787 when Richard Allen and other black worshipers stormed out of St. George's Methodist Episcopal Church in Philadelphia, Pennsylvania, in protest over a racially discriminatory seating policy. Rev. Richard Allen was kneeling in prayer when a fellow black minister, Absalom Jones, was forcibly lifted from his knees and told to leave the church.

Born into slavery twenty-seven years earlier, Allen was an itinerant Methodist preacher. After leaving St. George's, he started the fledgling African Methodist Episcopal Church, which he named Bethel Church, in a blacksmith's shop in Philadelphia. With an anvil as his pulpit, Allen declared independence from the Methodist Church:

> Wherefore, as from time to time many inconveniences have arisen from white people and people of color mixing together

Catherine O. Sweeting is the project manager at the New York office of Concerts of Prayer International. She lives in East Elmhurst, Queens, with her husband, William, pastor of Leverich Memorial Church, and two sons, Joshua and Timothy.

in public assemblies, more particularly places of worship, we have thought it necessary to provide for ourselves a convenient house to assemble in, separate from the white brethren.[1]

Richard Allen, who later became Bishop Allen, viewed the church as a means to uplift the black community and help his people gain freedom. For Allen, the church would best serve God by serving God's people, and Allen preached a doctrine of self-help and reliance on God. That message has found a new messenger in the person of Floyd Flake and in a church named for Bishop Allen.

FLAKE'S PASTORATE BEGINS

Floyd Flake began his ministry at the Allen A.M.E. Church in Jamaica, New York, 189 years after Allen left St. George's and added "African" to Methodism. The rich tradition in the African Methodist Episcopal Church of serving all the needs of the black community has advanced unabated since Pastor Flake became pastor in 1976. At that time, Flake was serving as chaplain at Boston University when Bishop Richard Hildebrand asked him to take the pastorate of Allen A.M.E. Church. The thirty-one-year-old Flake answered what he felt was the call of God. "I felt that it was time to take my skills in marketing, sales, social work, and education, and utilize them within the church," Flake recalled.[2]

Flake's theology, a holistic gospel that links Scripture with contemporary needs, has found practical expression in the ministry and outreach of Allen A.M.E. Church. Allen's model of ministry responds to the spiritual, political, social, educational, and economic malaise of urban America.[3] Literally tens of thousands of people have been fed in spirit, body, and mind through the ministry of Allen A.M.E. Church. The multidimensional ministries of the church addressing diverse spiritual and physical needs include the Ministry to Men, Ministry to Women, Ministry to Singles, Ministry to Single Parents, Marriage Enrichment Ministry, Spiritual Life Counseling Ministry, Family Ministry, and Hunger Ministry (feeding five thousand at Thanksgiving and serving hot meals every Monday).[4]

The church had a membership of twelve hundred and an

annual budget of $250,000 when Pastor Flake arrived in 1976. Many believed the growth curve of the church had reached its height and would taper off. "Where was there to go from here?" many congregants wondered.[5] Two services were held each Sunday in a beautiful church that was only eight years old, and all of its debts were paid! Instead of leveling off, however, membership grew. Nineteen years after Pastor Flake's arrival, Allen A.M.E. Church had grown to a membership of over eight thousand. The church sponsors nine thriving corporations with combined assets totaling over $25 million, a dynamic youth chapel, and a multitude of programs serving the needs of the church and community.[6] A church growth paradox is epitomized at Allen A.M.E.: one way a church grows is by observing its own growth. The pride that comes when a church accomplishes something visible leads to further growth.

Flake followed a legacy of ministers committed to evangelism and meeting the needs of its black congregants and the local community.[7] Evangelism is a hallmark of Allen Church. Upon Pastor Flake's arrival, evangelism took on new forms. Evangelistic preaching, a radio ministry, dynamic music, and youth ministry drew many to Christ—and to Allen Church. The radio ministry gave greater exposure to the church and drew many newcomers. Conservative music gave way to gospel music, and as the tempo increased and instruments such as drums were added to worship, more people—young and old—began to attend. Youth ministry programs such as Sunday school, choirs, and sports activities were the precursor to today's Shekinah Youth Chapel.

HOUSING FOR SENIORS

Before Pastor Flake arrived at Allen, an application to build Allen Senior Citizens' Complex had been sent to the Department of Housing and Urban Development. "It was one of those situations where you didn't have to wait to start working," comments Flake regarding his arrival. Although it was a monumental task, by the time the new minister completed negotiations for the building, the initial funding for one hundred units was increased to three hundred units. Flake notes that "it propelled us into the middle of the life of the community. These visible things have a way of *moving people.*"

Financed by funds from the Department of Housing and Urban Development, the $13 million complex is one of the largest housing projects for senior citizens developed by a single church congregation in the United States. The Allen Senior Citizens' Complex provided housing for three hundred elderly citizens in a comfortable environment within their own community. Since the complex was federally funded (Section 8-202), residents pay only a portion of their income toward rent, and those living on limited incomes could occupy the new apartments. The success of the complex thrust Allen Church into the life of the community and established Flake as a community leader.

A SCHOOL FOR CHILDREN

The main agenda item at the first meeting Pastor Flake had with the Allen Church congregation was education. The congregation's vision was to create a "learning environment focusing on teaching basic education in a disciplined environment with a Christian educational foundation." Even before the Senior Citizens' Complex was completed, plans were underway to build an educational and multipurpose center.

Early in 1977 a building committee was formed, and the land on which Allen Christian School now stands was purchased for $64,000. The congregation was so enthusiastic about building the school that they raised $1.5 million in two years. Each Sunday morning offering soon surpassed the monthly mortgage payment of $3,000. A series of fund-raising events was held over several months, culminating in Women's Day and Men's Day, and specific monetary goals were set and met.

Today, 475 children attend the four-story school building on the corner of Linden and Merrick Boulevards in Jamaica. The first school of its kind in the A.M.E. denomination, it now houses seventeen class and resource rooms, a computer lab, library-media resource center, music room, cafeteria, gymnasium, chapel, and children's play area.

Soon after the school's completion, Allen Church purchased stores adjacent to the new building. Pastor Flake said, "The buying of stores came in large measure as an economic reality. If we were going to invest $3.8 million in a school, then we ought to invest in whatever properties were around it . . . to protect the investment and to protect the children." At that time, drug dealers flourished on the corners of Linden and Merrick Boulevards. Driving down Merrick Boulevard today, one will see uniformly modern, well-kept stores, featuring dry cleaners, a pharmacy, and law offices. The rent from these stores helps pay the mortgages the church has on the properties. The arrangement is one of the many beneficial situations brought about by Flake.

When asked what accomplishment he is most proud of, Pastor Flake responded without hesitation: "The school—because it is institutional, and an institution based on the faith of people." Church members put their hard-earned resources into a project and saw it come to fruition. "It helped us early on to congeal the focus of this church," says Pastor Flake. "Well beyond the tenure of Floyd Flake, the institution will still be able to produce quality kids." Flake compares himself to Booker T. Washington, the founder of Tuskegee Institute, which still graduates students a century after its inception: "The feeling that kids will be graduating from Allen School one hundred years after I'm gone makes me really rejoice."

TWO ROLES—ONE GOAL

Ten years after becoming pastor of Allen Church, Floyd Flake was elected to Congress in New York's Sixth Congressional District. Seeing what the church could do, but also realizing its limitations, led him to make a bid for Congress: "I saw what could be done by using the resources of the church, and I wanted to tap into federal resources because so much more could be done."[8]

Congressman Flake, now serving his fifth term in office, is on the Committee on Banking and Financial Services and the Committee on Small Business. He currently leads House members of both parties from downstate New York in procuring lucrative federal projects.[9] Flake says, "I feel it is important to make the kinds of things my church is doing happen on a much larger scale." He successfully negotiated for five hundred units of housing to be built by Southeast Queens Clergy for Community Empowerment, Inc. in the poorest part of the

Sixth Congressional District; for the construction of a federal building in downtown Jamaica, which added three hundred jobs to an economically depressed area; and for a $48 million pilot project that trains tenants of public housing in management and maintenance functions to promote independence.

Flake feels no conflict between pastoral and congressional responsibilities. The first black congressman, Hiram Revels, elected in 1870, was also an A.M.E. preacher. "For us the distance between the sacred and the profane is shorter than that distance is in white America," says Flake.[10] Still, pastoring is his first love, and if ever a choice were to be made, he would remain in ministry and leave politics.

A DESTRUCTIVE SEASON

Tribulation struck Floyd Flake and Allen Church in 1988. Several church officers, whose goal was to take control of the church, brought inflammatory information to the Internal Revenue Service. Pastor Flake, who describes himself as nonconfrontational, believed this internal church conflict would pass without his having to make "decisions you generally have to make in a corporate setting but don't like to make in a church setting."

Pastor Flake was indicted in August 1990 on charges of conspiracy, fraud, and tax evasion. He was accused of embezzling $75,000 from the Allen Senior Citizens' Complex and diverting $66,700 in church funds for personal use.[11] Throughout the month-long trial, which took place in the spring of 1991, the church rallied around Pastor Flake and held daily prayer vigils. Many church members flocked to the church to pray, literally morning, noon, and night. Members also came to the courtroom an hour before the trial began and held on-site prayer and devotional meetings. Pastor Flake fondly recalled, "It will always be inscribed in my mind—what they did."

Eventually all charges were dropped by the Justice Department. The ministerial expense fund in question was determined to be a legitimate church account—not a personal fund to benefit Flake. After the court proceedings, many jurors revealed the government's case had been weak from the start.[12] Flake described the trial as the "lowest point" in his ministry.

But throughout the low points in his life, Flake has held on to God's promise in Habakkuk:

> Though the fig tree may not blossom, Nor fruit be on the vines; Though the labor of the olive may fail, And the fields yield no food; Though the flock may be cut off from the fold, And there be no herd in the stalls; Yet I will rejoice in the LORD, I will joy in the God of my salvation. The LORD God is my strength; He will make my feet like deer's feet, And He will make me walk on my high hills. (Habakkuk 3:17–19, NKJV)

PRAYER AND EVANGELISM

Allen, a church birthed in prayer, still clings to God with a vibrant corporate prayer life. Pastor Flake attributes much of the phenomenal growth in the church's prayer life to his wife, Elaine. When they first arrived at Allen, Elaine helped shift the women's group focus from fund-raising to spiritual enrichment. Today she is an ordained minister.

Prayer meetings and all-night prayer vigils have increased in frequency and fervor. The Allen Church family has begun regular fasting and prayer for the ministries and outreach programs of the church. On Wednesday through Friday before the first Sunday of each month, the entire church is encouraged to fast and pray. An intercessory prayer ministry links intercessors with prayer requests. On Tuesday evenings men gather for prayer, and on Thursday and Friday mornings from 6:30 to 8:00 A.M. members come together for prayer. On the Allen Prayer Line, someone is available to pray with phone callers weekdays from 8:30 to 9:30 A.M., while persons with AIDS or HIV and their loved ones may call "An Ear to Hear" on Fridays for prayer. All aspects of church life are touched by prayer, and it is understood by the people that prayer undergirds the entire work.

According to Pastor Flake, "The greatest evangelism program you have is a serious commitment to preaching and a commitment to service." Thousands of unchurched adults are reached through the services Allen provides, such as the school and the Allen Senior Citizens' Complex. Parents who bring their children to Allen School often have no relationship to the church, but when their children come home singing praise songs, many parents are drawn to church for the first time.

"Senior citizens who get housed wind up talking to their children and their grandchildren . . . they wind up being a part of the body."

SHEKINAH YOUTH CHAPEL

Pastor Flake notes that "our greatest evangelism tool of late has been the Shekinah Chapel." Led by the dynamic youth pastor Anthony Lucas, Shekinah Youth Chapel is a vibrant expression of worship by black youth. Over fourteen hundred young people are enrolled, and the church is filled beyond capacity during Sunday worship. African dance and step teams are as integral to worship as are the youth choirs.

During the "Shout Out" (short testimonies), children ranging in age from three to twenty-three come forward to the microphone to praise God for salvation and, some, for getting perfect scores in school. During "Say, Word!" each Sunday during worship service, children learn a new vocabulary word. Before the offering is taken, the worship leader asks the children to figure out 10 percent of their allowance, thus tithing is encouraged.

Shekinah is *for* youth and run largely *by* the youth. Young people serve as stewards, trustees, and ushers and learn the complexities of running a church. It is an excellent training ground for developing leadership and skills. On a recent Sunday, twenty-year-old Ibrahim, a former drug dealer, delivered a message to the youth. Like Ibrahim, who is the only Christian in a family of thirteen, most of the youth come from homes where they are the only churchgoers. Many of these young people have led their parents into the church. In fact, since 1992, when Shekinah was formed, Allen Church has gained twenty-five hundred new members.

EXPORTABLE MODELS

The predominantly black Jamaica section of Queens, New York, was labeled a "middle-class community on the decline" by local newspapers in 1976. Located in Community District 12, Jamaica has a population of about two hundred thousand, with over 20 percent of its residents receiving public assistance.

Allen Church's profound impact on the Jamaica community has not gone unnoticed. In addition to the school and housing complex for seniors, Allen has spawned six other corporations: Allen Housing Development Fund; Allen A.M.E. Neighborhood Preservation and Development Corporation; Allen A.M.E. Housing Corporation; Allen Home Care Agency, Ltd.; Allen Women's Resource Center; and Allen A.M.E. Transportation. Except for the transportation corporation, all of them are nonprofit.

Churches from around the country regularly call and ask for advice and help in starting similar programs in their communities. How can this be done? How can programs like Allen A.M.E.'s be started in St. Louis, Missouri, or Denver, Colorado? Community development starts with need. The pastor, or church member, defines the need. If the church sees its role as meeting that need, a vision is born, and the process of community development begins.

Note, for example, the Allen Women's Resource Center (AWRC). The congregation saw the need to serve battered women. Local services were poor or simply nonexistent, and there were no services with a Christian foundation. AWRC, a nonprofit corporation, provides temporary shelter for battered women and their dependent children. Crisis counseling focused on separation is provided to clients, along with medical and day-care services, support groups, legal assistance, and educational training. Medicare and Medicaid are accepted for payment, and fees are prorated according to client income.

Mrs. Q., the thirty-two-year-old mother of a thirteen-year-old daughter and two sons ages twelve and eight, sought admission to the shelter to allow her to separate from her physically abusive husband, who was addicted to drugs.[13] During their four-month stay in 1990, Mrs. Q.'s family received individual and family counseling to address their feelings of victimization. Upon discharge from AWRC, Mrs. Q. and her children were transferred to a supportive housing program developed for domestic violence survivors. Eight months later, she moved into her own private apartment. Mrs. Q. keeps in touch with AWRC staff, and she has secured employment. Her daughter is enrolled in college, and her sons are also doing well, but she must continue to help her children deal with the trauma of domestic violence, a process of healing that strengthens with time and communication.

AWRC, with a total annual income of $520,000, is funded primarily through government grants; only $8,000 comes from nongovernment sources. There are *some* limitations imposed when receiving federal government funds. No religious activities can be mandatory. For example, attendance at a chapel service cannot be required for shelter residents. However, providing voluntary Bible studies or Christian worship services is not prohibited.

The Fannie Lou Hamer Missionary Circle, named for a leader in the civil rights movement, is one of sixty-two auxiliary organizations in the church and has taken on the AWRC as its mission. The missionary circle raises additional funds to improve the quality of services offered by AWRC.

"Missionary" outreach at Allen Church, and at many black American churches, is devoted primarily to the black community. Lack of proper housing, quality education, a safe environment, and daily needs such as food and clothing are addressed by women "missionaries." At Allen, organizations like the Fannie Lou Hamer Missionary Circle alleviate suffering and improve the quality of life in the community. Another missionary circle, The Dorcas Society, administers the prison ministry. More than forty active members go to prisons each week to conduct worship services. Some ex-offenders have joined Allen Church upon their release from prison.

The Allen A.M.E. Neighborhood Preservation and Development Corporation addresses the need for better housing by overseeing the rehabilitation of existing homes and the construction of new ones. A consortium of business leaders and local government known as the New York City Partnership finds sponsors to build and sell homes in minority communities. For example, two-family homes valued at $219,000 are sold for $155,000, and the New York City Partnership provides subsidies to make up the difference. Allen A.M.E. Neighborhood Preservation and Development Corporation, having previously rehabilitated vacant housing units, was chosen to sponsor the building project. Fortunately, it did not involve any outlay of sponsor money. Allen A.M.E. Neighborhood Preservation and

Development Corporation selected the contractor and screened all potential buyers, who were chosen by lottery.

Through Allen's sponsorship, thirty-six homes have been rehabilitated, sixty-one homes have been built, and another forty-nine homes are currently under construction. Each home has a three-bedroom owner's unit with two baths, a full-size basement, and a rental unit. Private parking and separate entrances insure security. Prospective homeowners must be first-time home buyers with an annual income of $33,000–$53,000 and must be able to pay a nominal down payment of $5,000. The corporation also helps buyers obtain low-interest mortgages. Two-family homes are available to buyers, who may live in one part, rent out the other, and apply rental payments to their mortgage. Workshops provided by the Allen program prepare homeowners to become landlords, for example, by providing instruction on property maintenance.

New homes sprinkled throughout Jamaica raise the quality of life for both the homeowner and the community by eliminating vacant lots and instilling pride in the neighborhood. Inspired by the Allen A.M.E. model, smaller churches, though unable to take on large projects, might join with local associations in order to increase their ability to meet local needs. Thus, local clergy or church associations with common goals can take on projects jointly.

According to Howard Henderson, the corporate administrator of Allen A.M.E. Church, "Identifying funding sources is an important part of the process." Henderson advises churches to gather people who have expertise in community development. Next, they should find out what monies are available and when corresponding requests for proposals are issued. Some services may be provided by volunteers at little or no cost.

Other local churches have begun major community development projects in the past few years, largely inspired by Allen. Pride in the community has become infectious, and the resulting improvements benefit everyone.

WE'VE COME THIS FAR BY FAITH

What does the future hold for Allen A.M.E. Church? Pastor Flake is currently assisted by three full-time assistant pastors and sixteen unpaid staff ministers. These ministers have felt the call of God on their lives and have completed three years of Bible training and internship at the A.M.E. Bible Institute. Both men and women are ordained as itinerant deacons and are qualified to preach and administer the sacraments of the church.

Nineteen years after Pastor Flake's arrival, the church is filled to capacity and continues to grow. Sunday worship services are held at 6:30 A.M., 8:30 A.M., and 11:15 A.M. and were moved to the twelve-hundred-seat auditorium in the school building when attendance began to outgrow the church sanctuary. The first shovel of dirt on the future site of Allen Cathedral was lifted to God in praise on May 20, 1995. With a planned seating capacity of twenty-five hundred, the new cathedral should accommodate Allen Church's growing needs . . . for a while anyway.

One way money is raised at Allen is through tithing. A key principle in this regard is if people are tithing, other fundraising will probably not be necessary. Howard Henderson attributes the financial health of the church to the generosity of Allen members, "They have a lot of confidence that their resources are going to be well governed. They see how the money is being spent." Stewardship at the church today has as its motto, "Not equal giving but equal sacrifice."

With a heart for youth and education, can plans for a high school at Allen be far behind? Apparently not. Finishing construction on the cathedral and starting a high school are two of Allen A.M.E.'s immediate goals. Yet, vast numbers of young people in the community appear to have lost hope. Restoring hope to them is probably Allen A.M.E.'s greatest task. The task may be daunting. But Pastor Flake, like the members of Allen A.M.E. Church who have followed this far by faith, has only one declaration in the face of the challenge, "I ain't tired yet!"

7

Bethel Gospel Assembly

Ministry to Harlem and Beyond

Louis A. DeCaro Jr.

> In a community like Harlem, which has not yet attained
> cohesion and adjustment, the church is a stabilizing force.
> The integrating value of the churches in Harlem, where
> there are so many disintegrating forces at work, can easily
> be underestimated.
> —James Weldon Johnson, *Black Manhattan*

As Harlem continues to strive for "cohesion and adjustment,"
struggling with awesome internal and external forces, Bethel
Gospel Assembly is emerging as one of the most important
churches of the community. Harlem's many churches range
from moderate traditional structures and dismal storefronts to
fortresslike sanctuaries and majestic cathedrals. There are
mosques, too, and temples and many other religious meeting
places, for Harlem—like Athens in the days of St. Paul—is a

Louis A. DeCaro Jr. is pastor of Vroom Street Evangelical Free Church, Jersey City,
N.J. He holds a Ph.D. in religious education from New York University and is the
author of *On the Side of My People: A Religious Life of Malcolm X* (New York: New
York University Press, 1996).

most religious community. And if the prefacing comment by James Weldon Johnson was true in 1930, it seems to remain so in the last decade of the twentieth century. Harlem's religious backbone is the Christian church, and despite all the "disintegrating forces" that continue to assault this premier black community of the Western world, the church continues to represent its greatest force of stability and hope.

In Harlem it is rare to find a large church that is zealously evangelistic, thoroughly committed to holistic ministry, and globally oriented in its missions program. Indeed, it is rare to find such a church anywhere.

Bethel Gospel Assembly is situated in the heart of Harlem, its front doors facing Mount Morris Park (renamed Marcus Garvey Park in honor of one of Harlem's greatest leaders), a site immortalized in Ralph Ellison's classic novel *Invisible Man* as the scene of a hero's funeral. Bethel's structure was originally the James Fenimore Cooper Junior High School, a large complex situated on an entire city block between Madison and Fifth Avenues. Though Bethel cannot help but look like an urban school building constructed in the 1920s, it is an impressive church complex consisting of a spacious auditorium, abundant and roomy class and office facilities, double gymnasium, and a refurbished banquet area on the lower level that is easily as attractive as any dining hall in a Manhattan hotel. Indeed, Bethel has so much space that in addition to housing a variety of ministry and community-oriented projects, it also leases classrooms to the nursing program of North General hospital, which has recently raised its new building around the corner from Bethel on Madison Avenue.

Bethel is in the vanguard of gospel-preaching[1] churches in the black community, while at the same time its progressive evangelistic and ministry programs have caught the attention of white evangelicals, who are themselves increasingly desirous of establishing a ministry presence in the inner city. Bethel is a black church with a membership composed of North American, Caribbean, and African believers, and yet it is comfortably inclusive in its approach.

Bethel was born in the 1900s, ironically, after a German American woman named Lillian Kraeger formed a Bible study with a few Harlemite believers. Kraeger had been a member of a white congregation in downtown Manhattan but had heard of two black women converts who were refused membership. Apparently untouched by the rampant racial prejudice of the white Christian community, Kraeger defied her church and fiancé and ventured uptown to Harlem to disciple the young converts. When Kraeger's fiancé gave her an ultimatum, she chose ministry over marriage. The small Bible study grew, first taking a rented room, then a storefront, and finally purchasing their first church building, a private house on West 131st Street, in 1924. Kraeger married later in life, but she never had children. However, in a very real sense, her ministry was her progeny—a family that has grown and prospered and never forgotten her commitment to the gospel.

The pastor of Bethel is Bishop Ezra N. Williams, a Harlemite by birth and a son of Caribbean immigrants who were well settled in the great black metropolis by the time of his birth in 1929. Williams grew to maturity in a Christian home that was closely knit to Bethel Gospel Assembly through the evangelistic witness of Lillian Kraeger. A true son of the church, Williams once attended junior high school in the very same building where Bethel is now located. When he was a student there, no one could have imagined that many years later Williams would be preaching inside his old school building as pastor of the church that Lillian Kraeger had helped to start in Harlem. Another foreshadowing of Bethel's ministry was Ezra's early memory of his uncle and aunt, who committed themselves to pioneering gospel work on the Caribbean island of St. Vincent. He still remembers frequent trips to the seaport, where trunkloads of supplies were sent off to his aunt by his uncle, who stayed behind to provide the only missionary support available. "Missions was burned into my memory," Ezra Williams says with a tender smile, "even from that young age." [2]

SOW ABROAD, REAP AT HOME

Early in his pastorate, which began in 1966, Williams made his commitment to missions a priority, and Bethel members became familiar with their leader's motto, "Sow abroad, reap at home." Bethel launched evangelistic crusades in the Caribbean, thereby following the example of Williams's aunt and uncle, who decades before had organized Bethel's first missionary effort. Global missionary ties were established with Christian workers in a variety of fields, including South Africa, West Africa, and India.

By the early 1970s it was clear that Bethel was emerging as a vanguard congregation in terms of its missions commitment. Over the next decade the church fortified that commitment to global missions through the appointment of Ruth Onukwue as director of the missions program. Onukwue, a Nigerian physician with a lifetime commitment to world evangelism, brought her own zeal for ministry and Bible teaching to Bethel—as if to confirm the church's global identity. By the 1980s Bethel's missionary program could claim an annual budget of $150,000—an impressive amount for any congregation of its size. Presently, Bethel supports missionaries in the fields of Zambia, Cameroon, Sierra Leone, Nigeria, Israel, Japan, India, and the Caribbean (Antilles and St. Vincent) as well as urban ministries in the United States. In addition, Bethel has directly launched evangelistic crusades in South Africa, England, several Caribbean islands, and various cities in North America. Short-term missions teams have been dispatched on national and international projects, and the congregation has adopted its own unreached people group, the Bakka, who live in the rain forest of southeast Cameroon.[3]

By the 1980s Rev. Ezra N. Williams had become Bishop Ezra N. Williams, having served as national overseer in the United Pentecostal Council of the Assemblies of God (UPCAG), an East-coast-based denomination. However, Bethel has recently ventured out by launching its own independent fellowship, the Urban Global Missions Alliance (UGiMA), which is based on Bishop Williams's determination to foster a commitment to missions among African American churches. Williams points out that in many black churches in the United States, "missionaries" are little more than church auxiliary groups that have little or no focus on evangelism, either locally or internationally. With the inauguration of UGiMA in January 1997, Bethel's incorporated fellowship already has affiliate churches in New York City, the Caribbean, Africa, and even in Japan. Bishop

Williams serves as the president and superintendent of the organization.

As if to prepare Bethel for its mounting influence in Harlem, the new site at the former James Fenimore Cooper Junior High School was made available in the early 1980s. When Williams and the congregation found it, however, it was in disrepair. Years of neglect had left the structure an empty shell filled with filth, scarred by vandalism, and stripped of even its copper plumbing. By 1984, however, Bethel had overcome these obstacles, and the evolution of the present Bethel complex was underway. The auditorium was transformed into a beautiful sanctuary that can seat well over a thousand people, and offices and classrooms were provided for an array of ministries that activate the life of Bethel.

A HOSPITAL IN HARLEM

If Bishop Williams has a commitment to world missions, he has an equal passion for Harlem and urban ministry. Indeed, under his leadership, Bethel Gospel Assembly has become almost legendary for its success at developing and implementing evangelism and holistic ministries for the Harlem community. Williams likes to call his church a "hospital in Harlem" because Bethel has established itself as a healing presence in the community.

The entire church is encouraged to participate in one or more of Bethel's ministries. All new members, whether new converts or transfers from other churches, are instructed in the tenets of the Christian faith and Bethel's doctrinal distinctives. Members are then assigned to one of Bethel's prayer groups, each drawing its name from one of the mission fields supported by the church, such as Nigeria, India and—of course—Harlem. The prayer groups serve as small groups that involve participants in outdoor evangelism in Marcus Garvey Park or on 125th Street, the main thoroughfare in Harlem. During these evangelistic "invasions," food is provided for those who are hungry, though recipients are expected to listen to the preaching that is featured in every outing.

Though Bethel Gospel Assembly resides in the structure of a former school, the church has taken its own unique form as it has evolved into a ministry center. Bethel has many traditional church auxiliaries—such as a fine choir and other music ministries, along with a traditional Sunday school and children's ministry—yet the structure serves the church's holistic philosophy in more innovative ways. The twin gymnasiums, for instance, have been beautifully restored to provide young people a place to play basketball—and an opportunity to hear the gospel. The Beth-Hark Crisis Center provides Christian counseling services on the first floor, where there is also a clothing ministry.

Beth-Hark is a lay Christian counseling center that has existed for twelve years, originating as a joint effort of Bethel Gospel Assembly and a parachurch ministry in Harlem founded by Rev. Joseph Holland. Since 1988 Walter Wilson, an associate pastor at Bethel, has served as executive director. Wilson says that Beth-Hark is "geared to meeting the needs within the community of the local assembly. Its doors are opened to attract those who would not normally come to church on Sunday morning. Consequently, this enables the local assembly to reach out and encourage others in nontraditional ways to experience the love and the drawing of God." Wilson, who is an activist with a strong interest in community and economic development "through the body of Christ," is also a Harlemite by birth.

Beth-Hark has four paid staff members, including Wilson, and seven volunteers. The center is open Monday through Friday from 1:00 P.M. to 7:00 P.M. No fee is charged, and "there is an open door policy for 'whosever will.' It allows those who are unable to pay to feel as if there is a place to go just as those who can afford to go for advice and counsel have places to go." Wilson sees the involvement of volunteers as one of the center's strengths, and he ironically delights in the center's "lack of professionality"—which means that because Beth-Hark draws on a devoted pool of lay believers "who feel led of the Lord," there is no institutional standard that subjects clients to an inflexible measure of evaluation. "Instead, people reach out for the sake of love and the need to serve God."

Since Beth-Hark functions inseparably from the life of the church, the impact of lay believers on the clients often goes beyond their visits to the center. "A strength of this ministry," Wilson says, "is our ability to refer our clients to the local assembly and other local congregations in order to receive additional support—not in the form of 'treatment,' but ministry." Wilson adds that the body becomes part of the healing process with the clients developing relationships with others from a Christian perspective and that "this helps the clients to develop a positive view of life that enables them to overcome."

Wilson also speaks frankly about what he believes is another advantage of Beth-Hark's ministry in contrast to many Christian parachurch groups: "One strength of the ministry is the attachment it has to a local assembly, so that there's always a conduit of resources, human, spiritual, and financial." Having that as a foundation is very comforting and assuring. If it were not attached to a church, especially a type of church like Bethel, it might become unattached from the body. In fact, Wilson believes that "some parachurch ministries have gone too far afield of the church, and they often distract believers from the essentials of relationship with the body of Christ."

Wilson says that over the decade he has served as executive director, he has come to see the potential of God's provision, even with minimal resources: "This potential has been fully realized in my life and in the lives of so many of the staff and clients." But Wilson does not hesitate to underscore that much more could be done in the ministry if more resources were to be made available: "I would like to see a greater influx of resources to fill in gaps that have become more obvious to me, resources that would further enhance the competency of Beth-Hark's ministry of meeting the needs of others."[4]

On the lower level of Bethel's expansive complex, the Discipleship Program provides a residential ministry for men. Rev. Leander Harris, also a pastor in Bethel, serves as the director of the program along with his wife, Yolanda, who is a deacon and worship leader in the church. Participants in the Discipleship Program are provided dormitory facilities, meals, and religious education. Participants follow a course of study that is integrated into the program and must be completed if participants wish to graduate. Since the facility is within the church complex, the "Discipleship Brothers" are very active in the life of the church and are not only expected to attend services but become reintegrated into the community through participation in Bethel's ministry.

ENTER TO LEARN, GO FORTH TO SERVE

When Bethel's structure was still a school building, its doors were engraved with the challenge, "Enter to Learn, Go Forth to Serve." Williams often reminds the congregation of that statement, believing that God engraved those words for a time when Bethel would become a center for teaching and preaching the gospel. In a very real sense, in fact, Bethel is still a school, and many aspects of its ministry include educational endeavors.

Bethel's Christian education program provides a multifaceted educational experience to members and guests who can enroll in the Sunday school, the Bethel Bible College, the School of Urban Ministry, the church Bible study program, and the vacation Bible school program. The Christian education department of Bethel is directed by Joyce M. Ford, who is currently completing a master's of professional studies in urban ministry from Alliance Theological Seminary and is the former director of the Breast Examination Center of Harlem. While serving at Bethel and completing her seminary program, Ford, who is also a registered dietician, is currently serving as a research nutritionist for the American Health Foundation. She is quick to point out that the Christian education department's motto is based on Ephesians 4:12, which speaks of "the perfecting of the saints, for the work of the ministry, for the edifying of the body of Christ. Our mission in Christian education is to teach, train, and equip the people of God for ministry."

The vision of Bethel's Christian education department is not only being realized but is expanding to accommodate growing numbers of students. Currently Bethel's Sunday school has the standard classes ranging from nursery to adult, while also offering a variety of topics to adults and classes for new converts, both children and adults. These not only serve to instruct new believers but also to bring transfers and other new members into uniform understanding of Bethel's doctrine and instruction. Beyond the Sunday school program, Bethel offers an evening program that includes a systematic Bible study for church members and guests, while Bethel Bible College and Urban Ministry Center (BBCUMC) offers a Bible college curriculum in affiliation with the Vision Christian College of Pamona, California. Current student enrollment in BBCUMC is about seventy-five, either matriculated or auditing courses in theology, Bible history, and missions. The final aspect of the Christian education department is the annual vacation Bible school, which offers biblical training to students ages two through high-school age as well as crafts, field trips, and music. Throughout the year the department also provides an ongoing curriculum of training for teachers, including "equipping seminars" and classes offered in conjunction with the Evangelical Training Association curriculum and taught by Ford.[5]

Bethel also has other kinds of educational ministry endeavors, such as Project Step-Up, a tutorial program for literacy and general equivalency diploma (GED) instruction. Led by Robert Perkins, a native Harlemite and a teacher in the New York City school system, Project Step-Up is staffed by professional educators and capable teachers who provide literacy instruction to primary-level reading adults up through secondary-level readers as well as math skills instruction.

Another form of education and edification is *Bethel's Voice*, a free weekly paper distributed on Sunday mornings to the membership. Produced on site at Bethel, *Bethel's Voice* features news and announcements pertaining to the church, summaries of sermons, devotionals, and articles by the paper's editor-in-chief, Beverly Lane, and a staff of writers and artists. Bethel also runs its own Christian bookstore, managed by the pastor's wife, Dorothea Williams. The bookstore not only features an assortment of religious education and devotional literature but serves the needs of Bible college and study students.

Though it is an independent ministry, Soul Release Prison Ministries (SRPM) is intimately involved in Bethel Gospel Assembly. Recognizing the critical need to minister to prisoners in New York City and State facilities, Bishop Williams opened Bethel's doors to SRPM in 1987, offering free office space and telephone service. As Bethel continues to grow, SRPM has likewise developed, drawing many volunteers from Bethel and other urban churches.

Willie and Barbara Jarrell are the executive directors of SRPM. With the cooperation of Bethel and SRPM volunteers, the Jarrells are able to reach into a variety of prison facilities, conducting visitation, evangelism, and ministry to incarcerated Christians. SRPM has increasingly broadened its scope, developing or participating in crime prevention and aftercare programs as well as ministry to families of the incarcerated. Perhaps the most popular prison ministry event at Bethel is the annual "Angel Tree" Christmas party. The children of incarcerated parents are invited to Bethel for a party, an entertaining puppet and clown show, and a birthday party for Jesus. The Angel Tree Project, originated by Prison Fellowship, is a massive undertaking requiring year-round preparation and follow-up by the leadership and volunteers of SRPM, not to mention the generosity of many donors who provide gifts for the children on behalf of their incarcerated parents. In addition to developing prison awareness and prevention programs, Bethel and SRPM are working jointly to establish a postprison care facility, the Jericho Road House Project, which will integrate selected ex-offenders into the life of the church and the community through education, employment, and spiritual support.

The pastor likes to reflect that as a youth he spent many unhappy moments in the principal's office at James Fenimore Cooper Junior High School—waiting for his mother to arrive with a chastening for her mischievous son. Today Bishop Williams is again sitting in that office—a room that God has transformed into the office of a leader, just as God has transformed the leader himself. This theme of transformation is key to the continuing presence Bethel will have in a community that is struggling to transform itself against internal and external forces of disintegration.

ACHIEVEMENTS AND CHALLENGES

As illustrated in the story of Bethel Gospel Assembly, the church's achievements—though intertwined with ongoing challenges for the future—represent a significant success among churches in New York City. Key to this success has been commitment to evangelism and holistic ministry, a global as well as local vision, and support for other ministries.

A Firm Commitment to Evangelism

Bethel is indisputably committed to both local and global evangelism. Despite the fact that Bethel, like most successful churches, relies on a core of activists, the philosophy of evangelism permeates the church. Every service or ministry is based on the biblical mandate to present the gospel to the world. Bishop Williams has demonstrated his commitment to this witness for three decades, whether in community outreaches and crusades abroad or in smaller ministries that find shelter in Bethel's facility.

A Firm Commitment to Holistic Ministry

Bishop Williams recalls how "street people" have shown a greater degree of respect to Bethel than to churches that do not reach out to the community. Bethel is not guaranteed immunity from crime, but because the church is committed to meeting human needs, it has earned the respect of those who might otherwise feel contempt toward the church. By being attuned to the needs of Harlem, Bethel has developed a significant holistic ministry, including counseling, prison ministry and crime prevention, literacy and GED instruction, clothing and food provision, the men's Discipleship Program, and other manifestations of the healing presence of Christ. "We are Christ's hands and feet," Bishop Williams often reminds the congregation. And it is in this manifestation of Christ's presence that Bethel has made its ministry known in Harlem.

Thinking Locally and Globally

Bethel may be a church in the heart of Harlem, but it is also a church with an international orientation. Not relying on a denomination or a missions organization to advance the gospel, Bethel has taken the initiative in building international bridges. In addition to funding missionaries and indigenous ministries in nations like Nigeria and India, Bethel brings missions to Harlem—especially with its own missions conference.

One week a year, the church hosts delegates from various mission fields, holding seminars, workshops, and services in keeping with a specific theme. Keynote speakers are featured, and the entire congregation is expected to participate throughout the week. Bishop Williams even encourages his membership to take a week's vacation in order to attend. The commitment to missions as demonstrated in this annual convention has no parallel in any church in Harlem—indeed, the traditional churches tend to stress events like church and pastoral anniversaries, which have little or no value in terms of outreach and missions. A positive side effect of this commitment to missions is that many "Bethelites" are far more oriented toward cross-cultural situations than is the traditional urban church member.

A Supportive Role toward Other Ministries

One of the distinguishing characteristics of Bethel's success has been its embrace of other ministries, such as SRPM, that are not actually Bethel programs but have been adopted by the church and integrated into the church's ministry presence. By offering office space to SRPM and other ministries, Bethel has proven to be a critical resource without requiring remuneration from them. In so doing, these ministries have been relieved of the financial burden of overhead expenses involved in office rental while, in turn, Bethel has been strengthened by new types of ministry expertise.

Apart from long-term collaborations, Bethel supports other urban ministry endeavors, playing host to visitors, sharing experience, and participating in a variety of neighborhood and citywide crusades. The conciliatory tone set by Bishop Williams has created forums for guests to interact with Bethel's ministries at a grassroots level.

PART TWO

*New York City Mission
in the Latino Context*

As never before, Latinos are leaving their imprint on the religious and political life of America. Today, there are over 30 million Latinos in the United States, including 2 million of New York's 8.5 million people. Sixty-five percent of the residents of the South Bronx are Latino, and many traditionally black sections of the city are rapidly becoming Hispanic. Nationwide, Latinos are growing four times faster than the African American population and ten times faster than the white community. The religious life of Latino Americans is characterized by rapid growth in evangelical churches, often at the expense of Catholic churches. Many of New York's fastest-growing Protestant megaparishes would actually post no growth or negative growth if it weren't for their Latino members. And yet, Roman Catholicism still claims the allegiance of 70 percent of Latino Catholics. Whereas evangelical Latinos tend to shy away from involvement in political and social change, Latino Catholics are at the forefront of community organizing and advocacy on behalf of the poor.

This section presents three very different models of Latino Christianity—two evangelical and one Catholic.

The Latino Pastoral Action Center (LPAC) breaks out of the "celestial" mold of Latino evangelicalism to present a "holistic" model of Christian ministry. Its CEO, Rev. Ray Rivera, seeks to "challenge churches that are Christ-centered to develop a passion for social justice and liberal churches to develop a passion for evangelism." LPAC is located in the distressed Highbridge section of the Southwest Bronx and is a second home for hundreds of youth in its neighborhood. LPAC supports a variety of ministries that serve vulnerable populations, train people for ministry, and improve neighborhoods through community organizing and development.

Bay Ridge Christian Center defines its mission in terms of worship, discipleship, fellowship, and service. Luis Padilla, the pastor of Bay Ridge, is a Pentecostal minister who seeks to avoid the legalism that often accompanies Latino expressions of Pentecostalism. The scope of Bay Ridge's work ranges from a ministry to the homeless in Brooklyn to Radio Vision, with a daily audience of half a million people. The vision of Bay Ridge is to transform societies through reaching individuals with the Gospel and through planting churches. Concerns about the school system have, however, prompted Bay Ridge to open an academy to "serve the whole Bay

Ridge community." The academy currently enrolls 200 students in kindergarten through eighth grade.

The Roman Catholic parish of St. Barbara's is activist in promoting a political role for the church. "Jesus preached and healed on the streets and in the marketplace," Father Powis says. "Parents who accept the challenge to live the gospel also need to preach in the public forums of the community and attempt to heal the sickness of systems which leaves children no alternative to failure." At St. Barbara's, activism takes the form of political organizing to promote educational reform, safer streets, voter mobilization, and naturalization services. St. Barbara's is a member of the East Brooklyn Congregations, which has built thousands of affordable homes for the working poor and has opened two alternative public high schools.

8

Redeeming Babylon

The Latino Pastoral Action Center and the South Bronx

Robert D. Carle

A sharp deceleration thrusts seventeen-year-old Willie Ramos deep into the pilot's seat of the four-passenger Skyhawk aircraft. Willie turns the yoke slowly, tipping the wing of the small plane toward the ground. A lush New Jersey landscape of cultivated fields, farmhouses, and tidy suburbs bursts into view. Water shimmers everywhere beneath the blazing August sun—in lakes, canals, glittering swimming pools, and ponds dotted with pink water lilies. Willie rights the plane, and cows emerge from the green, plodding aimlessly in the blinding sunlight.

Willie radios the control tower through the microphone on his headset. "This is 6521 X-ray Cessna 210 inbound from the northwest with ATIS Gulf."

"6521 X-ray report on entry to the pattern," a voice answers back.

"Abeam the tower."

"Cleared to land."

Willie takes a deep breath and steers the plane into the wind for the final approach to the runway.

Blasts of hot summer air blowing through the vents make Willie and his passengers feel like they are inside a huge blow drier. As the plane draws level with the runway, Willie activates the brake flaps and pushes the yoke toward the dashboard. The plane slows down to forty-five miles per hour and lands with a thud on the tarmac. When the plane door opens, steamy air, heavy with the smell of flowers and gasoline, fills the cockpit.

Riding as a passenger back to the Bronx with his flying mates, fifteen-year-old Al Martinez and his fourteen-year-old brother, Jeremy, Willie views manicured lawns surrounding elegant homes that sell for $3 million apiece. As their car crosses the George Washington Bridge, they plunge into the poorest congressional district in the United States, filled with sirens, honking horns, potholed streets, and grimy, rattling subway trains, which pop out from underground when they hit the South Bronx.

No trees line the Grand Concourse where Willie lives in a massive beleaguered public housing project, called by residents the "hottest crack spot in the Bronx." The sidewalks along the concourse are crowded with children, some of whom have forced open a fire hydrant and are playing in the water gushing out of it. Idle clusters of teenagers smoke cigarettes, sip beer, and flirt with each other. Adults sit on folding chairs, playing cards and dominos on empty crates that serve as tables. Billboards advertising liquor, cigarettes, check-cashing services, and other "transactions of decline" color the side streets that feed into the Concourse. The interiors of *bodegas*, small food stores, are lined with bulletproof protective shields through which goods are exchanged for money. Burglaries, armed robberies, muggings, and rapes are so commonplace here that only the most outrageous among them qualify as news.

For Willie, the link between the elite world of aviation and the distressed world of the South Bronx is the Latino Pastoral Action Center (LPAC), located in a two-story white building whose five thousand square feet of space sits astride the busy intersection between 170th Street and Jerome Avenue. The center includes a full-court gym, a stage, a multipurpose room, classrooms, a weight room, computer rooms, a theater, and an auditorium.

The Latino Pastoral Action Center was founded in 1993 by the Reverend Ray Rivera. "We are here," Ray says, "to challenge churches that are Christ-centered to develop a passion for social justice, and liberal churches to develop a passion for evangelism." Ray has a history that is uniquely suited to this task. He has been at various times a community organizer for the Johnson administration's War on Poverty, a Pentecostal minister, and a Reformed Church in America administrator with ties to the National Council of Churches and the World Council of Churches.

The ministries at LPAC represent the breadth of Ray's background and the range of his interests. LPAC houses:

Youth Ministries

An after-school program offering 200 children after-school activities, including homework help, basketball, dance, karate, and art.

Greater Heights Program—an after-school program that trains 150 young adults between ages sixteen and twenty-five for college and career opportunities in addition to offering extracurricular activities and opportunities for spiritual growth.

Family Life Academy—a public alternative elementary school.

Training for Urban Ministry

Latinos in Ministry—a program that addresses the needs of Latinos who are serving people inside the church through various leadership roles or outside the church through their jobs.

Urban Youth Fellows Program—a nine-month certificate program in which youth pastors and lay leaders are trained to develop holistic youth ministries.

Pastoral Care Skills Program—a two-year training program that teaches pastors and laity how to provide pastoral care to church members taking into account psychological and biblical principles.

Community Development Initiatives

The Latino Housing Initiative Planning Project—a project for developing affordable housing in the South Bronx and East Harlem.

Parent Action Network—a community organizing/training institute for parents who seek improvements in the education of their children.

Nuestra Gente (Our People)—a community development project in the Highbridge area where community residents, community-based organizations, and local churches seek to effect change on concerns ranging from public education, community-police relations, lack of public spaces, welfare reform, and immigration laws.

La Iglesia y Comunidad (The Church and Community)—a cable TV program that focuses on church issues as they relate to the community.

Partnerships with *Marymont College* and *Nyack College* through which fifty students are enrolled in B.A. programs and receive scholarships.

Ministries of Mercy

Bruised Reed Program—a program ministering to persons with AIDS and HIV.

His Abundant Love Ministries—ministries to people with disabilities.

All these ministries seek to touch people with four principles: *liberation* from personal sin and from oppressive social structures; *healing*, as exemplified in the suffering servant image of Isaiah 53 (Ray says, "We all are called to be wounded healers."); an authentic experience of Christian *community (koinonia)* that issues in service *(diakonia)*; and personal and structural *transformation*, which represents "a call to perpetual growth." These principles—liberation, healing, community, and transformation—are displayed prominently on the front door of LPAC along with the slogan "Educating, Equipping, and

Empowering People to Transform Our City." The four principles aim to build a thriving community by strengthening the "four pillars": churches, community-based organizations, families, and schools.

The *Greater Heights Program,* in which Willie participates, is directed by Ray's son, Stephen Rivera. It serves 150 youth, ages sixteen to twenty-one, and meets Monday through Thursday from seven to ten P.M. Daily activities include a short motivational message followed by a time of reflection. Participants then have a selection of college and career-building activities to choose from (GED preparation, Writing That College Essay, Getting an A on a College Interview, Assessing Skills for Today's Job Market, Basic Office Know-How). They also have daily times of recreation that include body building, drama, karate, dance, and basketball. On a weekly basis participants attend leadership classes that address such issues as Achieving Success Regardless of Your Past, Volunteer for Character Building, Getting Along with Difficult People, How to Manage Your Time, How to Make a Budget.

One of the optional activities in the program is the Civil Air Patrol, which involves a rigorous schedule of training led by bespectacled seventy-five-year-old Major Rev. Jim Anderson. He tells his charges, "If you attend school every day, come to meetings on time, and stay away from all the sins of the world, you will fly." The Civil Air Patrol (CAP) is the part of the Air Force auxiliary that is committed to training civilians in the art of search and rescue. In CAP, youth aged fourteen to twenty operate global positioning satellite systems that "make all other computers old-fashioned," learn first-aid from the Red Cross, and make flying grids designed to locate lost airplanes.

"For teenagers who lack discipline, this training is a lifesaver," Pastor Anderson says. "Youth learn a whole host of activities that will lead to productive employment. The most outstanding participants qualify for Air Force scholarships."

Sixteen-year-old Beatrise Feliciano spends at least three nights a week at the Center. She participates in the Center's aviation, martial arts, and chapel programs. Greater Heights has enhanced her relationship with God, increased her physical and mental well-being, and taught her to do things that she never imagined possible. "Flying a plane is better than a roller coaster," Beatrise said. "It is a thrill I will never forget."

A HOLISTIC VISION

During an interruption in a steady stream of phone calls and demands from staff, Ray Rivera sits back in his chair and takes a deep breath. "The church," he says, "is the only indigenous Latino institution in this country dedicated to personal liberation and systemic transformation. Unfortunately, the liberal-evangelical divide during modernist controversies in the 1920s is reflected in many ethnic churches, depriving them of the vitality they need to play a transformative role in their contexts. Now we have churches that care about social justice that are empty, and 'celestial' churches that are packed."

Ray explains, "Liberal models are weak congregationally. Liberal churches have small membership, low morale, little success in stewardship. Indigenous Latino churches in the evangelical tradition focus on ministering to the individual. They have powerful organizational infrastructures and significant leadership and traditions of tithing.

"We seek to build an organization that combines the achievements of evangelism and the liberating vision of the best of liberal theology. Our organizing principle is the Word of God. We are holistic, Christ-centered, dependent upon the Holy Spirit, and focused on the realities of people. We are providing leadership for local churches to provide holistic ministry.

"Excuse me," Ray says, "I need to take this call." For fifteen minutes, Ray argues with a member of the board of education over the case of a youth for whom an arrest six years ago is blocking employment with the city.

"But he was only a kid, and he was only incarcerated for six months," Ray says into the telephone. "In the intervening years, he has had a life-transforming Christian experience, and he has been a completely reliable member of our team here."

The call ends inconclusively, with the person on the other line promising to speak to her superior about the case.

"Sorry," Ray said, as he returned to his explanation of "holistic ministry," which is the theological and practical foundation of Latino Pastoral Action Center.

Ray, fifty-one, holds together a variety of commitments and perspectives that appear at first to be contradictory. He speaks of systemic and structural oppression and of Pentecostal glossolalia. He is a pastor in the Reformed tradition yet is dedicated to building bridges between Latino Protestants and Catholics. He speaks the language of an academic theologian yet relates easily to kids on the street.

Ray grew up in a Roman Catholic family in East Harlem, "the capital of Puerto Rico in New York."

"This was a time of ethnic tension between Italians and Puerto Ricans," Ray says, "the kind of thing *West Side Story* was made of. I remember that as a child I could not go east of Third Avenue because First and Second Avenues were all Italian."

When Ray was fourteen, a move to Ocean Hill in Brownsville plunged him into a frightening world of interracial relationships. Ray was the only Latino in that Italian Brooklyn neighborhood, and he was derisively nicknamed Poncho. Making Italian friends in that painful context prepared Ray to reach out across the barriers of race and class that have been a hallmark of his ministry.

Shortly after Ray's move to Brooklyn, he attended a series of meetings that changed his life.

"I was walking on Fulton Street, and I heard this music coming out of a dance hall and thought it was a dance. But when I looked in, it wasn't a dance. Two evangelists had rented out the place and were having a crusade.

"The evangelists would pray for the sick, and my friends and I made out that we were healed. Everyone in the tent was praising God, and we were laughing at them. But something kept drawing us back. The evangelists rented the place for three weeks, and we went back every night. The last night of the campaign, the evangelists invited us to a deteriorated storefront Pentecostal church in Brownsville that held fifty people—when it rained outside it rained inside. It was there that I accepted Christ as my personal Savior.

"The church became my life," Ray says. "I came from an undisciplined life, and now I had rules and regulations."

When Ray was nineteen, the Pentecostals sent Ray to pastor

his first church, which had "ten members and three feuding families." He was there for six years, during which the church grew from ten to two hundred members. While serving in this pastorate, Ray became a community organizer for the Johnson administration's War on Poverty.

"Two pieces of my life were diametrically opposed." Ray says. "Pentecostal churches teach that you must separate yourself from the world. And here I was organizing people to change the world."

Ray's attempt to integrate his Pentecostal faith with his passion for justice became a creative struggle that, to this day, governs his life.

After earning a seminary degree from New York Theological Seminary, Ray was hired by the Melrose Reformed Church to pastor a church in the South Bronx. "Ten white people were left in the church," Ray says, "and the denomination wanted me to minister to the remnant and transition the church to Hispanic."

In the years that followed, Ray rose quickly through the structures of the Reformed Church in America, and in 1976 he became the national secretary for Hispanic Ministries in the Reformed Church in America.

"I was thirty years old and the top Hispanic executive in a mainline denomination, with an office at 475 Riverside Drive overlooking the Hudson River and Grant's Tomb. I traveled all over the country. I was a young Puerto Rican born and raised in East Harlem, dealing with people of Dutch extraction. I preached in places like Holland, Michigan, and Sioux City, Iowa. As I went around preaching, I lived in people's homes.

"At Riverside, I served on the World Council of Churches and National Council of Churches policy bodies that were reflecting critically on what the role of the gospel is in relation to issues in the world. I brought to these bodies Pentecostal experience and evangelistic zeal. It was a crucial contribution that they needed at that time."

In 1993 Ray went to the Pew Trusts, the New York Foundation, and the Aaron Diamond Foundation with a proposal to develop ministries for Latino and other urban churches that would combine evangelism and social concern. He started the Latino

Pastoral Action Center with a staff of two. Six years later, LPAC is housed in a $5-million building and has a staff of forty and an annual operating budget of nearly $1 million.

Ray says about LPAC, "I feel that working here is the culmination of what I started when I pastored that Pentecostal church and worked as a community organizer for the War on Poverty. Back then my two worlds did not meet in a very systematic way. Now, finally, I am integrating the personal with the social and the sacred with the secular to provide balance in ministry. That is where the Lord wants me to be.

"We want to lift this building up as a model of what can be done. We want to be a signpost for the twenty-first century that holistic ministry can be done. This is my best effort to present a model that addresses the historical dichotomy in the evangelical church."

SAVING THE CHILDREN

The schools in the LPAC's neighborhood (the Highbridge neighborhood of the Southwest Bronx) are among the most troubled schools in the United States. Students at City Elementary School 64 scored dead last in New York City in both reading and math competence. The locals grimly nickname Taft High School "Training Animals For Tomorrow." Gangs such as the Kings, Nieta, and Zulu Nation wield more authority in the halls of the school than teachers and administrators do. Taft made national news last year when a thirty-one-year-old English teacher, son of Time-Warner C.E.O. Gerald Levin, was murdered by a student in his Westside Manhattan apartment for an ATM card. Every year hundreds of students in the South Bronx do not even have a school building but are placed in abandoned buildings and trailers to ease overcrowding. Others study in makeshift classrooms in stair landings, coat closets, and bathrooms. The school boards in the South Bronx are so corrupt that in 1996 Attorney General Reno suspended them and placed their schools under the trusteeship of the Chancellor's office.

In 1997 the Latino Pastoral Action Center partnered with School District 9 to open the Family Life Academy under the New York City New Vision School Program. New Vision Schools are an attempt to upgrade the quality of public education in

New York by encouraging community-based organizations to open public schools. These schools are funded at the same level (around $7,000 per student per year) as public schools run by the city, but they are administratively autonomous. Churches are not excluded from this program, although religious education is not permitted in public schools run by churches.

Family Life Academy submitted a proposal to form a school that would function as an annex of City Elementary School 64, which is one block from the LPAC complex. The academy agreed to take the "overflow" of students that CES 64 and two other local elementary schools (CES 114 and 35) could not accommodate. The school would seek to create a "family" atmosphere in which values such as trustworthiness, care, respect, peace, and tolerance would thrive. Parents at Family Life Academy are expected to be intimately involved in the education of their children and in the life of the school. "Every opportunity I get," Principal Isabel Gutierrez says, "I tell the parents that they are the children's first teachers." Dr. Gutierrez gives each parent a packet of books for use at home to educate their children. Parents raise funds for the purchase of the books by selling candy and class pictures.

As the school day at the Academy draws to a close, Carlos Lopez (Carlito) presides over a kindergarten class of twenty four- and five-year-old children dressed in crisp yellow and blue uniforms. The tables in the bright classroom are littered with Lego sets as the children put together rockets, cars, and towers, their faces gilded in the late afternoon sunlight. Carlito goes from table to table, coaching and guiding in both Spanish and English, absorbed in the passion of instruction. Occasionally he speaks harshly to a student who is restless. The walls of the classroom are lined with children's books, one wall with books in Spanish, the other in English.

Carlito, twenty-six, has a bachelor's degree in Journalism from Baruch College and is currently enrolled in a masters of divinity program at the New York Theological Seminary. He is a graduate of LPAC's Urban Youth Program. The program, designed for youth ages sixteen to twenty-eight, offers a nine-month series of interactive workshops and conferences to "equip youth with the necessary tools to create their own holistic ministries." "Ph.D.s from all over the city come to LPAC to talk to us about issues ranging from strategic planning to fund-raising to sexuality," Carlito explains. After the program is over, LPAC helps graduates implement and manage their own holistic ministry projects. The program has seventy-five graduates who have started twenty holistic Latino ministries.

Carlitos' holistic project, which he is still in the process of developing, is RACHEL's Hope (Rebuilding Authentic Community Holistically Engaging one another in Love). RACHEL's Hope will set up support groups for men and women affected by violence (both abusers and abused), with psychological services and shelters to support such groups. Carlito's interest in the issue of domestic violence developed in response to the large number of his kindergartners who were traumatized by violence in their homes.

"Domestic violence is our nation's 'silent crime,'" Carlito says, "For every ten domestic violence shelters, we have twenty animal shelters."

"I practically live here," Carlito says of the Latino Pastoral Action Center. Carlito teaches from 8:00 to 3:00 on weekdays, and on weekends he serves as the executive director of the Urban Youth Program. On nights when he is not at seminary, Carlito stays at the center to help the staff with the large number of youth who pass through its doors to lift weights, play basketball, learn martial arts, or work on computers.

"I'll take a group of five of them for a pizza or ice cream," Carlito says. "Many of the kids who come here are in gangs, such as Kings, Nieta, and Zulu Nation. The brightest ones deal drugs," Carlito says pointing to a store up the street. "You will notice that the stores in the neighborhood carry $50 designer shirts and $100 designer pants. Drug dealers pay these prices."

Carlito leads Bible studies tailored to the roughest kids at the center. Ten surly youth shuffle into the five-minute Bible study that Carlito asks them to attend as the center closes. Several of the kids in the study wear beads identifying them as gang members. Nearly all of the kids carry knives.

Carlito reads a selection from Jeremiah:

"O LORD, you have enticed me,
    and I was enticed;
you have overpowered me,
    and you have prevailed.
I have become a laughingstock all day long;
    everyone mocks me.
For whenever I speak, I must cry out,
    I must shout, 'Violence and destruction!'
For the word of the LORD has become for me
    a reproach and derision all day long. . . .

Cursed be the day on which I was born!
The day when my mother bore me,
    let it not be blessed!
Cursed be the man
    who brought the news to my father saying,
'A child is born to you, a son,'
    making him very glad.
Let that man be like the cities
    that the LORD overthrew without pity;
let him hear a cry in the morning
    and an alarm at noon,
because he did not kill me in the womb. . . .
Why did I come forth from the womb
    to see toil and sorrow,
    and spend my days in shame?"
                        —Jeremiah 20:7-18, NRSV

"Jeremiah was called to be a prophet. He was called at a young age, probably sixteen. And yet he finds himself against a wall."

Carlito fixes his gaze on the cross above his audience's head: "God, you never told me that it would be this hard," he shouts. "God, you never told me that people would mock me, curse me, backstab me, leave me, hurt me, deceive me. You never told me these things, Lord. You never told me that my family would disown me. You never told me that my mother would disown me. You never told me that I wouldn't have a father for a good part of my life. You never told me that I would go through all this. God, you lied to me! How dare you, O God, do this to me?"

In a quieter voice, Carlito says, "Many times we feel in our walk that it is unfair. Why has God let so much nonsense filter into our lives?

"But it is not God making us go through nonsense.

"Through every school there is separation, preparation, calling, and then there is the anointing to work within the calling. I don't know what stage you are in, but know it is not going to be easy. There are a lot of things that you will not be able to understand, not now, not two years from now, not ten years from now. God never told us that we would understand at all. He only said that he would be with us.

"Cry out unto him, and he will respond. Call out to the Lord and he will be by your side. God is sufficient for us. God has a calling for you. He will not leave us or forsake us. Not even a leaf falls off a tree without having been ordained by God. Each and every thing in your life God uses for a purpose. If you let him, God will use even your pain to bless others."

Carlito lowers his voice still further as he winds down his homily. "God is not a God who failed to plan and plans to fail. God is a God who plans ahead of time. Even before you were born, God had ordained it for you to be here today.

"May I have an Amen?"

"Amen!" some of the youth shout before shuffling out of the center into the darkness.

"I tell stories that will hit home," Carlito says. "The woman caught in adultery; the Samaritan woman who had five husbands and now a lover; tax collectors making dishonest gains." To kids caught in a web of sexual license, violence, and drug dealers, these stories show God's love. The plethora of activity at the center offers them an alternative to life on the streets.

Richard Baldwin, a skinny sixteen-year-old who calls himself Piggy, is a former "street pharmacist" (drug dealer) and member of the Zulu Nation. Piggy is an alumnus of Carlito's Bible studies and attests to the transforming power of the gospel that he has encountered through the center.

"I used to hang out on the streets from 3 P.M. until 2 A.M. every day," he said. "Now I spend my evenings doing sports and listening to the Word of God. The center is my second home. They don't try to change you here. They accept you and treat you like an equal. You come here and you feel wanted, not unwanted."

For Piggy, and for many of the other kids at the center, LPAC is the only safe haven in their lives. Piggy lives in the same beleaguered building as Willie, the "hottest crackspot in the Bronx," where shoot-outs are a regular feature of life. Piggy, like all of the youth at the center, talks about the many friends he has lost to gunfire.

Of Taft High School, Piggy says, "I saw people get sliced there every day. You need army training to get through that school alive." Piggy was thrown out of Taft for fighting, but at the center he learned that "when you have to fight you don't need weapons, for the Bible says that 'the Word of God is living and active, sharper than any two-edged sword' (Hebrews 4:12)." After his conversion, he gave his knife to Pastor Rivera, who keeps it locked in a drawer, along with many other knives that kids have given up. At the Center's annual Victory Weekend retreat during which he committed his life to Christ, Piggy tossed his Zulu Nation beads into a fire to dramatize his shifted loyalties.

"The gangs respect Christianity," Carlito says. "If you leave a gang to serve Jesus, that's okay. If you leave for any other reason, you're life is in danger."

Homicide is the number one killer of children in the Bronx, and AIDS is second. LPAC is committed to a two-pronged effort to combat the epidemic. Through Bruised Reed Ministries,[1] the Center provides supportive services for people affected by AIDS, including hospital visitations, a referral network, advocacy for entitlement, a food pantry, and support groups for survivors. Bruised Reed also offers grief counseling and funeral services to families of the deceased. "HIV/AIDS is as diverse as the persons who are afflicted by it," Rosa Carballo writes. "The virus has touched our parents, sisters and brothers, children, relatives, friends, coworkers, and our community at large."

Through sex education, leaders at the center hope, in a modest way, to begin changing the machismo environment that promotes promiscuity and shuns the use of condoms.

Thirty-year-old Pastor Mitchell Torrez, leading an LPAC workshop, tosses an apple into his boisterous audience. "Pass it around," he shouts, and the apple soars around the room as hollering kids compete to catch it.

The apple returns to Pastor Mitchell, and he says, "Stephen, come here."

A small thirteen-year-old in a huge Tommy Hilfiger outfit approaches the stage.

"Eat the apple," the pastor says.

"No way," Stephen responds.

"What's wrong?" asks Mitchell.

"I will get sick," Stephen says.

"Something much worse will happen if you throw your sexuality around."

"Here at LPAC," Ray Rivera says, "we stress abstinence as the best possible method, and we teach that the Christian position is abstinence outside of marriage. But we are not so dogmatic that we won't talk about risk reduction. Kids who are sexually active should use condoms. Women who are married to sexually promiscuous men should use condoms. AIDS is growing faster among Latino women than among any other segment of our population."

Carlito believes that LPAC has created an environment in which abstinence is credible. "Teachers can talk to kids about sex until they are blue in the face, but some kids just won't listen. But when they come here and see that the youth counselors they admire are abstaining from sex until they meet that someone special, they get turned on. They want to try abstinence themselves!"

A THEOLOGY FOR THE URBAN CONTEXT

Ray Rivera explains how the preaching and teaching at the center express a biblical theology that is relevant to those who come there. "The minute Hagar was exiled she became an abandoned wife and single parent," Ray says. "Ishmael became the victim of an absent father. Here is a typology for the urban context, speaking to inner-city issues. Abraham and Sarah become abusers as their lack of faith victimizes Hagar."

Ray explains the Bible is not a book about the sanitized "heroes of the faith" that we study in Sunday school, but a book full of fallible, fragile individuals who, in atmospheres charged with aggression, anger, sexuality, and pain, are filled with God's grace. The Bible speaks candidly about how even the best of God's people get caught in syndromes of sibling rivalry, favoritism, theft, obsessions with being number one, and selfish individualism. Most of the Old Testament and all of the New Testament were written in "situations of captivity" in which Jews were a minority people struggling to survive in a hostile environment: Joseph in Egypt, Daniel in Babylon, Nehemiah, Ezekiel, Esther, Jesus, Peter, and Paul all address a captivity context that is directly relevant to the South Bronx.

Dr. Dean Trulear expresses this contextual preaching on a sunny Saturday afternoon at the center in an auditorium packed with teenagers. "When David went out to fight Goliath, the king had no confidence in David. I work with the government right now, and your government has no confidence in you. They have plans for you. They are building jails for you. The government had no confidence in David. King Saul did not think David could kill Goliath. His family didn't think he could do it, but God knew that David could do it. That is your solace and hope. This is your choice. Even if friends and family are not there with you; even if the government is not there with you, God is on your side. David was fighting for Israel. David was fighting for his community, for his neighborhood. Every victory you win is a victory not only for yourself but for your community.

"You have a Goliath in your neighborhood: drugs. Isn't that a Goliath in your neighborhood? If you conquer Goliath, your whole neighborhood wins. We have landlords who do not deal fairly with the tenants. Landlords keep raising rents and doing it in violation of the law, and we don't know that they are violating the law because we can't do our percentages. You kids need to get your math straight. Do you know why you need to get your math straight? You need to do the best you can in math so you can figure out how to do contracts in such a way that your people never get ripped off again.

"If you conquer math, you conquer Goliath. Like David you will not be fighting for yourselves, you will be fighting for your community. David cared, and he made a difference in the lives around him. He did not give up. He never stopped trying no matter how difficult things became."

PAINTING HAPPINESS

If you take the Cross-Bronx Expressway through the South Bronx, you will see out of your car window pleasant looking middle-class homes full of flowers, lace curtains, and smiling brown faces. These homes look real from a distance but are in fact pictures that the city of New York had painted on the side of buildings facing the highway to give tourists and commuters a positive image of the Bronx. Behind the pictures lie neighborhoods full of deteriorating buildings, toxic waste, dysfunctional hospitals, garbage-strewn lots, violent schools, and warring gangs.

But behind these pictures also lies the Latino Pastoral Action Center, vibrating with redeemed life, defeating the Goliaths in its midst. On weekday mornings schoolchildren in blue and yellow uniforms pour into cheerful classrooms. In the afternoons hundreds of youth engage in a myriad of programs to strengthen body, mind, and spirit. In the evenings activists gather for meetings to organize for better schools and against the environmental racism that produces the Bronx's alarmingly high asthma rates. On Saturdays the Urban Youth Program trains young adults in the art of holistic ministries, multiplying the effect of the center in the Bronx and elsewhere. A housing program at the center constructs three-family houses for home ownership, and an employment program trains welfare women to find jobs. The center offers technical assistance to more than fifty nonprofit organizations that are fighting child abuse, caring for AIDS patients and the handicapped, tutoring teenagers, and ministering to the homeless.

It is Ray's vision that, by the twenty-first century, every church will be engaged in holistic ministry. "LPAC is a challenge for our church, saying look what can be done. Every church, for example, can have an after-school center. It doesn't have to be for two hundred kids. It can be for twenty.

"Can you imagine what New York would be like if every church was tutoring kids or building homes or opening credit unions or training welfare mothers? This city would gleam."

And New Yorkers would no longer need to paint pictures along our highways to hide our neighbors.

9

A Reformation in Brooklyn

The Story of Bay Ridge Christian Center

McKenzie P. Pier and Louis A. DeCaro Jr.

> The evangelization of these young Puerto Ricans, difficult
> as it may be for any traditional missionary approach, may well
> hold the key to the future of Christianity in New York City.
> —Antonio M. Stevens Arroyo, "Caribbean Unity"

Seated in the front pew of Bay Ridge Christian Center (BRCC) one Sunday morning, I leaned over and asked Carlos Jimenez how long most sermons last in the Hispanic church. Carlos, the church administrator, said nothing but held up his index finger indicating "one hour." An Anglo with a Baptist background, I was preparing to speak in the second Sunday service at BRCC—a Spanish-language service—already having been in the English-language service for more than two hours. I was overwhelmed by the enthusiastic experience of Sunday morning worship that lasted for a total of five hours and a church that

McKenzie P. Pier currently works as the international director of urban strategies for Concerts of Prayer International (COPI). He has worked with COPI since August 1994. Prior to that, Pier served with InterVarsity Christian Fellowship for thirteen years as associate regional director for New York and New Jersey, area director for metro New York, and campus staff member.

ministered in two languages to a multiethnic congregation. That Sunday morning I was first exposed to the Hispanic Pentecostal experience, a day I will always remember for the powerful, joyful worship of a responsive and animated congregation.

BRCC is located on the corner of Seventh Avenue and Sixty-fourth Street on the west side of Brooklyn, New York. From the front steps of the church one can see the Verazanno Narrows Bridge, which connects Brooklyn with Staten Island, another borough of New York City. BRCC has a profound presence in the Hispanic community of New York City—an important presence indeed, given the fact that the Hispanic presence nationwide numbers more than 22 million, representing a 53 percent increase from 14 million in 1980. The Hispanic population is growing four times faster than the African American population and ten times faster than the white community. It has been projected that within fifteen years Hispanics will be the largest minority group in North America, with a population that will reach 30 million.[1]

New York City itself has become a home to 1.8 million Hispanics, though radio marketers predict that there may be as many as 3 million in the metropolitan area. Of this total number, 60 percent are Puerto Rican—arguably the largest minority in New York City.[2] In "Spanish Harlem," the Hispanic section of New York City's most famous village, the majority is Puerto Rican, while in Manhattan's Washington Heights section, the predominant Latino community is Dominican. In the borough of Queens, many Latinos are from various countries in South America, especially Colombia. And right across the Hudson River in Union City, New Jersey, there is a notable Cuban population. Given this marvelous diversity, it is no wonder that BRCC, though primarily a Puerto Rican congregation, includes Christians from twenty-six ethnic groups. Given its history, vision, and effective ministry, BRCC is clearly key to presenting an effective Christian witness in and beyond the vast Hispanic community of New York City.

HISPANIC AND DIVERSE

Luciano Padilla Jr. has pastored BRCC since 1970. Throughout nearly three decades of ministry, BRCC has undergone incredible transformation under his leadership, especially in moving away from being a traditional, exclusive Spanish-language congregation to a bilingual, multiethnic, multicultural church with an influence in ministry that reaches throughout the Hispanic world. Under Padilla's pastoral direction, BRCC's leadership is comprised of a board of eleven elders and trustees representing the Spanish- and English-speaking membership. The church board provides spiritual and administrative guidance to BRCC's forty-eight ministries, working cooperatively with each ministry's committee head. These ministries fall into one of four established categories: worship, discipleship, fellowship, and service. The diversity of BRCC's ministries is broad, ranging from outreach to the homeless of Brooklyn's streets to radio evangelism in the Caribbean.[3]

Padilla's vision for ministry is especially attuned to the needs of Puerto Ricans and other Hispanics in the world's greatest city. He enumerates these needs as critical areas of BRCC's ministry focus: (1) to combat fatherlessness by building up the family, (2) to combat poverty with education, and (3) to combat the lack of identity by building Christian community. However, Padilla says, "when we started a multiethnic, multicultural ministry to Hispanics of the second generation, this opened the door to others, allowing us to minister to the community at large." Of course, the preponderant culture of BRCC remains "Hispanic"—a term that Padilla prefers, believing it to be inclusive—in contrast to "Latino." Padilla says that those who prefer "Latino" tend to be more nationalistic and therefore less inclusive. Padilla feels that identifying himself and the majority population of the church as Hispanic emphasizes the "whosoever will" message of the Christian gospel. He feels it is important that non-Hispanics feel welcome at BRCC. "The large majority of our people are Hispanic in origin, but we have a representation of others. We try to promote a kingdom culture. I have seen what [nationalism] has done in the black church—indeed, some of our Hispanic brethren have been driven away from Africentric churches. We emphasize a common gospel, a common experience of salvation, and a common Lord."

PUERTO RICO COMES TO BROOKLYN

Of New York City's five boroughs, Brooklyn is the most popu-
lous, with more than 2.3 million of the city's residents. Besides
the Hispanic presence of Brooklyn, there are notable communities of African American (Caribbean and North American),
Asian, and Jewish descent. Of course, Brooklyn's diversity is
specially accented by its Puerto Rican population—a people
who, in themselves, carry a diverse heritage that includes
Spanish, African, and Taino Indian ancestries. In a society
founded by European domination of African labor on land
stolen from Native Americans, the Puerto Rican presence perhaps represents an ironic and providential bridge between
black and white. The origin of this marvelous blend of peoples
can be traced to the history of Puerto Rico itself, a Caribbean
island first taken in the sixteenth-century conquests of the
Spanish and loaded with stolen laborers from Africa. The
mixture of these three cultural forces, while entangled in oppression and domination, produced a new people who inherited a struggle for justice and national identity that continued
into the nineteenth century. With the close of the Spanish-
American War in 1898, Puerto Rico became a province of the
United States, and its people first immigrated to North America
in 1900. The struggles of the Puerto Rican people are still quite
relevant: the quest for national identity, hindered by marginal
economic and political power, remains a vital reality. This is
best illustrated in Puerto Rico's single seat in the United States
Congress—held by a *nonvoting* representative.

Luciano Padilla's family, like many other poor families in
rural Puerto Rico, fled the poverty of colonialism to seek a
better life abroad. Crossing through the Panama Canal, the
Padillas first settled in Hawaii. Later, the family was moved to
North America, where they settled first in East St. Louis,
Missouri, and, in the 1930s, finally in South Brooklyn. Arriving
with many other compatriots, the Padillas came to New York
in the first wave of Puerto Rican immigration, the "Pioneer
Era,"[4] which lasted from 1900 to 1945.

In those early years, the elder Luciano worked for nearly two
decades in a chocolate factory, while many Puerto Rican immigrants were working on New York's famous piers along the East

River. Like many contemporary Mexican immigrants in New York City, these Puerto Rican "pioneers" in New York struggled with poverty in a land of plenty, often being forced to share a single apartment dwelling with one or two other families.

Just as Luciano Padilla represents the advancing offspring of the Puerto Rican community, he is also a spiritual heir to the legacy of "pioneer" faith in that community. Indeed, he is a son of the very church he pastors today. At the age of eighteen, he heard a call to vocational ministry. However, his growing awareness of God's calling in his life also included coming to the realization that in the United States, racism was a sin that permeated the church along with the rest of society. Padilla recalls an eye-opening incident that occurred in 1955, when he attended a conference in Mingus, Texas, along with a group of hundreds of Hispanic youth like himself. This, he says, was the first time he experienced racism in the United States. "Before we even got into the deep South, just in Baltimore, we stopped into a local restaurant and were asked to leave. When we got to Texas, I got the shock of my life. I actually had a man tell me—quite sincerely too—that he believed in Jesus but did not believe in 'niggers.' In the South I was 'colored.'"

Two years later, he took his first pastorate at a mission church in New Britain, Connecticut. From 1963 to 1970 Padilla attended Manhattan Bible College, working toward a bachelor's degree in theology while pastoring a mission church in the East New York section of Brooklyn.

At age thirty Padilla was called to his home church, a Pentecostal congregation that originated in a Methodist prayer meeting in 1930. Like many others in the founding generation of the Pentecostal movement, Padilla's church had begun in rejection and religious controversy. Its founding members, led by a woman named Mercedes Lopez, were "excused" from the Methodist church for speaking in tongues. They found their own place of worship, where they remained until 1947, when the congregation relocated to a building owned by the Salvation Army. This was the foundation of the church upon which Luciano Padilla began to build in 1970, the church that would eventually be called "Bay Ridge Christian Center."

1970–80: BUILDING A TRAINING AND SENDING MOVEMENT

In the first decade of Padilla's leadership, the church dug deeply into its Pentecostal roots, particularly in its regard for the poor. The Hispanic Pentecostal church has always been a church for the poor, and this is particularly the case with Puerto Ricans, who, according to Manuel Ortiz, "have experienced a declining sense of well-being compared to Mexicans and Cubans."[5] Indeed, the Puerto Rican community is the poorest of the Latino communities in the United States, with an average annual income of $18,000 and 38 percent in poverty, the highest percentage. As noted above, an accompanying issue of great concern is fatherlessness, since almost half of all Puerto Rican families are without the presence and influence of fathers. In awareness of these needs, BRCC began to develop worship and prayer as a means of introducing people to the fatherhood of God, a heavenly Father who knows their every need and remains present and faithful to his children.

Between 1970 and 1980 Padilla's congregation grew from two hundred to three hundred members, a growth motivated by evangelism empowered by vibrant worship and prayer. In the early 1970s BRCC had forty-five daughter churches up and down the eastern seaboard and in Puerto Rico and Guatemala.[6] At this time Padilla was asked to serve as the bishop of the Pentecostal Christian Church. Serving as the movement's overseer, he traveled extensively throughout the regions of Central and South America and the Caribbean. Padilla held this demanding position until 1981, having functioned as a spiritual father and teacher to scores of international pastors. Besides enriching the spiritual vision of his own congregation with the breadth of his international ministry, Padilla sought to develop the educational ministry of the BRCC church.

BRCC hosted Emmanuel Bible Institute beginning in 1970 but in 1982 became affiliated with Logos Bible College. In 1989 this affiliation was transferred to Vision Bible College of Ramona, California. BRCC's Bible Institute provides training for lay leadership, offering forty-three courses in either Spanish or English and a nonaccredited bachelor's degree. Today there are as many as 150 students enrolled in the institute, sustaining leadership development in a transient urban environment. In almost thirty years of teaching ministry, BRCC has helped hundreds of students gain a greater intimacy and understanding of the fatherhood of God and the lordship of Jesus Christ.

1981–90: CONTEXTUALIZATION FOR A NEW GENERATION

In Padilla's church is an Asian named Johnny who serves as the cameraman at BRCC. Where did a Puerto Rican Pentecostal church get an Asian cameraman? Johnny's presence at BRCC, like the presence of many other non-Puerto Ricans, reflects another aspect of the church's development as a vital ministry in New York City.

Even though the church had grown in the 1970s, Padilla had become restless and concerned over the youth exodus from the Hispanic Pentecostal movement. Typically, many were moving to "American" churches, and some were dropping out altogether. Padilla studied the situation carefully and discerned three main reasons for this disturbing trend: (1) the Hispanic Pentecostal movement's binding legalism that emphasized issues of dress; (2) language; and (3) a loss of hope among youth, whose educational and employment opportunities were limited. Padilla knew the Hispanic church, and he recognized that youth were restricted by the older generation and at the same time had adopted English as their language of choice because of their experience in the city's educational system. The voice of the Hispanic Pentecostal church was fading in the hearing of the young generation.

In 1981 the church moved from Summit Street in South Brooklyn to its present location at Sixty-fourth Street and Seventh Avenue in Bay Ridge. During the first service at their new location, Padilla, who had resigned from his denominational position of bishop,[7] announced a new church philosophy that accompanied the church's new name, "Bay Ridge Christian Center." The church, Padilla declared, would take a stand against the prevailing legalism of the Hispanic Pentecostal church. As it turned out, the new name and stance of BRCC were complemented by its strategic new location. Now residing next to Eighth Avenue, New York City's emerging third Chinatown, BRCC began to attract Asians and Latinos. With a new building, a new philosophy, and a new diversity, BRCC introduced an English-language service (the second Hispanic church in New York City to do so). The initiation of an English-language service and the renunciation of legalism proved to mark a new point of growth for BRCC. During the 1980s the congregation grew from three hundred to six hundred members.

Representatives of the Hispanic community in New York City cite employment and education as their two greatest concerns. According to these sources, a majority of Hispanic New Yorkers have a negative assessment of their neighborhood public schools. More than a third describe these schools as "not so good," and more than a fifth actually describe the schools as "poor."[8] Among the top ten needs of Hispanic in the northeastern United States, Ortiz writes, is an increase of school attendance and a reduction of dropout rates.[9] The dropout rate among Hispanic is three times that of whites—a problem worsened by the fact that less than 3 percent of elementary school teachers in New York City are Hispanic.

In response to the educational crisis in the Latino community, BRCC opened Bay Ridge Christian Academy in 1984. The school provides Christian-oriented education for two hundred students, from kindergarten through eighth grade. The vision of the school is to serve the whole Bay Ridge community, not just BRCC; students from more than twenty local congregations have been registered.

AN ALTERNATIVE TO LEGALISM

According to Padilla, the nature of the legalism common among Hispanic Pentecostal churches is one focused on the outward, exterior person—"No makeup, no hair cutting, no excessive jewelry, shunning worldly entertainment, and an emphasis on these to the extent that it becomes repressive and oppressive." Padilla says that the younger generation of Hispanics in the church has strongly resisted this kind of legalism, and consequently many have left the Hispanic Pentecostal church. Padilla says further that "the person who does not conform to the norms of legalism becomes a scapegoat and may even be used to intimidate others in order to make them stay within those established norms." "It is a very serious issue that is keeping the church from expanding," Padilla says, "because there are so many positive aspects within the Hispanic church. It is a giving church—a church that is willing to invest time and effort in the Lord's work, but its legalism stifles the life of the spirit and keeps it from attracting people from the masses of our community."

Padilla has spearheaded what may very well be a reforming movement among Hispanic Pentecostals, since other churches are beginning to follow his lead in abandoning the old legalism. "In New York City over a dozen churches have broken the mold, so to speak, and they are the largest and most successful churches in the Hispanic Pentecostal community right now. The average Hispanic [Pentecostal] church has thirty to seventy members. On an average Sunday we have over a thousand people. Other churches that are attracting many hundreds of people are those that have also broken the mold." Padilla says that because they jettisoned legalism, "We retained the young people and formed a church to meet their needs." Even at the Sunday afternoon service, a service that is not very popular in any evangelical church, BRCC regularly has 450 people in attendance. "And this is very typical for nonlegalistic churches," Padilla says.

As to legalism itself, Padilla attributes its enduring nature in Hispanic churches to leaders of the various organizations with which Hispanic churches are affiliated, usually called councils. The hierarchies of these councils, says Padilla, keep feeding legalism to pastors, especially in conferences, which in turn is filtered down to local churches. "Pastors who deviate from the norm are viewed as apostate and liberal," and they are often screened and isolated as well. Padilla speaks from experience:

> As I was coming to an understanding of this problem, I experienced this treatment from our mother church at the time and from the Hispanic Pentecostal church at large in New York City. In fact, at the time I was like a superintendent of fifty or more churches, and despite the fact that we were a moderate church, most of the churches I supervised had been born into and influenced by legalism. Thus, when we became independent, I was not only isolated because of my stance toward legalism as a pastor, but I felt the isolation even

more because the churches I had overseen were alienated from me as well. It was like a "double whammy."

With time and a determined commitment to love and respect his legalistic brethren, Padilla proved himself. "By maintaining a biblical standard of holiness and a nonjudgmental attitude toward those who criticized me for leaving the traditional church, after many years I have been received by the Hispanic Pentecostal church at large." According to Padilla, this was most evident in the fact that he was asked to serve as president of Radio Vision Christiana (see below). Today Padilla and BRCC continue to lead a reformation in the Hispanic Pentecostal church. "We have been part of fifteen churches that have outgrown legalism. In fact, we have an informal group of like-minded pastors who support each other, and now we are in the process of organizing. We need to support and encourage each other."

One of the things that Padilla has done to facilitate this encouragement is to hold an annual pastor's conference, bringing in key pastors from Latin America who are not legalists. "We are seeing the beginning of a change in the Hispanic church," Padilla says. "We dealt with legalism as a barrier to growth and dealt with it openly. We have even had speakers on a panel debating this issue, and though it became heated, we maintained compassion in dealing with our legalistic brethren." Through the pastors' conference, Padilla concludes, the new movement is effectively challenging and changing the mindset of many pastors in the Hispanic Pentecostal leadership of the city.

Despite the challenge that Padilla poses to legalistic churches, he has not lost sight of the apprehensions and concerns of the traditional pastors. He understands the mindset of legalism and has consistently endeavored to demonstrate that sensitivity. Padilla believes that "the legalists fear falling into a worldly extreme. I constantly assure them that being nonlegalistic is not as bad as being worldly," and that the new nonlegalistic churches are just as committed to holiness and obedience to God's Word as are the traditional Pentecostal churches. Padilla also believes that legalism has become part of the Hispanic Pentecostal's sense of identity and tradition, and in clinging to legalism, the Hispanic Pentecostal legalist may also be trying to hold on to what has traditionally also provided a sense of security and stability in this society. "Try to take that away from them and you leave them feeling in limbo." Consequently, Padilla believes that the legalistic Christian must not be dealt with in drastic measures. "I tell my young people that the truth of the gospel must be received by revelation, but it cannot be imposed. The pastors' conference may be slow in making an impact," he continues, "but it is important that our pastors understand that our goal is to lay everything at the altar for the sake of truth. When I left my superintendent position, I left behind everything that I had achieved over many years. Many pastors are not willing to do that."

Another significant aspect of the reformation that BRCC and the other nonlegalistic churches have enjoyed is the renewal and refreshment of worship because of music that is "more contextualized to our reality." According to Padilla, prior to the renewal experience, "we sang hymns that we could not relate to, hymns born in a past revival. . . . Our experience today is transformed in that the focus of our worship is exalting Christ who is the One who has the answer we need." Padilla emphasizes further that "urban people can relate to our music—music with synthesizers, drums, percussion—music that expresses joyous celebration. We worship anywhere from forty-five minutes to an hour, and it is dynamic and uplifting, spiritually and emotionally. It releases joy in us and brings relief—and this is especially important for people who are often battered by urban pressures."

LEADERSHIP IN EDUCATION: TWO PROFILES

BRCC is equally committed to higher education. Profiles of two leaders in the church demonstrate that the church's presence in the community provides exemplary personal models of leadership in the attainment of higher education programs for the church.

Carlos Jimenez

Padilla met Jimenez in the Dominican Republic, recognizing in him great leadership potential for the church. BRCC provided

Jimenez a scholarship to attend Regent University in Virginia, where he eventually earned a master's degree in business administration and a master's degree in theology. Jimenez was able to return to BRCC and serve as the church's business administrator; in 1995 he established the Luis Montes Educational Scholarship Fund. Reflecting the need for education, and speaking from his own experience and attainment, Jimenez writes:

> If we take the time to look upon the state of affairs of the educational system of our city, and to truly understand the condition it is in and its implication for our youth, we would be awestruck at the incredible negative odds young people are dealing with. Education is the entry point of opportunity towards economic mobility, self-sufficiency, life skills, self-determination, and identity.[10]

In its first year, BRCC's scholarship fund reached $22,000 through a musical concert featuring popular gospel singers Alvin Slaughter and Helen Baylor. The youth of BRCC covered the concert expenses by earning money in car washes, and local businesses invested in advertisements associated with the event. The scholarship fund has benefited students enrolled at Princeton University, Brooklyn College, Manhattan Community College, and Moody Bible Institute. Jimenez is currently negotiating with a local Christian college to begin a satellite bachelor's degree program in church management at BRCC.

Luis Montes

Like Padilla, Luis Montes is also a son of the church, having attended between 1959 and 1994. His academic career in New York City, going from grade school to graduate level, culminated in a master's degree in secondary education from New York University. Montes taught public school for twenty-seven years and served as a track coach. Under his tutelage more than eighty athletes received scholarships (one of the most notable of his students was Cathalina Stage, who won the National 400 Meter Indoor Championships). In 1984 Montes helped to launch the Bay Ridge Christian Academy, and ten years later he planted a church on Long Island. A bivocational pastor, Montes exemplifies the experiences and accomplishments of many ministry leaders in the Hispanic church and reflects the philosophy and direction of BRCC.

RADIO VISION CRISTIANA: BUILDING BRIDGES OF FELLOWSHIP

Padilla's first move toward building bridges of fellowship across New York City took place in 1984 when he and a few other men of great vision bought radio time for the inception of Radio Vision Cristiana. This answered a decade of prayers among Hispanic Christians in the New York area for a Christian Spanish-language radio station. Padilla was the founding president of Radio Vision, and under his leadership in 1989 the entire radio station was purchased for the price of $13 million—the entire amount provided by individual and church donations. As David Greco, Radio Vision's executive director, says: "When people pray, God births not only a vision, but faith."

The purpose of Radio Vision is "preaching the gospel to the unsaved and edifying the body of Christ." Listeners number over a half million every day, and through additional outlets Radio Vision's listening area includes not only the New York area but also Puerto Rico, Haiti, Cuba, and the Dominican Republic. However, Radio Vision has a commitment to build a bridge to the whole body of Christ. On August 28, 1996, ten pastors from Korean, black, white, and Hispanic backgrounds came together for a three-hour Concert of Prayer on Radio Vision. In praying for New York City and the nations of the world, these leaders also made representative confessions of sins and insensitivities across ethnic lines within the body of Christ.

Padilla believes that Puerto Ricans, with their mixed ancestry of Spanish, Indian, and African are a unique community, along with other Hispanics, capable of bridging differences among the whole of the body of Christ. The Puerto Rican loss of identity is a result of the transient nature of the community, but connecting to the whole body of Christ is one way that Puerto Ricans may discover their identity. Consequently, since 1990 Padilla has been influential in bringing Hispanic churches together and reaching out to the whole body of Christ in West Brooklyn. BRCC has hosted semiannual Concert of

Prayer events for several years, with attendance exceeding seven hundred. Attending the Concert of Prayer event hosted by BRCC in the spring of 1996 were pastors from Hispanic, Italian, Chinese, Egyptian, and African backgrounds.

Throughout 1996 BRCC has functioned as a nerve center for seventeen initiatives in the West Brooklyn area. Spearheaded by Joe Mattera, pastor of Resurrection Church, congregations have been holding joint initiatives ranging from Communion services, a "March for Jesus," street evangelism, and the "Brooklyn Cities Campaign for Community Development." Hundreds of churches across the denominational spectrum have interacted through the medium provided by BRCC over the past year.

PRAYER AND BEYOND: BRCC TODAY

BRCC remains anchored by its commitment to corporate prayer. Each week three hundred people attend a bilingual prayer meeting on Wednesday; Monday through Friday a small group gathers for prayer for two hours in the afternoon; and two days a week another group gathers for three hours of prayer in the morning. In harmony with its intense commitment to prayer, BRCC implemented small groups in 1993. This program presently involves hundreds of people in forty-five home groups, further cultivating a vision of the church built upon a commitment to intercession and relationships within the body of Christ.

In the spiritual foundation and growth of BRCC, Padilla sees three signs of hope for New York City and beyond. First, he sees a coming together of pastors in the community across racial lines. Second, he sees a movement of churches praying for the condition of the city through Concerts of Prayer. Finally, he shares a sense of expectancy among Christian leaders that produces hope for a new move of God that will be far reaching. In this light, Padilla advises new leaders in New York City to spend quality time seeking the face of God for vision and for a growing love for the city. He also urges them to take time to do the necessary homework about the city—demographics, history, and the doing of theology in context.

Padilla believes the historical roots of Pentecostalism in

prayer provide the answer for Puerto Ricans who would seek to discover the fatherhood of God. He acknowledges that the challenge of the church is to be involved with education that empowers youth. He sees the need to embrace the whole body of Christ as the ultimate answer to the question of identity. Padilla believes that ministry is a call to serve, and he wants to be remembered as one anointed by God to serve.

When asked about his vision for Hispanics in the future of New York and the country in general, Padilla reflects: "I have heard it said that the Hispanic church is going to become a force that is going to be used of the Lord to bring renewal to the church at large. There is a life that is lived in the Hispanic church that, when it is released, is going to be a blessing." He believes the Hispanic Christian presence is vital in a society where, unfortunately, in many cases, the so-called mainstream church in the United States has become irrelevant. The evangelical devotion of the Hispanic Pentecostal church to the Scriptures, the vitality of its community and worship, and the promise of an inclusive diversity in the new Hispanic churches may serve as the greatest alternative to many Christians caught "between American traditional churches and liberal churches." Likewise, Padilla believes that Hispanics of the second and third generation in New York City and across the nation have a greater sense of responsibility to make this society a better place to live. "The new generation of Hispanics understands that we are Americans and that we are going to be here for the rest of our lives. We are thinking about living in America and investing ourselves to make this a better place, especially from the gospel's point of view. . . . That's where we are

The future of Christianity in New York City inevitably will be influenced by the Hispanic Christian presence, and this by the evangelization and training of second- and third-generation Puerto Ricans especially. Such a future will require a model of service in ministry exemplified in BRCC—a model that must be multiplied many times over.

Recalling his own family's experience, Padilla points out that the first generation of immigrants invariably thinks about going back "home." "My father's dream was always to go back home. My mother was born in America and would have stayed here, but out of loyalty she went back to Puerto Rico with him. My generation wants to educate our children so they will become successful in America and make the this country better, especially through the church."

The spiritual challenge of prayer is perhaps far more defined for Padilla and BRCC than for the suburban church, which tends to see the cities of our nation as places to be avoided. "We are to pray for the city, as did the prophet Jeremiah, and we ought not to flee the cities. Jeremiah was even to pray for those who were not necessarily his allies"—perhaps a reminder that the Hispanic Christian may at times feel alienated by a society that is at best ambivalent about the growing Hispanic presence in the United States. Yet, Padilla says, God told Jeremiah and the Jews in exile to plant themselves where they were, and in so doing, they became a witnessing community. This witness will not only shine in the European American community, but will prove to have great worth on an international scale. "One of the blessings of the bicultural Hispanic is that we have access to Latin America ministry, and in the Third World I am not viewed the same as whites are often viewed abroad. Yet, being Americans, we have a passport to go anywhere and present the gospel of Jesus Christ."

10

A Gospel of Power

The Story of St. Barbara's Church

Kathy Maire

From almost any place in Bushwick, a neighborhood situated in the northeast corner of Brooklyn and surrounded by Williamsburg, Bedford-Stuyvesant and East New York, you can see the spires of St. Barbara's Church. To those unfamiliar with the community, the sight of the recently-renovated baroque-style church towering over the area may seem an anachronism. To those who know better, it is a symbol of hope. St. Barbara's stands as a proclamation that life can triumph over death, that hope can spring up from despair and that a poor Hispanic community can achieve great things.

St. Barbara's Roman Catholic Church has just celebrated its 100th anniversary and looks over a community that is struggling to be reborn. Today, proud homeowners who have survived tumultuous changes in demographics speak of their

Kathy Maire, O.S.F., is an associate organizer with the East Brooklyn Congregations. She is currently organizing parents and students in Community School District 32 and in the two alternative high schools opened by EBC in 1993.

belief that their community is on the upswing. Most residents, however, are newer to the area and many live in one of the 92 buildings of public housing known as Hope Gardens. At the time the church was built, it served a German immigrant population; today most parishioners speak Spanish and represent dozens of countries in Central and South America. A hundred years ago, Bushwick was known for its mansions. Today, Bushwick is more likely to draw media attention for any of a series of problems that create headlines and sell newpapers.

The signs of life in the community are celebrated at the Sunday worship of St. Barbara's. The 9:30 A.M. English speaking community draws parishioners who hunger to create the Reign of God in their midst. They come to find a way to make moral sense of life and to create a future for their children. Following them, the Spanish-speaking congregation crowds into the church early, coming each week to reestablish its identity in a safe and familiar arena. Parshioners greet each other like long-lost friends, restoring their faith in each other and in their community.

Msgr. John Powis has served as pastor of St. Barbara's since 1989, but no one, including Father Powis, is quite sure how many people attend Mass on Sunday. One thing is certain, however. The church is bursting with life and vitality. An active RCIA (Rite of Christian Initiation for Adults) program attracts from thirty to forty adults each year to prepare for entrance into full sacramental life at Easter. Eucharistic ministers visit local hospitals, nursing homes, and the homebound. A flea market collects clothing and furniture to sell to those in need. Groups meet daily and compete for every available space in the church buildings. Those involved in leading a religious education program must keep up with a growing population of children, and the parish actively participates in community organizing activities of East Brooklyn Congregations (EBC).

Many of the parishioners have participated in local leadership trainings with EBC, and a good number have spent ten days in an intensive training program designed to develop skills for leaders who show great potential. These parishioners speak naturally and easily about meetings with police chiefs, mayors, council members, and other leading city officials.

Parish notices about rallies at city hall are as common as messages about religious activities. This church clearly sees itself as existing beyond the confines of its buildings.

RENOVATION

As the one hundredth anniversary of St. Barbara's approached, the parishioners met often to brainstorm events and activities for the year. The dream of renovating the church kept emerging in these meetings. Many years of water leakage had ruined the walls and the magnificent paintings that had adorned them. Two graceful bell towers rising to a height of 175 feet above the church had been repaired recently, but major exterior and interior renovation was still needed. The parishioners had compelling reasons for renovating the church. Of all the congregations in the diocese, St. Barbara's was unmistakably one of the most alive and vibrant, bursting with parishioners and yet still capable of further growth. Its lay leadership was among the finest in the diocese, and people in the church were deeply committed. All that was lacking was money.

During the times of discussion, an incident happened that dramatized the urgency of repairing the exterior of the church. A twenty-pound chunk of masonry fell from one of the towers, smashing through the roof of the parish vehicle used to make pickups for the flea market. While no one was hurt, the frightening reality remained that the next piece to fall might strike someone. Powis came to the next finance committee meeting dragging the twenty-pound chunk of masonry, and the shocked parishioners knew the time of decision had come.

The best estimates received indicated that the total package of interior and exterior work would cost over $550,000. This might not have overwhelmed a parish in better circumstances, but St. Barbara's struggled even to meet its payroll. The parish was proud that it had never been on subsidy from the diocese and managed to pay its bills. Parishioners had come through time and again when the boiler broke down, during harsh winters when heating oil was high, or when one of the buildings needed a new roof. The parish's financial struggle was a larger version of the struggle individuals and families in the parish experienced on a day-by-day basis.

However, the church was a symbol for the parishioners and for the entire neighborhood. Longtime residents remembered the 1970s when Bushwick resembled a bombed-out war zone, far different from the Bushwick detailed in *Brooklyn Is America* by Ralph Foster Weld describing the World War I period: "The neat and trim brownstone residences which spread through the quiet streets of Bushwick and Ridgewood were models for middle class America. They represented a German ideal—the ideal of respectable social standing in a well regulated community."[1]

Longtime residents remembered the tumultuous years of the seventies, including the 1977 blackout. The *New York Daily News* reported on August 1, 1977, that

> Bushwick is a place where people sleep with their clothes on and their bags packed, where parents often alternate on fire watch. It is a section of 120,000 souls and 6,000 fire calls a year . . . a section of blackened, abandoned homes . . . and weed choked lots where buildings once stood . . . a section that loses a house a day to fire.[2]

Throughout this time of despair when folks surely wondered if God had abandoned them, the church stood as a sign of God's presence in Bushwick. Father Ed Brady, pastor at St. Barbara's for ten years, tells of arriving at his new assignment in 1979 and finding that the church bells did not work. He immediately had them repaired and began to ring them on Sunday mornings to proclaim that God was still in the midst of the community.

After much prayer, serious consideration, and a great deal of research, the committee decided to present their suggestion to the parish stewards. They would seek a loan from the diocese for the exterior renovation and raise $250,000 for the interior work. In order to engage D'Ambrosio Studios to do the entire project, they determined to use a fund-raising company in a three-year fund-raising effort. The stewards approved the plan with full knowledge of the commitment it would mean to each of them in time and money. The parish received a loan from the diocese with the understanding that building safety issues had to be addressed first, especially the front wall of the church, which was in danger of imminent collapse. Powis was encouraged: "The diocese's putting money into the outside of the church is a sign to the community that the bishop is committed [to St. Barbara's]." Eager to support this effort, the parishioners pledged what they could, most of them pledging $720 to be paid over the course of three years.

When the parish celebrated its anniversary Mass in December 1995, the parishioners were ecstatic. The renovation was completed, and all the sacrifices made by the parishioners had paid off. Reporters called the church an architectural wonder, noting the Italian Renaissance style of its facade and other features of Spanish baroque. But the parishioners made their own appraisal of the church. It was home.

STATISTICS

Bushwick is a community of young people. The area surrounding the church, and from which most of its parishioners come, has a median age of 16.3 according to the latest census data. These statistics shock no one living around the church. Children play in the streets and on doorsteps and crowd the yard between the rectory and the former school building. Others look out apartment windows and call to their friends; still others ring the doorbell asking for jobs. Some come with their parents for counseling, and it is the young who swell the ranks of worshipers on Sunday. Children and young people are the life of the community, the hope of their families, and the reason why parents work so hard.

Nevertheless, statistics are also harsh. In the *Bushwick Neighborhood Profile,* Toby Sanchez notes that Bushwick is the poorest area in Brooklyn and is poorer now than in 1977, when riots following the blackout left much of the area devastated. Bushwick does not fare well in comparison with other areas of New York City. Although the poverty line is $12,290 citywide, the median family income in Bushwick is $9,200 as compared to $16,320 for New York City. The poverty rate in Bushwick is 40.5 percent, and the unemployment rate is 16.28 percent. Those receiving public assistance number 33.1 percent, while 44.6 percent of the households are single-parent households with children under eighteen. Bushwick is one of only four of Brooklyn's community districts that has more than 20 percent of its population on public assistance (1990 Census).

Popular opinion holds that conditions are now much worse

than when the 1990 census was reported. Regarding education, the Sanchez report says that only 28 percent of the population are high-school graduates, another 20 percent have some high school, and 42 percent completed only part or all of grades 1 through 8.

In addition to these statistics, the most recent reading scores for children in the district, Community School District 32, indicate that less than one-third of the children are reading at or above grade level, and in many cases schools have fewer than 20 percent of their population in grade level.

Bushwick High School, the zoned school for the youth of St. Barbara's Church, was built in 1913, and in 1996 had an enrollment of 2,389 students. By any reliable measure the school does not do well. A report in *New York Newsday* published in April 1995 indicated that fewer than half of the students met requirements in reading and U.S. history; only 4.7 percent of the graduating class received a Regents' diploma; and 32.9 percent received a local diploma while 21.6 percent dropped out. Furthermore, Bushwick High School has the distinction of being the most overcrowded high school in the city for the longest period of time.

EDUCATIONAL INITIATIVES

St. Barbara's Church could not ignore the issue of education. In the early eighties, Father Brady reported that virtually every parent who came through the door was fearful over his or her children's education. Even when children received good grades in school, Brady says, it was obvious to the parents that their children lacked the skills base that would enable them to make a future for themselves. Most of the stories were not even that positive, however. Parents referred to the schools as battlegrounds, and many feared for their children's safety more than their educational dilemmas.

This same educational scenario was also being played out in many of the churches that comprised East Brooklyn Congregations. When EBC pastors met in clergy caucuses and lay leaders met in strategy team meetings, it was obvious that education had to be addressed. The self-interest of every congregation included the serious educational neglect and mismanagement of the local school districts. Out of these strategy sessions was born the initiative that EBC named Nehemiah II, based on the work of rebuilding by the biblical Nehemiah. The hope was that Nehemiah II would restore the educational scene of East Brooklyn. Elda Peralta of EBC took on the major responsibility of putting together a plan by which church leaders could leverage change in six zoned high schools.

Bushwick High School was one of the schools chosen, and St. Barbara's leaders took the major responsibility for forging ahead to interview hundreds of high-school juniors and invite them into the plan. Any student who committed to have no more than five unexcused absences, passed required subjects, and graduated would be guaranteed either an entry-level position in a bank or a scholarship to college. EBC made the contacts with colleges and banks and made arrangements to facilitate student contact with prospective employers and colleges.

Carmen Morales, one of St. Barbara's leaders, still speaks fondly of that effort. The individual meetings with students were grueling, and Carmen felt hope and despair as a result.

> The kids were great. They were good kids who wanted to make something of themselves and who agreed to whatever we asked. The hard part was seeing that the school had done nothing to prepare them. They didn't know what they needed to graduate. They had no idea of what SAT meant, and they didn't know how to find out about college applications.

Morales tells of meeting many of the students she knew from religious education classes at St. Barbara's: "Many of the kids knew me and trusted me because I had been their teacher when they were seven or eight years old. It was so good to know they were still eager to learn. But the heartbreak was hearing them try to speak or write good English."

Morales's description was accurate. After five years of trying to pressure the high school to improve its teaching and guidance, EBC decided to terminate the project. EBC was doing all the work, and the school was just taking credit for getting kids jobs or scholarships. However, the St. Barbara's team was realistic about their efforts. The church leaders had learned a lot. They had gained practical knowledge that confirmed their intuitive belief in their young people. It was not the kids who were lazy or unable to learn. Rather there was an educational system in place that systematically denied their youth the right to learn.

BUSHWICK PARENTS ORGANIZATION

In the summer of 1989 the staff of St. Barbara's met with the lead organizer of EBC to discuss the educational reality of the parish. There was a list of "knowns": the students could not read; young people could not get into good high schools in the city; dropout rates were very high; Hispanic parents often lacked skills to fight the educational bureaucracy; and Hispanic parents were looking to the church for leadership. Knowing that achieving their educational goals would involve a long struggle, the staff decided to have a series of individual meetings with parents to determine if there was enough anger and energy to take on the immense work of organizing them. Each of the four staff members from St. Barbara's agreed to test things out with ten parents. They chose families with children in different schools and a variety of grade levels and parents with varied levels of education in the United States. When they met to evaluate their work two weeks later, they lacked clarity. People were angry, but the anger was unfocused, and no one seemed to have any idea how to address the problem.

The newest person on staff was Sister Kathy Maire, who spoke Spanish fluently and who agreed to take on this project. She recruited fifteen top leaders and set them on a course of hundreds of individual meetings over the summer. Each leader was to verify the level of anger people felt, whether they had interest or energy to move to action, and who were potential leaders among them. July and August 1989 were incredibly hot and humid, yet the leaders persisted in speaking to parents on doorsteps, in parks, and anyplace people gathered to escape the heat.

In September the leaders gathered to assess the results of their work. They had conducted over six hundred interviews, and it was overwhelmingly clear that parents were angry, frustrated, and confused. What was also clear was that there was no consensus about what parents could do or even about who was responsible for the educational quagmire. EBC taught people that "problems" could not be solved but instead had to be broken down into "issues" that were manageable and winnable. How to accomplish this was the question!

It was decided that St. Barbara's would work in conjunction with another Hispanic parish in Bushwick to achieve an understanding of the entire district. St. Barbara's leaders then began to work with small groups of parents, having them share information and experiences. Out of a long, tedious process grew a fledgling group that became known as Bushwick Parents Organization. The first task was to do major training that would give parents the skills to counter the jargon of the educational community, who called them apathetic, irresponsible, and unmotivated. As the parents came together to share their anger and frustration at trying to take on the educational community, they realized the injustice of the accusations from administrators in the district and in the schools.

The efforts of Bushwick Parents continue today, and their list of achievements is impressive. They were responsible for a series of repairs in five schools, they established a credible reputation as an effective force to bring city and state attention to the failure of the local school board, and they drew national attention to the ineffective and self-serving administration of bilingual education programs and the incompetence of the local superintendent.

From a parish point of view, however, the internal results were equally important. The work in education turned out to be a powerful tool for evangelization. Sessions often began with scriptural reflections on the meaning of parenting. The work of making the schools safe and educationally sound was spoken of on Sundays as the building of the reign of God, and "godly" parents were recognized for their care of children in the public arena. In sermon after sermon, Father Powis pointed out that Jesus had preached and healed on the streets and in the marketplace. Parents who accepted this challenge to live the gospel, declared Powis, also needed to preach in the public forums of the community and attempt to heal the sickness of a system that left children no alternative to failure.

Many leaders grew out of this educational initiative. Some have moved to other states, but they have carried a new understanding of their abilities with them. Rita Ortiz is an example.

She began very tentatively with Bushwick Parents, unsure as to whether she could face administrators as an equal, speak in public, or act as a spokesperson with the responsibility to make decisions on the spot. Ortiz learned that with training and support she could do these things and do them well. One night Ortiz was asked to address in Spanish and English an assembly of five hundred people. Trembling, she had to hold on to the podium, but her voice never faltered. When she went home, her daughter Carmen told her she had been standing at the back of the auditorium, and when her friends came by, she told them proudly, "That is my mother!" Ortiz now lives and works in Texas, still deeply grateful for her training at St. Barbara's.

Maria Perez is another parent leader who grew in understanding of her role as a responsible spokesperson. Initially, Perez resisted speaking English in public. Finally, she saw that no one else could tell her story adequately. Perez has since met with teachers, principals, superintendents, board of education members, and two chancellors. She now has a sense of pride and determination that makes her a valuable asset to the parish and to the community.

Other parents have taken courageous steps in speaking to the press about conditions in the schools and incompetence in the district. Some have given legal affidavits to support a lawsuit, and many now act as an inspiration to newer, more tentative parents. Unfortunately, the need for strong and focused leadership is as real as ever. Powis insists, "It is unbelievable that when education is achieving unprecedented success in Europe, in places like Bushwick politicians are able to control schools and preside over a culture of failure."

POVERTY

Over 40 percent of the Bushwick population is dependent to some extent on public subsidies. For children the rate is even higher; two-thirds receive public assistance. Given this reality, Powis speaks often and forcefully about politicians and how public policy affects the lives of his parishioners. On any given day a small vestibule leading to the rectory is filled with people who come hoping that the parish knows of a job or even the possibility of a job. "The question of work is the basic question of this community. No work means no hope," he says. "What we need are jobs. People here have few skills, but they want to work, to do anything that will allow them some measure of dignity. What do I think? I think President Clinton should come and spend one week here on Bleecker Street in Brooklyn. Then we'd see if he would sign that horrendous welfare legislation."

How St. Barbara's reacts to this situation is typical of its "don't just sit there and whine" attitude. The parish is gearing up to be part of a huge voter-mobilization campaign designed to show local and city politicians that communities like Bushwick are seats of power. "The only thing politicians understand is the vote," says a team spokesperson. The parish is mapping out its strategy. They have committed to get twenty captains, and each captain will pledge to get one hundred voters to the polls. They believe they can hold elected officials accountable if they have enough voters to change the results of future elections.

DRUG INITIATIVES

"I can stand at my window and watch the dealers selling," says Rita (whose name has been changed for her protection). She adds, "If I can describe the dealers and see them wreaking havoc on the young people of my block, I expect the police to be able to do the same." Rita's comments are echoed by the entire gathering of parishioners at the meeting of leaders called by Powis. This scene could probably be replicated in most of the churches in Bushwick. What makes St. Barbara's different is that this is a gathering of EBC leaders who know how to take action. They realize they must act together to exert sufficient pressure on police officials to prioritize their community and work with the team. They are also acutely aware that any person who can be singled out by the dealers or whose name is given as cooperating with the police can be in danger. While this knowledge could leave other communities feeling powerless, this EBC group knows that together they can achieve safety for their families and neighbors.

Safety has been an issue of long standing, and leadership training has given this team an idea of the skills they need to make changes. They will not demand a meeting to complain or appeal to the police department's sense of duty and honor. They will present specific requests and locations that need to be watched, and they will demand accountability by requesting a response from the police by a certain date on what progress has been made: "We won't leave the meeting with the chief until we have a date for the next meeting and we know exactly who will be there from the police. We don't want to deal with someone who has no answers and no power to do anything."

These leaders know that they need to deal with the person who has the power to bring about change, not with an underling who needs to report and get permission before a commitment can be made. They need to get to the person in charge, so they set about strategizing with the pastor about how to arrange a meeting with the chief in charge of the Brooklyn North Drug Initiative. The team will do its part and in turn will demand results. "We are tired of hearing how many arrests the police make," says one of the leaders, adding, "We don't care how many arrests they make if the situation isn't cleared up. What we want to hear and see for ourselves is that the sites are clean and the dealers haven't moved down the block."

The team members were pleased that the meetings promised to provide a good working relationship with the police on a continuing basis. They were cautious, however, about letting down their guard by thinking that the police would continue if they were not consistent in their role. Powis pointed out that an article in the *New York Times*[3] made "it sound like the police have the whole thing cleaned up. We know the only way to make sure our community is safe is to have the community itself accept responsibility for making it so."

"It comes back to the issue of hope," says the pastor. "As long as parishioners believe they can do something about their streets, their homes, and their parks, they can see signs of resurrection. Without that, the gospel doesn't make much sense." The gospel does, however, make sense to this team of leaders. "Jesus didn't have a problem talking about power," says one of the women. "People are afraid of the word 'power.' I believe that Jesus came to teach us that we need more of it to make the world look a little more like the kingdom he spoke so much about. The power to transform this community has been won for us. Now it's up to us to use it."

NATURALIZATION

Because of the recent anti-immigrant sentiment sweeping the country, legal residents are pushing to seek citizenship. For years, St. Barbara's sent those seeking naturalization to a neighboring parish that has run citizenship campaigns for years. Recently, however, the parish perceived the need to do something closer to home. One of the long-time parishioners, herself recently naturalized, has taken on the task of helping applicants fill out the forms and gather the necessary documentation. Concepción Rodriguez speaks about her valuable assistance quite matter-of-factly, "There was a need. I could do something and I did. I believe this is the way I can minister within my church community."

Presently, applicants come to the parish three times a week to complete the forms, to be fingerprinted, and to have photos taken for the process. They also seek reassurance about the civics test and the interview. Since the test can be given in the community, much of the intimidation of entering government buildings in unknown neighborhoods is mitigated. "We don't advertise," says Concepción. "Folks just tell their friends and family members. I just hope we can keep up with the volume."

Concepción and those who help her with this effort are aware of the importance of voting for the new citizens. "Part of what we tell people," she says, "is that now they will have a voice to express their concern for all the members of the community."

THE CHURCH

For some, St. Barbara's Church is a place of safety. Recent immigrants come on Sunday to find worship in their home language and to sing hymns they have known since childhood. For others, St. Barbara's is the place they congregate to be reminded of who they are in an anonymous and frightening city. Some parishioners seek counsel and help with the overwhelming and confusing papers that make them feel powerless. Still others come to escape their problems for an hour or so on

Sunday mornings before plunging back into a never-ending struggle for survival. There are the peripheral parishioners, the ones no one seems to know by name but who come to worship and find solace in a beautiful church. There are others who come in time of crisis, like the loss of a loved one to AIDS or other illness or homicide, to seek comfort and support. To all of these, the parish reaches out, providing prayer or a funeral service that relieves them of isolation and bewilderment. Of course, some call only when a relative is ill or hospitalized or when they need placement for drug or alcohol treatment or when depression becomes unbearable. Still others simply wander in looking for food, lodging, or just someone to listen to them.

These are part of the picture but not the heart and soul of the parish. The vital center of St. Barbara's is comprised of the relationships that unite the parishioners in their determination to live as a sign of hope. The real parish is people committed to living out the Word of God on the streets and in the institutions of the community. St. Barbara's is people finding strength in God and in each other, and then proceeding to proclaim that God is with us indeed.

PART THREE

Church-Based
Community Organizing

The Industrial Areas Foundation (IAF), based primarily in churches, is the largest and oldest institution for community organizing in the United States. The IAF's mission is to "train people to organize themselves and take responsibility for solving the problems of their own communities, and to renew the interest of citizens in public life." There are now twenty-eight IAF organizations nationwide, representing more than 1.5 million families. For the most part, IAF organizations are made up of members of multidenominational groups of religious institutions.

The IAF now has nine affiliates in Manhattan, Brooklyn, Queens, and the Bronx. These affiliates address fundamental elements of community life in the city's poorest neighborhoods. As a result of IAF organizing, New York City has thousands of units of affordable owner-occupied housing, family health centers that serve the working poor, three charter schools that provide an alternative to failing high schools, cleaned-up and fenced-in lots, signs and traffic signals at appropriate intersections, safer subways, mail that is delivered to correct addresses, and innumerable other proofs of improved quality of life.

The next two chapters tell the story of South Bronx Churches. This organization was formed by a group of Protestant and Catholic clergy amid the burned-out buildings, vacant lots, and rubble that characterized the South Bronx in the 1980s. Their goal was to create an organization with power, one that could stand against the political, social, and economic forces that were devastating the South Bronx. Their successes have been impressive. In ten years South Bronx Churches has worked collectively to build five hundred homes that are now owned by the working poor. It has renovated seven buildings, started a high school, and mobilized to improve security in public housing.

The motto of Harlem Congregations for Community Improvement (HCCI) is "Empowered Congregations Rebuilding Harlem." HCCI has, since 1986, committed itself to the redevelopment of the Bradhurst section of Harlem by rehabilitating vacant buildings for low-income occupancy, promoting commercial development, and offering the supportive services essential for a healthy community—child care, space for artists, services for senior citizens.

Although this section of the book focuses on the achievements of community organizers in the South Bronx and in Harlem, organizing is a significant part of ministry in other chapters of the book. St. Barbara's Church, for example, is a member of Brooklyn's IAF affiliate, the East Brooklyn Congregations, and is active in working for affordable housing and educational reform in that borough.

11

"Come, Let Us Rebuild the Walls of Jerusalem"

Broad-Based Organizing in the South Bronx

Lee Stuart

South Bronx Churches (SBC), an affiliate of the Industrial Areas Foundation, is an organization of thirty congregations now approaching its tenth anniversary of collective action. Its mission is to train local lay and clergy leaders as agents for change and community transformation. The leadership of South Bronx Churches is black, Latino, and white. Recognizing diversity as a primary strength, SBC is held together by relationships forged over a decade of struggles for practical

Lee Stuart has been the lead organizer for South Bronx Churches since April 1992. As lead organizer, she has supervised the construction of 512 new units of housing in South Bronx Churches' Nehemiah program and the establishment of a new public high school in the South Bronx. Prior to working for South Bronx Churches, she worked as director of development for Augustine Fine Arts for two years. From 1985 through 1989 she served as the founding executive director (as well as other roles) for SHARE–New York, an ecumenical food assistance and community development program now serving eleven thousand families a month in the metropolitan New York area.

goals including construction of affordable housing, renovation of apartment buildings, installation of lights in subway stations, the requiring of good food in supermarkets, the opening of a new public high school with an emphasis on community leadership, the demand for responsive and respectful policing, and the end of gross political interference in public education. South Bronx Churches recognizes that fighting for justice is a constitutive part of the gospel. The fight for justice must be as vigorously pursued by the church as is preaching, teaching, evangelizing, charity, worship, and prayer.

SOUTH BRONX CHURCHES:
DIVERSE, ECUMENICAL, POWERFUL

"Mi nombre es Rosa Madrigal. Mi iglesia es San Jeronimo, y yo soy de México." "My name is Angel Bonilla. I am pastor of Second Christian Church, and I am from Chile." "My name is Felix Santiago. I am from St. Luke's, and I was born in Puerto Rico." "My name is Milton Duhaney. My church is St. Simeon's Episcopal, and I am from Jamaica." "My name is Father Skelly. I am pastor of Immaculate Conception, and I was born on 150th Street a few blocks away from here." "Mi nombre is Maria Rodriguez. Mi iglesia es La Iglesia Luterana de la Transfiguración, y yo soy de Guatemala." "My name is Elba Barnes. I am from Immaculate Conception, and I was born in Venezuela." "Mi nombre es Antonio Torres, de Cristo Rey, y de Ecuador." "My name is Theodora Brooks. I am pastor of St. Margaret's Episcopal, and I was born in Liberia. . . ."

By the time the roll call for the 1995 winter retreat of SBC ended and the sixty people present had identified themselves, they announced sixteen countries of birth and represented thirty congregations, nine Christian denominations, a Muslim mosque, two tenant associations, and a homeowner association. They were gathered on a rainy Saturday in January in the basement hall of Immaculate Conception Church in the South Bronx to pray, to reflect on Scripture, and to develop strategies for the coming year.

The leaders of SBC were gathered to do more than talk; they knew they had to continue concrete action to build on their successes. In the previous four years they worked collectively to build five hundred new homes—the most affordable in New York City—as part of the nationally recognized Nehemiah project. They renovated seven buildings for rental occupancy; they worked with the board of education to start an innovative high school focused on community leadership. They were in the middle of a campaign to mobilize at least a thousand parents to work on improving the local public schools. Many of their congregations were involved in hard local struggles for neighborhood improvements, such as community policing, demolition of derelict buildings, and improved security in public housing.

The participants in this retreat had a very different vision for the city of New York than is documented in the media by reports of crime, police brutality, wealth aside great poverty, municipal scandals, and corruption. They also had a very different vision for the United States than the fearful, divisive, and uncivil conversations being trumpeted from Washington, Albany, and city hall. In the heart of the South Bronx, they wanted what generations have wanted before them: respect, a safe home, good schools, decent health care, spiritual nurture, a chance to earn a living, and the opportunity to raise their children free from want. And they desired these things for their neighbors as much as themselves. They knew that these goals—simple, moderate, and certainly included in "life, liberty, and the pursuit of happiness"—are not inalienable today in the South Bronx. They gathered at this winter retreat in the context of their religious and civic traditions in order to do their part to build New York City in the direction of a city of God.

Ten years before, Protestant and Catholic clergy were brought together by the Reverend John Heinemeier, pastor of St. John's Evangelical Lutheran Church, and Jim Drake of the Industrial Areas Foundation. As they began to discuss the need for a new kind of organization in the South Bronx, the prophet Isaiah's descriptions of the devastation and fall of Jerusalem seemed to have been realized in the brokenness of the community:

> O city full of noise and chaos. O wanton town! Your slain are not slain with the sword, nor killed in battle. All your leaders fled away together, fled afar off; all who were in you were captured together, captured without the use of a bow.
>
> (Isaiah 22:2-3, NAB)

Lo, the LORD empties the land and lays it waste; he turns it
upside down, scattering its inhabitants. . . . The earth is
utterly laid waste, utterly stripped, for the LORD has decreed
this thing.

(Isaiah 24:1,3, NAB)

Broken down is the city of chaos, shut against entry, every
house. In the streets they cry out for lack of wine; all joy has
disappeared and cheer has left the land. In the city nothing
remains but ruin; its gates are battered and desolate.

(Isaiah 24:10-12, NAB)

In 1986 the slain of the South Bronx were being killed, not
in military conquests, but by firearms, brutal beatings, crack
cocaine, and the scourge of AIDS. The leaders had indeed fled
and been captured: both members of Congress, the head of the
Bronx Democratic Party, and the borough president were on
their way to federal indictments, criminal convictions, and
prison.[1] The people were scattered; the South Bronx had lost
over half of its population—nearly 450,000 residents moved
away—in the days of the fires and "planned shrinkage" of the
1970s.[2] The land was utterly laid waste, utterly stripped, how
much so is clear from reports of the New York City Department
of Housing Preservation and Development—thirty-five thousand new and rehabilitated dwelling units have been built or
rebuilt in the South Bronx since 1986.[3] Vacant lots, rubble, and
burned-out buildings throughout the South Bronx became national symbols of poverty and urban decay. Window and door
guards; triple locks; razor wire; gates; steel doors; armor-clad
pit bulls; thousands of homeless men, women, and children;
and a murder rate soaring with the onset of crack—the South
Bronx was indeed a city of chaos.

The ministers who gathered to give birth to SBC felt the
pangs of this devastation. Most had lived or worked in the
South Bronx for years. They came to the South Bronx by choice
or assignment, spurred by experiences in the civil rights movement, the call to urban ministry, a special desire to work
particularly with Hispanic and African American people, or
simply a faith that encouraged full service wherever they were
sent. These ministers had seen the neighborhoods around their
churches demolished and the exodus of those who were able
to flee. For those who remained, they had developed new

programs for the homeless, the hungry, and the addicted. They especially tried to make spiritual homes for the people who remained in the ruins. These ministers were veterans, the remnant who had not lost their vision in the midst of blinding ruin and despair. They wanted to build an organization with power, one that could stand against the political, social, and economic forces sweeping the South Bronx and make changes for the broadest possible common good rather than narrow political interest.

Although their congregations were successful and they (and their denominations) had exemplary social service programs, the pastors realized that they were actually in the business of the service and maintenance of poverty, and they wanted to be in the business of really transforming their neighborhoods. To do this would require new kinds of relationships with each other, with city officials, and with public and private interests operating in the South Bronx. The South Bronx was politically, spiritually, and economically divided, black from Hispanic, Protestant from Catholic, homeless from housed, Spanish speaking from English speaking. The clergy who founded SBC recognized that the exploitation of these divisions by politicians, service providers, and the media was also a symptom of the area's poverty. By 1986 the leading Protestant and Catholic clergy in the South Bronx wanted to act on, not react to, the forces of poverty.

The pastors realized that a "clergy association" was not the answer—they understood that the members of their congregations must be developed as leaders. They had seen enough in the course of their ministries to know that group-identity politics, narrow focus on a single issue, and reliance on government funding would eventually cause the downfall of any organization. Most importantly, they wanted to win. To win against the forces facing them in the South Bronx, they were unequivocal—they needed to enter the arena of power in a new way and to exercise the demand of the gospel for justice.

Guided by the Industrial Areas Foundation,[4] the clergy and lay leaders of the South Bronx spent two years in meetings, relationship building, and struggle to form SBC. As do all the affiliates of the Industrial Areas Foundation, SBC learned to adhere to a policy of institutional membership and generating support primarily from membership dues. Denominational and foundation grants helped fund the organization's start-up and special projects; no government money was or ever will be solicited or accepted. SBC became a nonpartisan, highly diverse, multi-issue organization, fundamentally focused on the accrual and exercise of power to make changes consistent with civic and religious values. The "Iron Rule" undergirded the formation of SBC and is dominant in its philosophy today—never do for others what they can do for themselves.

At the organization's founding convention in February 1987, over two thousand people were present. Hundreds of thousands of dollars had been pledged to the new organization from the Lutheran, Catholic, and Episcopalian judicatories. Member congregations each pledged annual dues ranging from $200 to $2,000. The lay and clergy leaders of the South Bronx stood together to announce a new force in the South Bronx; diverse, ecumenical, and organized for the long haul, SBC was prepared to act on the wide array of problems that ravaged their community.[5] Subsequent to its founding, a mosque, two tenant associations, and a homeowner association have joined SBC.

SOUTH BRONX CHURCHES NEHEMIAH HOMES: USING POWER

The South Bronx Churches Nehemiah Homes are the most visible project of SBC. Inspired by the words from the prophet Nehemiah and by the twenty-three hundred Nehemiah homes built by the IAF-affiliate East Brooklyn Congregations (EBC) in the early 1980s, SBC leaders dedicated themselves to rebuilding their troubled Jerusalem.

> Afterward I said to them: "You see the evil blight in which we stand: how Jerusalem lies in ruins and its gates have been gutted by fire. Come, let us rebuild the walls of Jerusalem, so that we many no longer be an object of derision!" Then I explained to them how the favoring hand of my God had rested upon me, and what the king had said to me. They replied, "Let us be up and building!" And they undertook the good work with vigor. (Nehemiah 2:17-18, NAB)

The construction of over five hundred units of affordable Nehemiah houses tested the relationships, commitment, and patience of participating leaders and required the denominational support and political clout of thirty congregations working together over many years.

The principal aims of the Nehemiah project were (1) to build ownership housing affordable to the typical working family in the South Bronx by maintaining a minimum income requirement of $20,000 per year, (2) to build a critical mass of new housing so that a community could be reborn, (3) to promote a humane scale of development through low-density construction,[6] and (4) to train new homeowners in the skills of public life so that, working with SBC, they could continue the revitalization of their community. Four things are required to build housing in New York City: a builder, money, land, and power to bring the builder, the land, and the money together. Finding the builder was easy. The visionary builder responsible for the Nehemiah construction in East Brooklyn, I. D. Robbins, was eager to repeat his success in the South Bronx. He brought years of experience and wisdom in the peculiarities of building large-scale projects in New York City. In addition, Robbins was able to contract on favorable terms with the construction crews from the Brooklyn Nehemiah project for work on the South Bronx Nehemiah.

Finding the money for South Bronx Nehemiah depended on the deep denominational relationships developed during the formation and early years of SBC. Construction financing for South Bronx Nehemiah was provided by a revolving trust fund that mirrored the broad-based composition of SBC. The construction capital was generated from $3.5 million in no-interest loans from Trinity Church on Wall Street, St. James Church on Madison Avenue, the national office of the Evangelical Lutheran Church in America, Roman Catholic religious orders, Jewish and Roman Catholic individuals, and SBC's sister organization, East Brooklyn Congregations. Loans varied in size from $25,000 to $1 million and were made on terms ranging from one to five years. The construction trust revolved approximately thirteen times during the course of construction, with the trust being replenished each time with mortgage proceeds. At the conclusion of construction the loan principal will be returned to the lenders. Mortgage loan financing was provided through the State of New York Mortgage Agency and Fleet Bank.

The struggle for land was more difficult. The Nehemiah project in Brooklyn was entirely comprised of single-family homes, and SBC wanted to build single-family homes too. The position of the Bronx borough president, however, was that higher-density housing was required to rebuild the South Bronx, even if higher density meant higher costs, higher income requirements, and higher subsidies.[7] The issue became polarized, and an eventual compromise was reached, which allowed construction of 224 single-family homes and 288 condominiums in the first phase of Nehemiah.

Before the compromise was reached, the largest piece of empty land in the South Bronx, known as Site 404, was the location of an eight-thousand-person rally for South Bronx Nehemiah. During weekly meetings, hundreds of SBC lay and clergy leaders became expert in land-use regulations and procedures, construction financing, and all phases of housing development. They visited the Brooklyn Nehemiah project and learned from the experience of the Brooklyn leaders. They walked the entire South Bronx looking for the land to make their dream of Nehemiah housing come true. They visualized gardens and yards where they saw only rubble. When they surveyed a landscape scarred by dumping grounds, gutted buildings, and rampant drug dealing and prostitution, they imagined row upon row of new homes, clean streets, flourishing small businesses, flowers, and laughing children.

The Nehemiah project became, for them, a kind of burning bush, reminding them of God's promises, calling them to take a prophetic stance in the face of repressive city policies and providing encouragement when things got rough. Years of common struggle bound the participating churches and leaders together in a manner superior to any ecumenical service, philosophical discussion of pluralism, or diversity workshop. In fighting for land and the right to build, SBC came of age, and the Nehemiah project became the only housing in the South Bronx to grow out of the hearts of people rather than visions of profit or political favoritism. Though they did not win the right to build on Site 404, SBC won control over nearby land for the construction of over five hundred new homes and condominiums.

It took three years of negotiation with the city before the first foundation was finally poured in October 1991. Thousands attended the groundbreaking. In May of 1992 the first homes were dedicated, and the first twenty-four families moved in. The first phase of Nehemiah, 512 homes and condominiums, was completed in the spring of 1996. Throughout this time, SBC overcame bureaucratic barriers and withstood attempted shakedowns and political forces contrary to the Nehemiah project. The modern equivalents of Sanballat, Tobiah, the Ammonites, and the Ashdodites, the enemies of the biblical Nehemiah, used similar threats, ridicule, misrepresentation, and internal division against SBC's Nehemiah project.

No stranger to struggle, SBC has remained clear in its vision: homes built in the South Bronx must be affordable to the people who live in the neighborhood. New homes must be priced so that people living in public housing can purchase them, making available room in public housing for those in need of that form of assistance. SBC maintains that scarce subsidy dollars should be used for those most truly in need. Furthermore, wherever possible, people must be allowed the privilege of ownership. In order to rebuild communities, people must feel invested in them; they must feel that efforts will be rewarded and cumulative and that their community is capable of resisting destabilizing influences.

SBC's Nehemiah project has reclaimed thirty-five square blocks for single-family homes and condominiums. Gardens now bloom where once was rubble. Families have individualized their homes and yards with decorative gates, walks, and religious shrines. Neighbors know one another, children have a safe place to play, and other parts of the community are coming back to life as well. The local Carnegie Library, once slated for closure, is receiving financial support to expand its programming from St. James Episcopal. The library, once nearly deserted, is now a pleasant mix of children reading, drawing, using computers, and doing homework. Additional land is being negotiated for a second phase of Nehemiah that will include 250 single-family and two-family homes. Laundromats and other commercial activities are also beginning to return to the neighborhood. The collective investment of nearly $40 million in the Nehemiah project provides a base of equity for long-term economic development.

The original goal of SBC's Nehemiah project—to provide affordable housing for the ordinary working people of the South Bronx—has been achieved. The average family income of the purchasers of Nehemiah single-family homes is under $30,000. Very few would qualify for the higher income required for all other new housing in the Bronx. In fact, most Nehemiah home and condominium owners now pay less for their mortgage than they did for rent. For example, one family required a Federal Section 8 subsidy for a two-bedroom apartment in the South Bronx but now pays less than half their former rent while building equity in a Nehemiah home. Their two children, a boy and a girl, have separate bedrooms—an impossibility in their former apartment. Similarly, another family saves several hundred dollars a month over the rent they formerly paid in public housing. For both families, the Nehemiah project was their only option for housing ownership.

Mary Martinez, a young legal secretary who lives in a Nehemiah home with her daughter, her mother, and her younger sister, succinctly summarizes the effects of Nehemiah on her life:

My family has been at St. Jerome's Catholic Church for four generations. We are Bronx through and through. My grandparents, parents, and I saw the Bronx burn down, but we didn't want to leave. My father was killed in a mugging about fifteen years ago. Earlier he had been badly beaten for trying to drive out drug dealers from our neighborhood.

Before Nehemiah, I lived with my daughter, Theresa, in public housing, and it was awful. Crowded, noisy, dirty, dangerous. I was scared for her. She couldn't go outside, the drug dealers were trying to take over, and I was working long hours. Theresa was only five—I wanted something more for her. I wanted her to grow up safe. I wanted her to have a yard. I wanted her to have quiet. Is this too much? I couldn't afford to move out of public housing if it hadn't been for Nehemiah. I couldn't afford that other new housing.

When South Bronx Churches finally won Nehemiah, I put in my application. Now I have my house. It took a few years, but it was worth it. Theresa and her little friends play in the yard. Nehemiah is the best thing that ever happened to my family. Now we are working to make the neighborhood even better. On my street we are beginning to work with the tenants who still live in the apartment buildings on the street to make it better for all of us. I can say it again—Nehemiah is the best thing that ever happened to my family, and Nehemiah only happened because of South Bronx Churches.

Despite the enthusiasm of its leaders, much is still required to rebuild and transform the South Bronx in the likeness of the New Jerusalem envisioned in Isaiah 26: a strong city, a nation that is just, one that keeps faith and maintains a firm purpose, and a city kept in peace, where the inhabitants know justice. The member congregations of South Bronx Churches know that *only part* of their mission is fulfilled in their denominational traditions of teaching, preaching, music, worship, and social service. Part is fulfilled in their prophetic role, and it is this prophetic, public stance of the religious communities against the principalities and powers of dominant forces in New York City that unites the members of SBC and empowers them to continue their work.

12

Redefining the Public Sphere

South Bronx Churches and Education Reform

Lee Stuart

The four young mothers praying in Transfiguration Lutheran Church were nervous. They had been preparing for weeks, but they were still nervous. They asked God to help them and to melt a heart of stone if necessary. Their children would be entering school in the fall for the first time, and the mothers had arranged a meeting with the local elementary school principal as part of the South Bronx Churches parents organizing project. The mothers were eager to put the training they had received from South Bronx Churches (SBC) and the Public Education Association[1] to work—they planned to survey nearby schools, interview the principals, visit classrooms, and evaluate which school would be the best place to send their children.

They went as a team; they knew they would be too intimidated if they went individually. Only one had completed high school; principals, teachers, and schools were not their usual turf. They went with prepared questions on safety, curriculum, and policies. They dressed up for the meeting to show how important it was for them. An organizer from SBC went along, not to run the meeting, but to support, observe, and evaluate with the mothers afterward what happened.

The mothers arrived ten minutes early for the meeting. The principal was late but came within the fifteen minutes that the women had agreed to wait. When the principal finally arrived, the mothers introduced themselves and thanked the principal for meeting with them. It was time for the first question: "My child is going to enter the first grade in this district next year. Can you please explain your safety and security policies so that I can be sure that my daughter will be safe if she goes to this school?"

The principal hesitated. "I don't have to answer that question. I am not going to answer that question, and this meeting is over." The mothers were stunned. They had, however, planned for this situation in one of their role plays prior to the meeting. They announced that it was now clear that their children would not attend the principal's school, that it was clear that the principal had no respect for parents or children, and so meeting any longer would be a complete waste of their time. They left with dignity. They also left with a deepened anger and commitment to work even harder to reform the underbelly of public education as practiced in the South Bronx.[2]

South Bronx Churches' work on behalf of education was sparked by the anger of parents who worshiped in SBC member congregations. Their approach to school reform is long term and dual focused: (1) the mobilization of parents to be more directly involved in their children's elementary and middle-school education and (2) the establishment of a new public high school in the South Bronx. The primary leader in the parent organizing strategy is Antonio Torres. His story reveals the specific strategy and the pattern of leadership development in South Bronx Churches.

ANTONIO TORRES—PRIMARY LEADER OF
EDUCATIONAL REFORM

One of SBC's goals is to train local lay leaders as effective advocates and agents of change in the South Bronx. The lay leaders of SBC must be members of congregations that pay annual membership dues to be part of SBC. The role of the clergy is to identify, support, and encourage lay leaders to engage in public-life issues as part of the prophetic witness of the church. A different type of pastoral care is often required for lay leaders newly engaged in public life. The exposure, the tension, the setbacks, and the victories require theological interpretation, spiritual counsel, and personal support.

Antonio Torres, a parishioner of Christ the King in the South Bronx, moved to the United States six years ago. Trained as a locksmith and electrician in Ecuador, Torres works as a home health aide in the Bronx. He learned activism from his grandfather, a man of great faith, who, with Antonio, was involved in land-reform efforts in Ecuador. Torres's continued inspiration comes from his five-year-old son.

Torres's development as a leader in South Bronx Churches began in SBC's Institute for Public Life, which he attended when an ordinary experience made him very angry and spurred him to action. "One day," Torres recounts, "walking around the neighborhood in the area of William Taft High School, I saw a group of students who were drinking and smoking pot. After they finished, they went into the school. This made me think about my son who would start kindergarten in a few months, and I wondered what kind of future my son would have if we parents did not start working hard to make changes. In those days in my church, they were announcing training for leaders of public life. The experience of observing those kids at Taft motivated me to participate in this training and get to know SBC."

In the institute, Torres learned the basic skills of public life—how to engage other leaders in dialogue about their visions and motivations, how to form relationships with a broad array of people, and how to practice social analysis, theological reflection, and evaluation in the course of direct civic action. After Torres completed the institute, he worked with the pastor of Christ the King on formulating SBC's strategy for school reform.

Christ the King is in notorious School District 9, where thirteen schools are under review by the State Department of Education and are threatened with closure by the current chancellor. Election irregularities, illegal fund-raising schemes, false residency documents, and lack of financial disclosure among board members are commonly under investigation.

As part of SBC's overall school-reform efforts, Torres mobilized a march of over two hundred members of Christ the King to a South Bronx Churches' rally in the spring of 1994 where an anticorruption program was announced. He led two busloads of leaders to Albany to meet with state legislators and convince them to enact legislation that would eliminate election fraud. He organized teams from Christ the King to deliver thousands of signatures on public petitions calling for the prosecution of all school officials who committed corrupt or criminal acts. He was part of the SBC leadership who met with the teachers' union, public-school advocate organizations, and citywide parents' organizations to bring about legislative reform and a massive mobilization of parents. Antonio Torres personally led the action when ten key leaders met with Chancellor Ramon Cortines and presented him with a petition of twenty-five thousand signatures. Torres personally asked the chancellor to add his signature, which he did.

In recognition of his work on the educational campaign, Torres was nominated to attend the Industrial Areas Foundation's (IAF) National Training in the summer of 1995. Three times each year, the IAF offers ten-day trainings to outstanding local leaders. These sessions allow leaders to interact with their counterparts across the country, as they discuss their organizations, their agendas, and their actions. The trainings focus on leadership skills, the art of public relationships, organizing strategy and tactics, reflection, and action.

Reviewing the educational situation back at Christ the King, Torres realized that, the chancellor's promises aside, there was no serious intent to increase the involvement of the local community institutions and resources to help reform P.S. 64, a failing local school attended by over two hundred students from Christ the King. Torres and the other leaders from the church turned their attention to building a new and powerful organization made up of public-school parents who were members of SBC parishes. Over the course of eight months, Torres and the other parent leaders mobilized parent groups in fifteen congregations. They organized workshops on the rights and responsibilities of parents and school boards, and they began to take direct action to improve safety and physical conditions in the schools. They also learned how to evaluate budgets, curricula, and the educational environment. They attended district meetings to study the way in which the meetings were used to discourage parental involvement. Hundreds of parents visited public schools for the first time.

On June 10, 1995, Torres cochaired a meeting attended by parents and leaders of SBC to announce the public birth of POWER: Parents Organized to Win Educational Reform. Torres stood before one thousand people and recalled their faith in God, their ability to transcend racial, ethnic, language, religious, and ideological barriers for the sake of their children, and their ability to tackle the gargantuan bureaucracy of the New York City Board of Education. That afternoon, in St. Jerome's Catholic Church, Roman Catholics, Lutherans, Episcopalians, Baptists, Disciples of Christ, Presbyterians, members of the Church of God in Christ, Muslims, and others raised their voices in hymns and prayers of thanksgiving. In the unity of these voices was the hope that together they could reverse the twenty-five-year course of official neglect and inaction caused by a failed public education system. Torres and the other parent leaders continued to work hard since that June assembly. During the summer and fall of 1995 they registered twenty-five hundred new voters and gained pledges from thousands more to vote in the 1996 school board elections. They continue to visit schools in an attempt to form respectful relationships between parents and school administrators.

The SBC parent leaders have testified at several hearings called by the Bronx borough president on the integrity and function of the local district school boards. School officials have attempted to discredit, threaten, and intimidate the parents, but they persevere. After leaving a meeting with the principal at a troubled school in District 9, parents were told by a school security guard that perhaps they should not come back; the school was in a construction zone, and perhaps some bricks would fall off the building onto their heads. When SBC raised important issues at a hearing held by the Bronx Commission on the Integrity of School Officials, the president of District 9 charged that the parents were not from District 9, that they had no children from District 9 and were just a front for the Catholic Church trying to pack the parochial schools.[3] At the time of this writing, the board of District 9 has been suspended by the chancellor and is now under investigation by the special commissioner for schools investigation for possible illegal fund-raising activities.

The parents are determined to outlast the staying power of the board members and the bureaucracy. They understand that they must act together and collectively; they must not allow themselves to be distracted or divided. Their children's futures are at stake. Antonio Torres is clear about his role as a leader in his family, his church, and his community. In an evaluation of his participation as a leader in SBC, he wrote:

> My family is very happy and supports my participation in these activities in favor of social justice. One of the most important things that I have learned in SBC is that in the unity and diversity of races and belief lies our power to bring about change, to promote justice. This power motivates me, keeps me participating, and challenges me to give more of myself to the community, today, tomorrow, and forever.
>
> My participation as a member of Christ the King is important for my spiritual life and is one way I live the gospel. I also try to do this in a different way as a coordinator of a base community as part of the Charismatic Renewal movement. I take the Word of God to the homes of people; I give baptismal conferences to parents and godparents. As a member of the Holy Name Society I participate in the masses and help the priest. I am also a lector. All of what I do, I do with great love and honor to Jesus Christ.

BRONX LEADERSHIP ACADEMY HIGH SCHOOL

The second focus of South Bronx Churches' educational reform platform has been the creation of a new public high school in the South Bronx. In 1991 Schools Chancellor Joseph Fernandez, reacting to the murders of several students inside New York City schools, called for community organizations to collaborate with the board of education to establish fifty small, thematic high schools. He felt, as did other educational leaders, that by forging closer ties with the community, by keeping the scale of schools small, by providing a unifying theme for each school, and by placing more of the authority for the school with a team of directly involved educators, parents, and community leaders, school function and student performance would improve. South Bronx Churches and its sister organization, East Brooklyn Congregations (EBC), took up the chancellor's challenge to develop new neighborhood schools.

A team of leaders from South Bronx Churches and faculty members from Fordham University designed the proposal for SBC's new high school. The founding premises of the school were simple: the school would be small (maximum enrollment of five hundred students), the curriculum would have a college preparatory focus, and the curriculum would include special leadership development courses to teach students to participate in the public life of the Bronx. Most public high schools in the South Bronx do not have the preparation of the majority of their students for higher education as an explicit goal; the Bronx Leadership Academy does. The decision to make the school college preparatory for all students while not restricting admission to only the students with top averages in middle school is one of the distinguishing marks of the Bronx Leadership Academy.

The leadership curriculum, jointly designed by academy faculty and SBC leaders and organizers, stresses the academic skills of research, writing, and analysis as part of the preparation for active engagement in civic life. Including SBC's leadership training as part of the curriculum was a natural outgrowth of the experience of adult leaders in SBC's Institute for Public Life. They often stated in their evaluations of the institute, "I wish I had known this when I was younger." The new high school enables teenagers to be trained in community leadership during their formative years.

A difficult internal decision for SBC dealt with the alignment of the school within the board of education. Although significant financial and technical assistance was available through a school development consortium of foundations called New Visions, SBC decided not to be part of this program because of the stated requirement that the local school districts would have to be involved. SBC had enough experience with local school boards not to want to form any alliances with them. SBC began a series of meetings with school board officials in both the regular and alternative high-school divisions. They visited schools under regular and alternative jurisdictions and decided that what they wanted to accomplish could best be done under the regular high-school division, and in particular with Joseph De Jesus, superintendent of high schools in the Bronx.

SBC also had to come to terms with school board policies directly opposed by several of its member denominations, specifically the distribution of condoms in New York City high schools. After weeks of deliberation, a position paper developed by the Roman Catholic clergy within SBC was adopted unanimously by all the clergy. This paper essentially claimed that the establishment of a new high school with an academic and value-focused curriculum would be the greater good and that SBC and the school staff would develop an environment in which the need and desire for condom distribution would be minimal.

It took nearly two years of negotiations, meetings, discussions, proposals, counterproposals, advice, and reactions to develop a proposal mutually acceptable to the board of education and South Bronx Churches. SBC's education task force, including lay and clergy leaders, faculty from Fordham, and other professional educators, began to build its competence in issues related to school formation, governance, and curriculum. It was a time of intense growth for leaders from both South Bronx Churches and the board of education as they struggled through the negotiations. But something wonderful happened—through persistence, through hard work on both sides, relationships were forged between the SBC leaders and key personnel at the top echelons of the board of education's high-school division.

On February 17, 1993, three school buses full of leaders from South Bronx Churches packed the board of education chambers in preparation for the final votes authorizing the new high

school. Several hundred leaders from East Brooklyn Congregations were also present, as their schools would be authorized
the same night. A request from SBC to be first on the board's
agenda was honored. SBC leaders testified eloquently, having
practiced their speeches in support of the school for several
hours before the hearing. Enough preliminary work had been
done to be certain that the board vote would be in favor, but an
unresearched area was who would speak against the new
schools. It was important to the leaders not to react to the
opposition but to state their goals and vision clearly.

As it turned out, the few speakers against the schools were
worried about a conflict of church and state. They were worried
that the churches, mosques, and synagogues making up South
Bronx Churches and East Brooklyn Congregations would some-
how teach doctrine as part of their curriculum. The board of
education had earlier had to decide this issue for themselves,
and it was they who countered the opposing speakers. The
board realized that SBC could never come to a decision about
which of the doctrines held by its members to teach without
tearing the organization apart. The thirty congregations (representing nine Christian denominations and a mosque) involved
in SBC had long ago agreed that their solidarity was around the
issues of public life and social justice values common to their
various religious traditions, not doctrine nor place on the
partisan political spectrum.

SBC never intended to establish anything but a public
school, consistent with the laws of the United States with
respect to separation of church and state. This did not mean,
however, a surrender to common assumptions that have too
often removed religion from public life. SBC assumed that, in
their school, values would be taught and that faith and religious
traditions would be lifted up as important factors in personal
and societal decisions. The vote was unanimous in favor of the
Bronx Leadership Academy. The SBC leaders went home
deeply satisfied that they had capitalized on a moment of
innovation within the New York City Board of Education, that
they had put their best efforts forward to design a high school
that would meet the needs of their children, and that their

efforts had been recognized. The more seasoned among them knew that the vote was just a beginning.

The years of building relationships between the board and SBC paid off during a series of crises that beset the school in its first year. For many reasons, no permanent site had been identified for the new school at the start of the 1993 term. A proposed temporary site was not ready. Other temporary sites located in intermediate schools with low enrollment fell through because of tensions between the central and local board. The school opened eventually in a wing of another high school in the South Bronx, but ongoing construction inhibited the first weeks of instruction.

A second crisis had to do with the relationships between the staff of the new school, the Bronx superintendent's office, and South Bronx Churches. In hindsight, much more preliminary work should have been done with the staff to develop a common vision for the school, a common set of standards, a common way to approach problems. South Bronx Churches felt that its wishes were being ignored or countermanded by school staff; the school staff did not understand SBC's involvement, and some actively resisted it. These misunderstandings created a great deal of tension between newly hired school staff and SBC leaders, who had devoted thousands of hours over several years to bring the new school into existence. The one hundred ninth-grade students admitted to the school were disappointed with temporary quarters in an existing school instead of a school of their own. Parents were concerned about the safety of their children and the general confusion of starting something brand new. Everyone was struggling with newness, and the conditions were not auspicious for success. The Bronx superintendent assigned a senior member of his staff to mediate with the school staff and South Bronx Churches to find common ground and to fulfill the collaborative mission of the school.

When relationships with some of the school staff remained acrimonious, SBC leaders put the board of education on notice that they expected the charter agreement to be honored. If it was not so honored, then SBC would withdraw from the partnership in a public, and not necessarily quiet, way. At issue were the development of the community leadership curriculum, assurance that the academic curriculum was college preparatory, and the recognition of SBC's role in the development of the school. To make their position clear, they met with the school staff, with the Bronx superintendent of high schools, with the leaders of the division of high schools, and with the new chancellor, Ramon Cortines.

Eventually, in the spring of 1994, the board of education assigned a new project director to lead the collaborative development of the Bronx Leadership Academy. Some parents, students, and staff members objected; some left the school; others decided to stay and make it work. The new project director, Katherine Kelly, immediately implemented policies to work more closely with the Bronx superintendent of high schools, improve teaching, build student morale, raise curriculum standards, and incorporate South Bronx Churches' vision into the school. She began to recruit faculty who were committed to the extra work it would take to create a new school.

In the fall of 1994 a second class of ninth graders was admitted, and the enrollment stood at nearly 150. The two primary challenges of the 1994–95 academic year were curriculum development, both to bring the academic subjects to regents' standards and to create the South Bronx Churches leadership class, and to find and deliver a permanent site for the school. The first phase of the leadership class was essentially a weekly seminar led by the SBC organizer and adapted from the curriculum developed for the Institute for Public Life. The students began to learn the basics of how power is used in public life and were engaged in the Industrial Areas Foundation's efforts to establish a living-wage standard for New York City.[4] An evaluation of the course, however, indicated that in subsequent years the course should meet daily, not weekly, and that there should be additional reading and writing assignments for participating students.

The issue of a site remained most vexing. The school moved into the church community center in midyear, and while that was an improvement, it still left something to be desired. Faculty, staff, and students worked hard to make a functioning school community in a building that was never designed for it.

Standards of academic performance and behavior were set high. Protesting a lack of "action," a school security guard requested reassignment!

School officials and SBC leaders inspected over twenty buildings in the South Bronx before settling on a newly constructed cinder block building just south of the Cross Bronx Expressway as the permanent home of the Bronx Leadership Academy. Architects from the board of education were able to design a state-of-the-art school, including a gym, music room, large art room, scientific laboratories, and computer facilities, within the existing structure. The cost of construction included an investment of $1 million from the owners and an allocation of approximately $5 million from the board of education. The board agreed to lease the building for fifteen years. Thus, the second year of the Bronx Leadership Academy ended on a high note—student achievement was up, faculty morale was high, Katherine Kelly had been named principal, a private benefactor for enhanced programs in athletics and the arts had been found through the board's "Principal for a Day" program, and the papers had been signed for a permanent site.

Over the summer of 1995, the new site for the Bronx Leadership Academy came under the gaze of the city budget cutters. The $5 million looked easy to cut; after all, the school hardly existed. It had fewer than two hundred students, and plenty of empty seats were available in existing schools for students to attend; why not just call the whole thing off? The SBC lead organizer and primary leaders engaged in the school effort were out of town when the budget cutters took action. Here again the tremendous efforts made by South Bronx Churches and the Bronx superintendent's office paid off. The budget cutters got the word from the Bronx superintendent's office that the $5 million was not an easy cut, that it was off-limits, actually, and that if they continued on their course, then *they* would have to deal with South Bronx Churches about it. The $5 million stayed in the budget.

The third year of the Bronx Leadership Academy has been marked by hope and the completion of the new building in February—three years after the school was first chartered by the board of education. The academic performance of students is encouraging, yet with plenty of room for progress. In a recent analysis of standardized examination results from the twenty-five Bronx high schools, the Bronx Leadership Academy ranked ninth in reading, eleventh in math, and sixth in science. SBC and the guidance staff at the Bronx Leadership Academy have begun connecting the academy students with local, regional, and traditionally African American colleges.

The leadership class has expanded to a study of citizen action including various historical liberation movements— Gandhi, the American civil rights movement, the labor movement—and of course including the current work of South Bronx Churches and the other IAF affiliates to build grassroots power to improve housing, health care, citizen participation, government accountability, policing, and schools. The students have continued to participate in hearings on the living wage and have identified local actions they might take near their new school. They participated in a meeting with SBC and the Bronx borough president to line up his continued support of their school. They are beginning to see that if they stick together, if they plan their actions, if they analyze the circumstance and amass enough power, they can bring about changes. They do not have to play the role of victim. There is an alternative to whining, and that alternative is deliberate, concerted action on a commonly agreed-upon goal. They are gaining a new sense of themselves: they see themselves as agents of change; they have an alternative to violence, passivity, and apathy. They are learning to act.

On April 21, 1996, as part of its tenth anniversary celebrations, South Bronx Churches dedicated the new site for the Bronx Leadership Academy in a celebration attended by over five hundred people. The new school has become a symbol and a challenge for the entire city of New York of what is possible when the best parts of the public, private, and voluntary sectors work together for a common goal. That thirty diverse religious congregations could stand together and work out a mutually acceptable relationship to the New York City Board of Education is little short of a miracle.

13

Raising Lazarus

The Resurrection and Transformation of Harlem

Roger N. Scotland

Harlem is distinctly an American community, a replica of which could not be found anywhere on earth except in this country . . . it is what it is because of American customs, habits, environment, prejudices, and conditions.
—*The New York Age* (April 9, 1932)

The economic distress of America's inner cities may be the most pressing issue facing the nation. The lack of business and jobs in disadvantaged urban areas fuels not only a crushing cycle of poverty but also crippling social problems, such as drug abuse and crime. And, as the inner cities continue to deteriorate, the debate on how to aid them grows increasingly divisive.
—Michael E. Porter,
"The Competitive Advantage of the Inner City"

It's a scary thing when you have a vision, and people don't necessarily think it's going to happen, and then it happens.
—Rev. Dr. Preston R. Washington,
in a conversation on the redevelopment of Harlem

Roger N. Scotland worked at Harlem Congregations for Community Improvement for almost three years. He assisted in strategic planning and coordinated the organization's special projects and fund development initiatives.

Anyone unfamiliar with the condition of Harlem might ask,
How could one community need so much revitalization? Those
familiar with Harlem, and Harlemites in particular, would
respond, "You don't know the half." Although some communities in Harlem prospered, the community as a whole needed
much more than was visible to the naked eye. Harlem may still
have been remembered as the cultural mecca of black America
early in the twentieth century, but in reality the devastated
community had long since lost it glory.[1] The rich legacy was
almost replaced by a reputation for rampant crime, drugs, and
poverty.[2] Its economic vitality, the feeling of pride, and the
hustle and bustle were all but extinct. The dreams of many
Harlemites had long since exploded. Harlem's residents, like
many other inner-city constituents around the country, had lost
hope. They were disenchanted with society and knew all too
well what life had to offer. Past generations had the opportunity
to be optimistic. Recent generations only had reason to be
cynical. Each day that passed brought the same reality: poverty,
subhuman living conditions, and societal debasement of their
lives. Although many have developed attitudes of skepticism,
despair, and resignation, the resilience of Harlemites have
never faltered. In the midst of great adversity they still found
meaning in life, managed to survive, and in many instances
blossomed. For these reasons the brightest, most visible, and
endearing aspect of Harlem to me will never be its legendary
aura, but its people.

At the turn of the twentieth century, W. E. B. DuBois asserted
that the problem facing America was that of the "color line."
In the 1960s and 1970s many inner-city blacks would argue that
it manifested itself as a geographic line, a divide, a border
between two worlds, two realities. Some may have overcome;
however, *we* did not overcome. This sentiment, shared by many
of Harlem's working poor, could be attributed to the deplorable
housing and environmental conditions. Many of Central Harlem's residents have to live without basic amenities, such as
heat and hot water. Some landlords neglect to make repairs or
provide exterminator services. Hallways are most often unsanitary and gloomy, and entrances to buildings unsecured. Many
Harlem residents live in dilapidated, congested arrangements.

There is a shortage of housing in the area and even less standard-quality, affordable living options.[3] Widespread was the belief that no one cared enough to spend the time, effort, or money to relieve them of their suffering. Residents of this community have for a long time been exploited through promises of improvements for the area, which have resulted in little or few changes. As one man, who identified himself as a "Vietnam veteran," said, "Tell them we are human too."[4]

Many residents found solace in the religious community. Historically, the church has been an integral, stable institution in the black community. In times of crisis, the church had always opened its doors and was active on a grassroots level in organizing community members and assisting them in their hour of need. If nowhere else, at least one could always find comfort and a place to lay his or her burdens. To many residents of Harlem, unlike society, the church had never turned its back or closed its doors. However, individually, the local churches were sometimes overburdened and only capable of so much. According to Preston Washington, Harlem clergy and laypersons wanted to help their neighbors to "initiate change and control their environment." To combat the crisis in their neighborhood, the local clergy and laity created an "interdenominational think tank" to devise a strategy to uplift the community.

In 1986 the ecumenical group of Harlem clergy set out to form a group that would "influence what priorities were set for the Harlem community and what plans are developed and approved for our community."[5] Harlem Churches for Community Improvement (HCCI) was the organization that came out of the initial clergy meeting. In their original statement to the Harlem and the larger New York community they stated, "[We are] very much concerned about the lack of affordable housing for the people of Harlem . . . [and are] also determined to prevent displacement of the members of our churches through the gentrification of our neighborhood." The group's initial motto was "Empowering the Church and the Community to Make Housing a Right for All." The motto has since been changed to "Empowered Congregations Rebuilding Harlem." HCCI is governed by a twenty-one-member board of directors comprised of members of the organization. The organization represents the member congregations in its consortium.[6]

It was not uncommon for churches in Harlem to address the individual needs of community residents. It was and is most uncommon for so many to work for so long without dissent on a common purpose. Yet, it seemed like a natural extension of their calling for the clergy to assist directly in the revitalization of their community. The Reverend Doctor Preston Washington, president and CEO of Harlem Congregations for Community Improvement, proclaims that "for years there had been nothing of consequence." To many developers and top city administrators, the redevelopment of Central Harlem was almost impossible since it was really a resurrection that seemed in order. This appeared especially true in the upper Central Harlem community of Bradhurst. One local newspaper asked whether Harlem could be "born again." Although other developers had failed, HCCI had a vested interest as well as faith and commitment. Besides, if Christ could raise Lazarus from the dead, was it not within HCCI's collaborative means to follow his example and try to raise their community or at the very least have a clear voice in the revitalization efforts? In 1987 an article written by Rev. Washington appeared in Harlem Urban Development Corporation's *HUDC Reports* that signaled to the Cuomo and Koch administrations the identity and intentions of Harlem Churches for Community Improvement:

> Our membership is interdenominational and reflects a broad cross section of the Harlem clergy community. Our purpose is to advocate and agitate for low- and moderate-income housing for Harlem families. We are particularly interested in a program whereby city-owned multiple dwellings in Harlem can be renovated and turned into cooperative apartments *managed by churches and community organizations* [emphasis added]. We are committed to being active participants in the struggle to revitalize the Harlem community.[7]

The city's administration seriously doubted the capacity of this "new umbrella group" to be successful in such a large endeavor. Nevertheless, HCCI remained committed and determined to the realization of its vision for a second renaissance for Harlem.

Although HCCI was concerned with all of Harlem, it decided to concentrate most of its efforts on Bradhurst (a forty-block neighborhood within Harlem with identifiable boundaries).[8] Bradhurst was a devastated neighborhood with characteristics of physical deterioration as well as economic and social isolation. Bradhurst is a state-designated Economic Development Zone and Distress Area and is located within a federally designated Empowerment Zone.[9] The community is marked by deprivation and poverty; sociologically, its residents can be branded with the loaded sobriquet "underclass." In press reports concerning Bradhurst, the community was labeled as "a blighted war zone," "a desolate wasteland," and a "downtrodden community in dire need of massive economic revitalization." In describing Bradhurst, the *New York Times* stated:

> The buildings, vacant for years, are at the heart of Bradhurst.... The neighborhood became a symbol of the decay that has blighted Harlem for decades, with some areas looking as if they were reduced to rubble by shelling. . . . For decades much of the bustle and vitality that made Harlem a center of black America was lost, as people left and buildings fell apart.[10]

DEMOGRAPHIC OVERVIEW

In 1987 approximately 64 percent of the households in Harlem had incomes below $10,000 annually, and only 8.2 percent earned more than $25,000.[11] One-third of the population received public assistance. Based on 1980 census information, the median income of Bradhurst residents was $6,152. By 1994 the median income dropped to $6,019. Since 1970 Central Harlem's population has withered by more than one-third. In 1990 Bradhurst's population was documented at 91,480 residents; the 1970 census estimate placed the population at 159,300.[12] The Census Bureau reported that there were 101,091 residents in Central Harlem in 1980.[13] From 1970 to 1980 Bradhurst's population declined 37 percent, 17 percent more than the rate for Harlem overall within the same period. The *Bradhurst Revitalization Plan* attributed the population decline between 1970 and 1980 to housing abandonment and implied that the resultant population has changed the social demographics.[14]

Thirty percent of the families in Bradhurst are single, female-headed households, many of which have incomes below the poverty line. In 1988, 46 percent were reported under the heading of single-headed households (presumably inclusive of both male and female); families comprised the remaining 54 percent. The community was characterized by a large concentration of very low-income and dependent households, with high percentages of unemployment, single female-headed households, children living in poverty (70 percent), criminal activity, low levels of labor-force participation, and deficient educational attainment.[15] Shifts in the type of employment resulting from fundamental, economic, and structural changes are considered the major elements that produced the "underclass" phenomenon and accelerated the ghettoization process.

COMMUNITY ASSESSMENT AND NEEDS

Although rehabilitating the housing stock was an essential goal in the revitalization of Harlem, it was apparent to HCCI that much more than bricks and mortar was needed. HCCI's board chairman, Canon Frederick B. Williams, had a clear understanding of the tremendous mission before his organization. He knew that to be successful, HCCI would have to develop Bradhurst holistically: "We understood you couldn't just reclaim the buildings." Williams said, "We had to rebuild the spirit and the moral fiber of the community, and we had to add all of the supportive services people need when they come into a community—economic development, child care, space for artists, ways of looking after senior citizens. We'd seen the failure of bricks and mortar only."[16]

HCCI sought to develop the community economically in part by promoting commercial development, offering entrepreneurial opportunities to minorities, and promoting the expansion of businesses that historically stayed clear of neighborhoods like Harlem. This endeavor would attract more investment in the community and create additional employment for local residents. The construction efforts also created employment opportunities for community members and gave many residents the opportunity to take a part in the physical rehabilitation of their community.[17] This succeeded at further linking the community's residents to the future success of the redevelopment efforts. It was unlikely that individuals would destroy buildings they had helped to build. HCCI's strategy for comprehensive development was given further credence by the results of a study of Bradhurst by the Harlem Urban Development Corporation (HUDC): "HCCI Community Improvement Housing Report." The study recommended that nothing short of a comprehensive endeavor be initiated.

The HUDC report on housing in Bradhurst coupled with the data on the physical condition of the community made it apparent that the majority of existing households were inadequately housed. To be inadequately housed is to be one step from being "houseless." The inadequacies were found primarily in the area of housing that is substandard, unaffordable, and socially and environmentally deplorable from blight and lack of community wholeness.[18] The report also found that commercial and retail activities were underdeveloped and unevenly distributed by type and location. The existing conditions suggested that residents had limited access to quality goods and services. There was a near nonexistence of professional services for area residents in the form of medical offices and legal and financial services. The neighborhood's physical appearance was a factor in disabling it from capturing investment and generating employment and business opportunities.[19] In addition, the community fell victim to redlining and disinvestment.[20]

According to an analysis of 1990 census data by the Program for Applied Research at Queens College (as reported in a 1994 *New York Times* article), there was a distinct difference between the economic vitality of Bradhurst in relation to a neighboring community. The report found that the Dickensian breach between Manhattan's richest and poorest areas had widened in the last decade. Both the city's richest census tract and the poorest were in Manhattan, the richest bound by Fifth and Park Avenues and by East Eighty-sixth and Ninety-first Streets on the Upper East Side. The poorest was bound by Bradhurst Avenue and Frederick Douglass Boulevard and by West 145th and 150th Streets in Harlem. Average family income in the richest was $301,209, approximately fifty times more than the $6,019 average in the poorest.

Many of Bradhurst's residents were in dire need of social services. The neighborhood was seriously deficient in terms of the type of services available and their capacity to meet the basic necessities of those in most critical need. Programs geared toward creating economic independence, such as educational preparation and job training, did not exist. In an area with an extremely high concentration of dependent households, unemployment, and a low labor-force participation rate, professional services (i.e., employment training and educational preparation programs) would have to be established. Among the limited services available, the majority were child-care facilities. In the case of child care, less than half of eligible children were served by the limited number of spaces, while nearly 316 children were on waiting lists. In addition to much needed child-care facilities and programs, the area lacked health care and services for senior citizens. Bradhurst had a large middle-aged and senior citizen representation in the community; 43 percent of the population was forty-five years and older, 21.5 percent of which was over 65.[21] This group had *no* facilities or appropriate programming in the community. Furthermore, neighborhood youth did not have quality open space for recreation. Although the neighborhood's playgrounds had long been slated for rehabilitation, the parks remained the same—decrepit and unsafe. Crime reached unprecedented levels, particularly among youth. There were abandoned cars on the streets, numerous vacant lots littered with debris, and an even larger number of vacant and unsealed buildings that almost certainly housed drug activity.

Blighted conditions were common throughout the area. To be successful in its revitalization efforts, HCCI had to address all the factors devastating the community. To ameliorate the physical decay, social problems, and economic isolation, a comprehensive and coordinated partnership was required between the community, the public, and the private sectors. In this context, the Consortium for Central Harlem Development (CCHD) was conceived and formed.

COULD FAITH MOVE A MOUNTAIN IN THE COMPANY OF POLITICS?

When the "umbrella group" CCHD was first organized, it also included various other community organizations and business leaders, thus further solidifying its base in the community. HCCI was portrayed by the *New York Daily News* as a coalition, consisting of seventy ministers, forty businessmen, and members of various artists' groups, on a collision course with the city. The anticipated "collision" between the city and the Harlem coalition would occur over who would develop the plan. The coalition had voiced its preference for a Harlem-based group to provide technical assistance and serve as the overall construction manager, the expressed preference being the HUDC. The city's housing preservation commissioner, Abraham Biderman, did not rule out HUDC as Bradhurst's developer but conceded that he was "not comfortable with the level of expertise possessed by the Harlem group." It was reported that beyond acknowledging there was a plan to redevelop "that general area," Washington and Biderman agreed upon little else.[22]

Biderman suggested that the two-year-old Harlem-based coalition develop 175 units of housing (about six buildings) on a "pilot project basis."[23] If the pilot project went well, he would then give the group more projects to develop. Harlem's *Amsterdam News* reported that the issue was really that the city's housing preservation commissioner questioned whether blacks were capable of doing what they proposed. The Catholic Dioceses of Brooklyn and the Archdiocese of New York (Manhattan) had spearheaded similar efforts in Brooklyn, Queens, Bronx, and parts of Manhattan with the city administration's approval. Now that the black churches of Harlem were leading similar initiatives, the *Amsterdam News* questioned why their efforts were not equally welcomed.

The Housing Preservation and Development (HPD) proposal called for the creation of twelve hundred units (apartments), all rental housing, for residents with $25,000 maximum income—there was no economic mixture or home-ownership options.[24] The HPD plan was projected to cost the city $78 million. The HCCI-backed development plan called for 2,256

units of mixed-income housing for families earning from
$11,000 to $35,000. The HCCI plan reserved 834 units for
families already residing in the area, 364 units for homeless
families (the same figure proposed by the city), 646 units of
middle-income condominiums, and 412 cooperatives for
moderate-income families. The total cost was about $119 mil-
lion and would be the largest rehabilitation effort in New York
City history. According to the *Amsterdam News,* the Harlem-
based coalition proposed to find around $57 million through
private investments and looked for the city to invest almost $63
million in the form of grants to subsidize the tenants' rent.

The city housing preservation commissioner stated that he
did not believe any one group was capable of developing the
entire project, but conceded that he was considering the New
York Urban Coalition, a private multiracial organization not
based in Harlem. HCCI and the commissioner had held discussions since the previous summer (1987), but HCCI felt there
was not sufficient progress and decided to involve Mayor
Edward Koch in the discussions.[25] However, according to
Washington, "Koch didn't believe that we had the capacity as
churches to pull off this massive plan and he took our plan to
another developer, a white developer, . . . we fought tooth and
nail."[26] In a 1992 *City Limits* article, Washington said, "Koch
fought us like you wouldn't believe, . . . it was like a personal
vendetta."[27] After three years of intense negotiations, the Koch
administration agreed to let the Harlem-based groups, CCHD
and HCCI, develop eighteen hundred units. Additionally,
CCHD members conceded that the city housing commissioner
could require the Harlem group to include the New York Urban
Coalition in its consortium in order for the city to support the
redevelopment effort.

Mayor Koch approved the first phase of construction and
named the consortium the developer in his last month of office.
Koch credited Mayor-elect David Dinkins and Representative
Charles Rangel with helping to forge the compromise that
resulted in the agreement that secured Harlem's $150 million
"heart surgery." Under the terms of the compromise, the city
retained responsibility for rehabilitating the city-owned buildings and issued the criteria that developers had to meet to take

part in the plan.[28] Lionel McIntyre, author of the *Bradhurst Revitalization Plan,* commented that Bradhurst was a "complex political piece of work." He took the complications in stride and stated that he had "yet to see a project without political turmoil."

As far as residents were concerned, Harlem was finally slated to get a sorely needed redevelopment boost. Although Mayor-elect David Dinkins was supportive of the Bradhurst project and committed $65 million to the first phase of development, many Bradhurst residents were still cynical and publicly said that they would not "believe anything until they saw it." Unfortunately, outside of Bradhurst there were many potential predators. The value of Harlem property immediately increased due to the forthcoming development efforts. Many speculators invested in an attempt to resell the newly acquired property at exorbitant prices. Consequently, the development of many blocks in the initiative would be further complicated and delayed. Eight years later there are still clusters of abandoned properties belonging to speculators, and many blocks still await rehabilitation due to unscrupulous investors.

HCCI: BUILDING TO SECURE TOMORROW . . . TODAY

The Dinkins administration was significantly different from the Koch administration. The city experienced an accelerated housing development boom with more than $200 million spent in Central Harlem over a four-year span. Under Mayor Dinkins and his housing commissioner, Felice L. Michetti, the city began a variety of new programs citywide that allowed community-based organizations to build more easily, either by developing projects themselves or by acting as community sponsors, with substantial say in the final product. It was this political climate that enabled HCCI to make its greatest strides toward comprehensive rehabilitation and remedying the "underclass" phenomenon among Harlem residents.

Initially, HCCI's mandate was to lobby on behalf of the community for decent housing and to revive the spiritual condition of the community (CCHD was to coordinate the physical rehabilitation). However, by 1992 HCCI's scope was increasingly taking on wider dimensions. In the past, HCCI had provided community residents with much-needed social services—primarily through the efforts of their member congregations—and served as organizers and community activists. In addition to the aforementioned responsibilities, there was increased need for direct social service intervention, and they found themselves directly serving in the capacity of a "developer," a function that absorbed additional resources but did not generate development fees for the organization. HCCI's fervent commitment to the community often left it in a financial predicament. They often initiated and financially maintained programs on a wing and a prayer knowing the community had come too far to be let down.

Since 1991 HCCI has grown from a staff of two and a budget of $100,000 to thirty-two employees and a budget of more than $2 million. Through its Housing Development and Marketing Division, headed by Greg Watson, HCCI has aggressively initiated affordable quality housing units throughout Harlem. In the span of three years (1993–96), HCCI has admitted over four thousand persons into the community who did not formerly reside in Bradhurst (one thousand of whom were formerly homeless families and individuals). In addition, they have (or are slated to soon have) ownership of nearly one thousand apartments. HCCI plans to be the owner or management coordinator of the majority of its housing and social services collaborations. Currently, HCCI markets all of its rental housing units and is currently in the process of developing a management company—the HCCI Property Management Company. The mission of the company is to provide efficient maintenance, security, and management for the longevity of HCCI housing developments, create employment opportunities, while simultaneously providing income to continue HCCI's community development endeavors.[29]

With respect to the various development efforts, the community's daily needs and concerns change. To keep abreast of larger community concerns, HCCI hosts a monthly General Assembly meeting. The General Assembly is a community-wide forum that meets bimonthly at the HCCI Family Life Center. The General Assembly was established to allow clergy, laity, local residents, and a cross section of professionals to have a voice in issues facing Harlem.

UPLIFTING THE PEOPLE: COORDINATION OF SOCIAL SERVICES

To augment the *Bradhurst Revitalization Plan,* HCCI created the *Bradhurst Social Service Delivery Plan.*[30] HCCI established supportive linkages with other Harlem social service agencies to deliver effective interventions to the residents of Bradhurst. Over fifteen community agencies joined in this partnership. In an effort to minimize repeat homelessness, HCCI developed specific interventions for former homeless families selected to move into Bradhurst. A social service coordinator met with all formerly homeless families prior to their moving into HCCI housing. The orientation assessed the needs of families, identified appropriate services, and evaluated their general mental health. Families who were considered "high risk" for returning to a homeless condition were provided with intensive case management for six months. Those relocated families who were not considered high risk were monitored with special attention given to their specific needs. All tenants received community-based support. Self-help groups and family mentoring programs met weekly and offered supportive, educational, and recreational activities to help reduce the isolation that many families experience in new communities. Volunteers from HCCI member congregations provided child care for tenants while they attended the self-help group.

Another component of the mentorship program linked families living in Bradhurst with a family from one of HCCI's member congregations. This component was specifically designed for young parents and their children. Church families were screened and were required to complete a comprehensive training program before being paired with a tenant family. Church members assisted with tutoring, parenting skills, housekeeping, and referrals for congregational interaction and involvement. The program was viewed as a vehicle for tenants to experience a smoother transition into their new community.

HCCI has two centers that serve as the Harlem "community hub" for educational and vocational training: the Family Life

Center and the Empowerment and Training Center. Both facilities offer programs for HCCI's Bradhurst Academy of Excellence (BAE). The centers host adult literacy programs (including General Equivalency Diploma [GED] and basic education programming); computer literacy training courses that teach participants typing skills and various computer programs relevant to securing a job in today's job market; tenant organizing workshops; and after-school tutorial programs featuring classes in United States and world history and exposure to the arts.

MEETING THE CHALLENGE: TOWARD A HEALTHY HARLEM

HCCI is committed to improving the general health of Harlem residents. Harlem Hospital and the World Health Organization (WHO) have independently identified Harlem as equivalent to a Third World country. The life expectancy of black males residing in Harlem is less than that of men in Bangladesh. Infants and children in Harlem are cited by WHO as an "endangered species" due to such problems as high incidences of drug dependency, HIV/AIDS, and physical and sexual abuse. Since its inception, HCCI has consistently advocated for preventive health services in Harlem. HCCI is currently working to develop outpatient health-care facilities and prevention programs through local congregations to establish and strengthen existing linkages with agencies that provide residential treatment where there are gaps in direct and preventive services in Bradhurst.

HCCI frequently incorporates new programs to meet the needs challenging the community, such as the HIV/AIDS epidemic. In 1993 the Manhattan borough president's office reported that AIDS is the second leading cause of death in Harlem and the third in the borough. The rate of deaths from AIDS among women residing in Bradhurst was nine times that of an affluent neighboring community. HCCI recognized the devastating significance of HIV/AIDS long before 1993. The member clergy saw victims of the epidemic daily—on the streets and in their congregations. To assist in combating the deadly disease, HCCI secured a $1 million contract with the city's Human Resources Administration (HRA), Division of AIDS Services, to provide an array of housing and support services. The program provides housing, furniture, clothing, counseling, and medical referrals and assists with entitlements (many individuals living with HIV/AIDS have difficulty locating quality housing due to bias). The program also provides apartment maintenance, pastoral care, and funeral assistance.

A CROSS TO CARRY:
THE PROBLEMS OF COMPREHENSIVE DEVELOPMENT AND DAY-TO-DAY MANAGEMENT

HCCI has come a long way in improving the overall physical appearance of Harlem. Its social service offerings have made a considerable impact, substantially changing many current social conditions facing Bradhurst residents (program offerings are open to all interested community residents). However, though the community has been resurrected, the transformation is not yet complete. For fiscal year 1995 Mayor Giuliani's housing plan slated city funding to be cut in half over six years from $153 million to $95 million. The ten-year, $5.1 billion housing plan that was initiated in 1987 under Mayor Edward Koch, but largely realized under Mayor David Dinkins, resulted in new and rehabilitated housing, from single-room occupancy hotels (SROs) to apartment buildings and small homes. However, Giuliani's housing agenda called for refocusing. His strategy shifted away from massive development projects like Bradhurst and toward the rehabilitation and sale of city-owned apartment buildings.[31] In the 1994 article "Reality Strikes," the stark realities facing New York City not-for-profits similar in scope to HCCI were detailed: "Some of the deepest reductions are levied on programs designed to assist homeless New Yorkers and tenants of the worst privately owned housing stock in the city. . . . Giuliani is seeking to eliminate city funding for the SRO Loan Program, which provides non-profits with loans at very low interest (about 1 percent)."[32]

In light of the altered political climate throughout government, HCCI found itself competing for much-needed funding from increasingly sought-after private-sector grants. Foundation support was not always forthcoming, and HCCI was in the midst of an uphill battle. During these uncertain years, funding for the organization was secured through committed, thorough, and innovative fund development. Furthermore, HCCI would have to maximize funds. To secure large grants and blossom, they needed enhanced financial credibility. Toward achieving this end, the Ford Foundation (one of HCCI's strongest supporters) funded HCCI to hire a chief fiscal officer. With respect to cutbacks in funding housing development, HCCI refocused its priorities to further addressing the immense social service needs of the community.

HCCI has made tremendous strides in Harlem in a short period of time. Some maintain that HCCI is in over its head. Cynics maintain that comprehensive development is a pipe dream, noting that the strategy dates back to President Lyndon B. Johnson's War on Poverty and holding up empirical evidence that the approach has proven ineffective. Still, HCCI's commitment to the long, arduous task of restoring Bradhurst and the larger Harlem community is unquestionable. By HCCI's undertaking of the tremendous task of resurrecting and transforming the community, there's a strong feeling that the churches run a high stake and "have put themselves on the line."[33] However, Steven Williams, the organization's economic development coordinator, sees the reality of a failed effort, regardless of sincerity and commitment: "The churches have to be responsible to the community in a more real way than anyone else. For someone you have special faith in to put up a building and let it go to hell would feed into the stereotype that churches are the biggest crooks in the neighborhood. A lot more is at stake than balance sheets. Their reputation is there."[34]

Some city administrators and community residents have forgotten or simply do not know how far along "development's road" Harlem has traveled. One tenant, discouraged by an inoperable elevator, asserted that HCCI "made you think this is going to be a new Harlem and it made you want to be a part of it." The tenant elaborated: "The commitments they made to the community aren't within their reach in such a short time."[35] Yet even though the resurrected Harlem may be obscured by the work that remains, it cannot be denied that strides *have* been made. In Harlem's case, the road has twisted, traveled endlessly in the valley of obstruction and unfulfilled promises, and fallen from precipitous cliffs, only to ascend at a rate often not satisfactory to community residents, activists, or developers. Community-based organizations, religious or secular, are often held accountable for their publicized intentions, plans, or visions for their respective communities. With frustration, it becomes harder to distinguish what has been accomplished.

In a recent article concerning HCCI's work in Central Harlem, Robin Epstein asked whether a "church group could be developer, landlord, social worker and tenant organizer—all at the same time."[36] The question illuminates HCCI's predicament. In some respects, to sustain the community, a locally based group wearing numerous hats may very well be needed. However, as a religious-based group there is a definite risk of straining communal relations, especially when business must take precedence. When all is complete, the legacy of HCCI should be written as one of activist, developer, and advocate.[37]

PART FOUR

*New York City Mission
in the
Asian American Context*

Ray Bakke has called our era the "age of the Asian Pentecost." For two thousand years, the Western church has struggled to share the gospel in Asia. Luke, in fact, records Christianity's first unsuccessful mission attempt: the apostle Paul's dramatic left turn into Europe, "having been forbidden by the Holy Spirit to speak the word in Asia." For much of church history, missionaries met with only limited success in the Asian interior, where more than half of the world's population lives. This century has witnessed a dramatic reversal of this pattern. *Operation World* estimates that the number of Asian Protestants more than doubled between 1980 and 1990, from 58 million to 127 million.

Korea and China have been the centers of the most dramatic Asian church growth. The first Protestant church was planted in Korea in 1884; by 1984 there were nearly thirty thousand churches. There are today more churchgoers in Seoul on Sunday morning than in any other city in the world. Seoul is home of the largest church in the world and ten of the twenty largest congregations in the world. In the last fifteen years, the number of Korean foreign missionaries grew from two hundred to three thousand. The church in China is growing at a rate unprecedented in its history. Under brutal repression, the number of Christians in China has increased at least tenfold. The exhaustion of old traditions, the sterility of life under communism, and the meaninglessness of monolithic political chants have created a cultural vacuum in China that Christianity is filling.

The chapters that follow bear witness to the fact that Asian Christian growth is not confined to the Asian continent. In New York, there are now sixteen hundred Korean churches and eighty Chinese churches. These churches are virtual clearinghouses for new immigrants, providing emergency shelter, job training, English-language instruction, and naturalization services. These churches also challenge New York's Christian community by presenting us with exemplary models of prayerfulness and evangelical zeal. The Korean Church of Queens, for example, consistently attracts hundreds of worshipers to its daily 5:30 A.M. prayer meeting. On Fridays, a group of ninety of these prayer partners fan out to various parts of Queens to hand out tracts in four languages.

14

The Seoul of New York

The Korean Church of Queens

McKenzie P. Pier

The Korean Church of Queens is located on the corner of Eighty-ninth Street and Twenty-third Avenue in Jackson Heights in the shadow of LaGuardia Airport. This morning, just as every morning during Lent 1995, hundreds of worshipers arrive before dawn. The sanctuary is dimly lit, and people are scattered throughout the bottom floor of the two-thousand-seat auditorium. Many are kneeling. The meeting begins promptly at 5:30 A.M.

Fifty choir members, attired in white, climb the stairs of the stage. In a stunning spectacle, they lead out in intricately arranged choral music. The first thirty minutes of the service also includes corporate singing and an exhortation from Pastor Han. During the second half hour, the congregation erupts into simultaneous corporate prayer, the worshipers having now become intercessors. The noise level of the meeting jumps several decibels, and an intensity envelops the sanctuary that is so real one can almost touch it. Prayers are offered for the sick of the church and then the youth. Intercession is made for the city, nation, and the world—the petitions reflecting the scope of the pastor's global vision.

During the 1995 Lenten season the Korean Church of Queens placed a special emphasis on mobilizing for early morning prayer. Attendance peaked at six hundred people, and the spirit of prayer was so strong that the church continued on a twenty-four-hour prayer vigil until June 17. Six times a week, 120 to 150 people meet at the Korean Church of Queens for prayer at 5:30 A.M., yet there are no fewer than eleven opportunities for corporate prayer during the week. Corporate prayer includes a Friday-night meeting from 10:00 P.M. until the early morning hours on Saturday and prayer meetings on Monday and Thursday evenings.

The Korean Church of Queens is the oldest of three hundred Korean churches in the borough of Queens. It is also one of the largest Korean churches in North America. Indeed, Pastor Han has a worldwide speaking ministry. Of course, the Korean Church of Queens was not always like this. In 1977 Jin Kwan Han was completing his eighth year as a struggling pastor. Largely dependent on his wife's income as a social worker, he was discouraged by the lack of fruit in his work. He had come so far, yet the kind of success he desired in ministry eluded him. How did he eventually attain the size and scope of ministry that is enjoyed by the Korean Church of Queens today? This question cannot be answered adequately apart from the context of the growth and development of the Korean American community itself.

THE KOREANS ARE COMING

Between World War II and 1965 Korean immigrants in the United States were largely found in three groups: Korean students studying in universities, Korean women who were war brides, and Korean orphans who were adopted. Still, the number of Koreans on American soil was small. This changed in 1965 after President Lyndon Johnson signed the Immigration Act, which allowed 250,000 people to immigrate to the United States annually. Since 1973, 20,000 Koreans have immigrated every year. In New York City most Koreans settled in the Flushing, Jackson Heights, and Woodside sections of Queens. In 1980 there were 33,260 Koreans in New York City and 13,000 in New Jersey. More than 2,000 Koreans immigrated into New York City annually between 1982 and 1990, the peak of the immigration being 1989 with 2,717 people arriving.[1] In the 1990 census Koreans were the fourth largest Asian presence in the United States behind the Chinese, Filipinos, and Japanese.[2]

KOREAN LIFE IN AMERICA

Korean life in America can be characterized by entrepreneurship, education, and church life. In parts of Los Angeles, California, and Queens, New York, the Korean community has taken over whole city blocks. Many streets near Main Street in Flushing, Queens, have business signs that are exclusively in Chinese and Korean.

Entrepreneurs

Many Korean immigrants came to America with university education, yet the language barrier was so great that many professionals exchanged suits and ties for aprons. Advancement in the corporate arena of South Korea gave way to starting grocery stores in urban United States.[3]

Korean-owned grocery stores, laundromats, and dry cleaners sprinkle urban neighborhoods. Grocery stores yield the tightest profit margin, while dry cleaners provide greater income. Import/export businesses are strong in both New York and Los Angeles. Los Angeles has six thousand Korean-owned stores, twenty-five hundred of which were affected by the 1992 riots.[4]

A powerful dynamic in Korean economics is the *kye*. The *kye* is a loan system in which a pool of money is used for one year. The profits from this money are then added to the money being transferred to another friend or family member. Community economics based on the *kye* provide explanation for the rapid growth of Korean businesses in depressed urban areas.[5]

Education

The English language has been described as the great prohibitor for many Koreans.[6] English has created a continental divide, often within the same home, between first- and second-generation Koreans. Accompanying this language difference are the thousands of cultural influences the younger generation receive through English-language communication.

According to the 1990 census, 48 percent of naturalized Koreans struggle with the English language. Among Koreans living in America (but not as citizens), 72 percent have great difficulty with the language.[7] The severity of the language barrier is no better exemplified than by the fact that Seventh Avenue in Manhattan is lined with three hundred Korean sweatshops: immigrants are forced to work sixteen-hour days because poor language faculties prohibit other types of employment.[8]

The Church

Of the first seven thousand original Korean immigrants only four hundred were Christian. By 1918, 40 percent of all Korean immigrants were Christian. The global explosion of the Korean church had begun.[9] Among Korean immigrant communities, the church has functioned as a community center. Churches have helped immigrants with reading, history, and geography and have also served as employment agencies and places of language study. The church also provided the headquarters for national liberation during the Chinese occupation of World War II.[10]

The influence of the church is so pervasive that 70 percent of Koreans surveyed in Los Angeles identified affiliation with evangelical ethnic churches. In Philadelphia the percentage was 50 percent. In communities like Flushing, New York, new Korean churches are being built every year.[11]

The Korean church is largely Presbyterian; that is, 50 percent of all churches in Korea are Presbyterian, while 40 percent of Korean churches in America are Presbyterian. Of the 378 Asian congregations of the Presbyterian Church (U.S.A.), Koreans belong to 305 of them—an astounding 80 percent.[12] In America, the Korean churches that are growing in influence are nondenominational, Baptist, and evangelical. The nondenominational Korean churches in America, which include charismatic and Pentecostal churches, have a 300 percent growth compared to native Korean churches.

THE TRANSFORMATION OF PASTOR JIN KWAN HAN

Before His Conversion

Against this backdrop of Korean immigration to America, Pastor Han arrived in Berkeley, California, in 1956. He studied in Chicago from 1957 to 1961. He arrived in New York in 1961 to study theology and received a master's degree in sacred theology in 1969 from Union Theological Seminary.

Upon graduation from Union in 1969, Pastor Han started the Korean Church of Queens. At the time there were only two hundred Korean families in Flushing. The church was located near the corner of Bowne and Roosevelt in Flushing. There were no agencies to help Korean immigrants with housing, education, or employment. Pastor Han viewed the primary role of the church as meeting the social needs of these immigrants and described the church as a social club.

In 1977 there were two hundred members attending the church. Pastor Han was discouraged and overwhelmed by all of the needs in the church. His sixty-minute services were characterized by dry sermons and lifeless worship. He had never read through the entire Bible. Unable to satisfy his congregation, he was also largely dependent on his wife's income to sustain them and their two young boys. He grew pessimistic.

At that time Korean churches were sending outstanding evangelists to America with a vision to preach to the exploding immigrant population. Pastor Han was invited to a revival meeting at the Korean Presbyterian Church of Queens. The guest speaker talked about his experience as a discouraged minister who had nearly quit the ministry but had a vision of Christ that renewed his vision for ministry. While listening to this account, Pastor Han received an identical vision, which he believes was his true conversion.

After His Conversion

The effect of that revival meeting in Han's life was dramatic. He began to read the Bible from cover to cover in a matter of weeks. His personal prayer life was revolutionized as he spent hours in God's presence. His sermons became energized and inspired.

Two years later, in 1979, Han's congregation had dwindled to fifty people. He felt that he had to literally start over and that God had done "housecleaning" by causing 150 people to leave. With his remaining 50 people, Pastor Han issued a fivefold challenge to qualify for leadership. The five expectations of a deacon would be (1) to pray an hour daily, (2) to read through the Bible annually, (3) to evangelize one person a year, (4) to tithe, and (5) to keep the Sabbath. Of the fifty who remained, eight accepted the challenge. With these eight deacons Pastor Han would rebuild the Korean Church of Queens. By the end of 1979 two hundred people were attending the church. From that group twenty-four agreed to be deacons.

During 1980 and 1981 the church doubled in size. By the end of 1980 the church had four hundred people with seventy deacons. At the end of 1981 the church had eight hundred people. The facility on Bowne Street was filled to capacity. From 1981 to 1986 the church remained the same size at eight hundred members. After moving to their new facilities, the Korean Church of Queens experienced steady growth from eight hundred to its current two thousand regular attendees.

FOUNDATIONS FOR CHURCH GROWTH

Why did the Korean Church of Queens experience such dramatic growth from 1979 to 1981? What were the dynamics at play? What was happening in addition to the immigration dynamics at the time? The four keys to the growth of the church were transformation of the pastor, evangelism, facilities, and leadership deployment. Each is predicated on a dependence on the supernatural power of the Holy Spirit.

Pastoral Transformation

Pastor Han says God has to begin by transforming the pastor. After his conversion Han dedicated himself to reading twenty chapters a day of the Bible. He reads the Scriptures from cover to cover six times a year. Shortly after his experience in 1979, Han and his wife came under criticism by church members. They began an all-night prayer series that continued for twenty-three consecutive nights. All-night prayer has become a hallmark of the church.

Pastor Han has an Old Testament view of pastoral leadership, rooted in Numbers 1–4 and 8–18, that draws an analogy between the church and Old Testament Israel. In Numbers, strong emphasis is placed on God's speaking to Moses on behalf of the people. Numbers also provides a leadership structure of Moses delegating to seventy elders.

Evangelism

Since 1979 Han has emphasized the need for spiritual transformation through personal evangelism. Many of the members at the church have come through personal evangelism. Others have been attracted from thirty-nine different denominations. People from Presbyterian to Roman Catholic backgrounds have been drawn to the spiritual food of the Korean Church of Queens.

Facilities

By 1981 the eight hundred members of the church had filled the space at the Bowne Street location. There would be no room to grow without relocating. God was setting the stage to do something dramatic. Providentially, Pastor Han had been saving funds since 1969 through an annual Founders Day collection. By 1984, $1.2 million had been saved. The church went in search of property. Three acres were found on Twenty-third Avenue in Jackson Heights. On the land was a Chinese health club for sale. Though the actual value of the land was $6.4 million, the owners were asking for only $2.5 million.

A contract was made for 10 percent down with the church paying $250,000. They had one year to raise the $2.25 million or forfeit the property. The contract was signed in October 1984. The church had requested a provision that they could assume ownership of the land if funds were raised ahead of schedule. The health-club owners were skeptical. As a result of fasting, prayer, and sacrifice, the funds were raised by March. To the overwhelming astonishment of the health-club owners, the church was ready to take possession seven months ahead of schedule.

With all their money spent on the land, the church was unsure how to proceed. Two months later God sent a former Assembly of God pastor to the church. He had become a building contractor. This man developed a plan to raise $1.5 million by which a sanctuary could be constructed. The two-thousand-seat sanctuary was completed by July 1986. The completed facility has dozens of classrooms, a gymnasium, and extensive cafeteria. The church can hold dinners for over five hundred people at a time. By faithfully meeting its weekly mortgage commitment, the church completely paid off the facility within nine years.

Leadership Selection

Han has surrounded himself with a strong leadership team of pastors, elders, and deacons. He currently has fifteen pastors, ten elders, twenty-four ordained deacons, and four hundred deacons. To implement the work of the church, these leaders oversee twenty-eight committees ranging from worship to hospitality and education.

The church has seven district pastors, each of whom oversees a district of families. The districts are found in Queens, Long Island, Brooklyn, Manhattan, Bronx, and New Jersey. Approximately 50 percent of the church lives in Queens, with Long Island providing residence to the next largest segment of the church. Other staff members include administrative pastors, youth workers, and education pastors. The staff team meets for a short time daily after the prayer meeting. This system of leadership enables Pastor Han to keep a pulse on the church in all of its breadth and activity.

THE PROGRAM OF THE
KOREAN CHURCH OF QUEENS

The ministry initiatives of the Korean Church of Queens emphasize prayer, leadership development, missions, and local outreach. It is very clear in the mind of Pastor Han that prayer is God's power to change the world. Emerging from an aggressive corporate prayer life, the church engages in aggressive ministry locally and worldwide.

The Prayer Ministry

When asked to identify one passage of Scripture that captured the motivation behind the church's prayer ministry, Pastor Han said that he was driven by Mark 1:35: "Very early in the morning, while it was still dark, Jesus got up, left the house and went off to a solitary place, where he prayed" (NIV).

Han believes that the early morning prayer meeting is the measure of the church. He purposely holds his pastoral staff accountable to be present and model a commitment to the prayer life of the church. The whole life of the church is rooted in this commitment to prayer. Pastor Han said, "Prayer is like breathing. If you breathe, you live; if you stop breathing, you die." He draws from the admonition in 1 Thessalonians 5:17 to "pray continually."

Street Evangelism

Every Friday after early-morning prayer, ninety members participate in street evangelism. Members fan out to Main Street, Flushing, and busy subway stops in Jackson Heights and Elmhurst. The vision behind this effort is to proclaim the gospel visibly and broadly to the masses of New York City. Those participating in the outreach wear vests that identify them as members of the church. For an hour they pass out tracts in four different languages. People entering and leaving the subway have been receptive and appreciative toward these Korean evangelists. Reaching out to people before the workday begins has been a strategic choice by the church.

Another dimension to this outreach has been street cleaning. As members pass out tracts, other members take broom and pan to the streets at the point of outreach. The efforts to beautify these little corners of the city have not gone unnoticed. The Flushing city council gave the church an award in appreciation for their care of the community.

Churchwide Outreach

Three times a year the church offers special programs as a vehicle for outreach. This past year programs were done at the church during Thanksgiving and Easter and again during the summer. The programs involve a theme with music, testimony, and speaking. These outreaches allow the church to give community exposure to their outstanding choirs. Pastor Han has training in music, and his influence is seen through the multiple choirs, which perform traditional as well as contemporary music.

These church outreaches have proved to be an important vehicle for friendship evangelism. This key strategy has annually drawn as many as thirty new families to the church.

Missions

The church fully supports four Korean missionaries. These missionaries have been working in the Chinese world, Russia, and Equador. Pastor Han's vision has been to link his missions team with indigenous leaders in these countries. The church also has an ambitious commitment to help twelve Korean churches worldwide. The vision of Han has been to empower other Korean ministries and churches to reach other Koreans and the rest of the world.

The Korean Church of Queens supports thirty agencies and missionaries. Many of the church's students have gone on to study in prominent evangelical Christian colleges and seminaries.

Education

The church has a preschool which currently enrolls sixty students. Pastor Han desires to provide a Christian foundation in the lives of small children. Accordingly, he would like to see a Christian grade school established in the facilities of the church. During the summer, scores of students are involved in a summer-school program at the church, which is made possible by the outstanding facilities and cafeteria. Students ranging from first to twelfth grade attend classes ranging from music to art to learning the Korean language.

The church has recently inaugurated Queens Theological Seminary, drawing its adjunct professors from the pastoral and missionary community. Currently, eleven students are involved. Pastor Han's vision is to produce laborers fully equipped for the pastorate and mission field.

Cell Groups

Each of the seven district pastors is responsible for visiting thirty to forty homes weekly, and each district is divided into cells with cell group leaders. Since the cell groups meet in homes, they provide an especially important strategy for reaching members who live farther away, for example, those who live in Brooklyn and New Jersey.

Cell groups provide a time of Scripture study, prayer, and worship. They also provide a place where members can invite their friends and contacts into a safe and intimate setting to learn about God and the church.

Youth Ministry

Friday night and Saturday afternoons are the times when the various high-school and junior-high groups meet. Their program includes Old Testament survey, social events, prayer, and service projects. Students are trained in leadership for worship and the conducting of meetings. Evangelistic coffee houses are sponsored by the youth groups.

Social Ministry

Small groups within the church have taken on social ministry projects. Within the English-speaking community a strong outreach to nursing homes has developed. Church members visit nursing homes, providing music programs and building friendships with senior citizens throughout northern Queens.

Within the last year, after associate pastors and members visited the prison on Rikers Island, the church has developed a ministry to prisoners. A ministry of friendship, sharing Scriptures, and testimony has been performed in this community.

CHALLENGES FACING THE KOREAN CHURCH

The Korean American church throughout the United States is facing great transition. The number of Korean immigrants has dropped off in the last decade. In order for the Korean church to maintain a strong presence, some Korean pastors believe that something dramatic must happen.

Leadership Transition from First Generation to Second Generation

It is estimated by Korean sociologists that as many as 80 to 90 percent of Korean young people leave the church after high school. The cultural gap between parents and children has resulted in deep alienation. Many Korean churches are desperate for English-speaking youth workers. Many first-generation Korean pastors are concerned over the fate of the Korean church in American in the next twenty years.

Many Korean Christians who are now in their twenties and thirties are striving to develop Korean churches to meet the needs of second-generation Koreans. Various new church models are being developed. English-speaking Korean services with young Korean pastors are being planted. Asian American services that bring together the Chinese and Japanese along with Koreans are being attempted.

Many believe that the future of the Korean church lies in its ability to relate to non-Korean churches. The Korean church has much to offer the broader church with its emphasis on prayer and evangelism. The Korean church has much to gain from the broader church in its need for reconciliation along racial and generational lines.

Addressing Social Needs

In order for the church to be relevant within its urban context, Korean churches need to be increasingly involved with urban needs. The call to fulfill the Great Commission needs to be married to the needs Jesus talked about in Luke 4—giving sight to the blind, release to the captives, and good news to the poor.

Korean churches often have great facilities and leadership to mobilize ministry initiatives. If the resources of the Korean church could be coupled with many black and Hispanic churches, tremendous ground could be taken in working with urban youth, homeless ministries, and outreach to prisoners.

Young People's Ministry

Perhaps the greatest challenge to the continued strength and survival of the Korean church is its ministry to Korean youth. The difficult challenge lies in maintaining respect for the first-generation Korean family and tradition while perceptively caring for youth in the transition from high school to college.

SOUL OF NEW YORK

It was a warm Friday evening at the church. The dining hall had been set to accommodate four hundred people. Beautiful tablecloths and decorations had been arranged throughout the hall. The Korean worship team was practicing. People began streaming in from all across Queens. Believers belonging to Baptist, Pentecostal, Episcopal, Mennonite, independent, and Presbyterian churches gathered. Many were wearing ethnic dress from African and Korean backgrounds.

The church had prepared Korean food for the evening. People brought salads, desserts, and drinks from their own ethnicity. So many people came that the church ran out of tables to seat everyone. As the participants enjoyed dinner together that night, Pastor Han shared that the church had been praying for five years for such an evening. The church had tried by sending letters to other churches, but there had been little response. That night, however, was different, for God had broken through in a powerful way.

Following the dinner, everyone moved to the sanctuary, where a banner strung across the front of the platform welcomed them to an "Evening of Unity." Roderick Caesar, an African American pastor, led in worship, along with a choir. Pastor Han then gave his testimony and exhorted the congregation to a life of passionate prayer. Ray Bakke from International Urban Associates also spoke that evening, inviting the audience to consider what God was doing throughout the city of New York and the entire church. New York has become the leading city in the world. God has placed the multicolored church in New York to be his witness.

Bakke pointed out that the gifts of the Korean church to the rest of the body are its prayer and evangelism commitments in a new land. The gift of the rest of the body to the Korean church is its diversity and history of being in New York. Together we can be the soul of New York.

15

Equipping the Saints for the Work of the Ministry

The Oversea Chinese Mission

Bobby Watts

One of the largest church-growth movements today is among the Chinese people. Indeed, we are witnessing perhaps the greatest evangelistic move of the Holy Spirit in history. Since the expulsion of missionaries from China in 1951, and despite brutal oppression, poverty, and lack of Bibles and trained leadership, the number of Christians in mainland China has increased from one million to perhaps as many as seventy million. The Lord's current harvesting of Chinese is not limited to the Asian continent, of course, but reaches to North America. There are approximately 750 Chinese churches in the United States and Canada, and the number is increasing rapidly. According to one source, there are seventy-nine Chinese churches

Bobby Watts is an African American who grew up in Brooklyn and has lived in Asia and Chinatown. He presently works with homeless people in New York, and his long-range hope is to serve the Lord with his wife, Deatra, in Asia.

in New York City alone,[1] one of the leading ministries being the Oversea Chinese Mission (OCM).

The Oversea Chinese Church is located in the center of an expanding Chinatown. On a Sunday morning, one enters to find a beehive of activity—there are children, teens, and senior citizens talking, laughing, and shouting in several Chinese dialects and in English. As the familiar aromas of steamed rice, noodles, and peanut and sesame cooking oils waft up from the basement, the young press past each other going up and down the staircase heading to and from services, classes, or meetings (seniors are the only ones who can use the elevators). In the afternoon, a medical clinic provides health services. Before the day is over, fourteen hundred people will have attended three worship services conducted in Mandarin and English, Sunday school classes, and small-group meetings. And in four other communities across the metropolitan area, an equal or greater number of people will have worshiped in churches that OCM has planted in the last ten years. Ministry outreach to seniors and children, ten radio programs, and English classes, all emanate from this building in the heart of Chinatown.

The 1990 census recorded more than 1.6 million people of Chinese ancestry living in the United States, which was almost twice as much as that recorded in the 1980 census. Though more than half of all Asians in the United States are located in the West,[2] New York City, with a Chinese population of 238,919, has more Chinese people than any other U.S. city—even more than the combined populations of Chinese in San Francisco (127,000), Los Angeles (67,000), and Chicago (22,000), the cities with the largest Chinese populations after New York.

Chinese Americans, like other Asian Americans, are not the "model minority," an often inaccurate, one-dimensional stereotype. By many measures, such as family size and per capita income, the Chinese community is similar to the overall U.S. population; however, a closer look shows that few groups in the United States possess as much internal diversity as the Chinese community. Chinese adults are slightly less likely than all Americans to have graduated from high school but are twice as likely to have graduated from college.[3] While the median Chinese family income is 15 percent higher than that of all families in the United States, the proportion of families that live below the poverty line is 14 percent.[4]

Part of the diversity may be explained by immigration. Of all Chinese in the United States, 69 percent are foreign born, and as of 1990, 57 percent of the foreign-born Chinese arrived between 1980 and 1990.[5] The immigrants and their reactions to the United States are as diverse as their reasons for coming to the United States. Many of the twenty thousand mainland Chinese students and scholars in the United States came with advanced degrees and especially since the Tiananmen Square Massacre of June 1989 have been reluctant to return to China, indeed viewing the United States as the "Beautiful Country" (the Chinese translation of *America*). Some immigrants from Hong Kong (a city that in many ways is more modern than New York City) came to establish citizenship here and/or to invest significant amounts of capital in anticipation of the return of Hong Kong to China. Some students from Taiwan take a step down in living standards to earn their degrees, with the intention of heading home immediately. Some newcomers are family members (often parents) who come to join those who have preceded them.

Census data do not reflect the large numbers of Chinese that are illegal aliens. While it is impossible to know with certainty, some estimate that one-third to one-half of the adults in China-towns throughout the United States are undocumented aliens, many of whom took desperate measures to come to this country. This country's attention was focused briefly on this fact when seven people died in June 1993 in the sinking of the *Golden Venture,* a ship smuggling nearly three hundred Chinese people into New York.[6] News accounts increasingly document the involvement of Chinese gangs in the lucrative smuggling of human cargo.[7] Those desiring to come to the United States via smugglers pay as much as $30,000 up front (usually obtained from loans from family or friends, who expect to receive money sent back from the United States) or defer payment with a promise to work it off upon arrival in America. The newly arrived indentured servants often have to work as laborers in illegal sweatshops or become involved in other criminal activities, including prostitution.[8]

What does this mean for the church? First, there are significant subpopulations in the Chinese community with huge cultural gaps between them that must be recognized and addressed. Individuals are often classified by whether they are ABC (American-born Chinese), OBC (overseas-born Chinese), or ARC (American-raised Chinese, that is, an OBC who was raised here). There is also an issue of language. Many of the Chinese dialects are mutually unintelligible (though the written characters are understood by all literates). In one Chinese church in New York, Mandarin-speaking worshipers shout good-naturedly, "Jiang Guoyu!!" ("Speak Mandarin!!") because the Mandarin-speaking majority cannot understand Cantonese.

Second, there are those in the Chinese community who are facing hardship and need material, social, and legal assistance as well as spiritual guidance. On average, the Chinese in New York's Chinatown are poorer than the Chinese in other New York City communities. A disproportionate number of new arrivals (especially those who do not speak English well) still come to Chinatown first. As such, Chinatown is largely a blue-collar community.[9]

Though significant Chinese populations and shopping districts have sprung up in Queens, the Bay Ridge neighborhood in Brooklyn, and in Parsippany and Madison, New Jersey, New York City's Chinatown is the center of the Greater New York area's Chinese community. As such, Chinatown reflects the diversity of the Chinese community—its strengths, weaknesses, hopes, dreams, and problems. Chinatown is home to approximately one hundred thousand hardworking Chinese people,[10] countless shops and restaurants, (until recently) the most active city-run Off-Track Betting gambling parlor, several illegal gambling dens and brothels, and several sweatshops and rooming houses, all interspersed among buildings with some of the highest per-square-foot rents in New York City.

Despite the growth of the Chinese church, most Chinese have not yet been exposed to the gospel. The dominant ideology in mainland China is Communism, whose basic supposition is that God does not exist. Taiwan has more idol altars per capita than any other country, and the average length of time from first exposure to the gospel to baptism for Taiwanese believers is eight years. Chinese secular culture is associated with Confucianism, Taoism, and Buddhism, but especially ancestor worship. In almost every store in Chinatown a small statue is placed on a shelf for good luck and prosperity. In most homes, there is a small altar to one's ancestors. A stark example of the task of the church can be found on one block on Madison Street. There are three solidly evangelical growing churches—and a Buddhist temple between them. It is in this context that OCM has been carrying on its ministry to Chinatown and Chinese people around the world.

HISTORY OF THE OCM

The Oversea Chinese Mission, located at 154 Hester Street in the heart of Chinatown, draws about fourteen hundred worshipers to its Sunday services, making it "the largest Chinese church east of the Mississippi." Founded in 1961 by Rev. Torrence (Torrey) Shih, an unusually gifted evangelist, the church exerts an influence that extends far beyond its size.

Torrey Shih was converted at a revival meeting in southern China and later became an itinerant evangelist in China. After serving as a pastor in Singapore, Shih came to the United States in 1958 with his wife, Evelyn, and their family. Concerned about the need for a greater witness among the Chinese in New York City, he began holding Bible studies among college students, many of whom he led to the Lord. These small-group fellowships became the foundation of OCM.

In 1966 the small congregation took a crucial step of faith and bought its own building, a vacant ten-story building that was then in Little Italy, adjacent to Chinatown. Other churches and businesses were convinced that the congregation would not be able to support the mortgage on the church. Even Evelyn Shih thought the undertaking too big: "As soon as he saw the solid brick walls and wide stairways, he ran back home and dragged me there to look at it too. . . . We went in this dark, filthy, cold and spooky building. I was so scared. But Torrey was in high spirits, telling me his plans to utilize each floor. I could only follow him in silence and shudder."[11]

Needing to raise $80,000 of the $100,000 down payment within thirty days, members formed and sold shares in an independent corporation to develop the lot adjacent to the building. Some members moved into apartments in the building and paid rent to the church to help defray building expenses.[12] To this day, some staff, including the senior pastor, live in the church building.

From the beginning, Shih and his wife placed a great emphasis on writing and distributing tracts and evangelistic literature targeted to restaurant and other blue-collar workers in Chinatown. This led to the establishment of *Fuying Monthly*, an evangelistic and teaching periodical, which is currently distributed to twelve thousand homes and businesses in thirty countries.[13]

Shih's vision for OCM was to reach overseas Chinese in the United States and throughout the world. Through his preaching and commissioning of other preachers, Shih was instrumental in establishing several churches outside New York City—in the cities of Chicago and San Francisco, as well as the countries of Taiwan, Trinidad, and Brazil.[14] The strong emphasis on local evangelism, church planting, and foreign missions remains a vital part of OCM's ethos. Approximately $320,000 of its 1996 budget of $1.58 million (21 percent) is to be devoted to missions.[15]

STRUCTURE AND LEADERSHIP

OCM is firmly and unashamedly rooted in the evangelical camp. Typical of many Chinese churches, however, OCM is independent of any denomination though it is a permanent member of the National Association of Evangelicals.[16]

Chinese churches in general (like African American churches) tend to be influenced heavily by the personality of the senior pastor, perhaps more so than in the case of predominately Caucasian churches. Though Torrey Shih's style has been called by one member "appropriately dictatorial for a founder," the original constitution he drafted is one that provides a series of checks and balances and active participation by the laity.

One of the most unique aspects of OCM's governance is its definition of membership. Members are "those who have accepted Jesus Christ as their personal savior, regularly participate in the worship and offering of the church, are willing to abide [by] the constitution of the church and its main goal." Thus, there is no "joining the church" or official membership roll. Members who "truly serve" in any department can be elected as the department's representative to participate in quarterly "coworkers' meetings," where the coworkers determine the implementation of each ministry.

The planning committee (the equivalent of the trustee board) is made up of seven elected laypeople and chaired by the senior pastor (who has no voting rights). The senior pastor is responsible for the pulpit and for supervising the ministries of each department. All other committees are chaired by a layperson and staffed by one of the ministers, which is led by the senior pastor (Rev. Dean DeCastro—a Chinese Filipino) and two associate pastors (Rev. Fred Pei, the pastor for caring, and Rev. John Ng, the English pastor). In addition, there are two elders and six full-time ministers.

MINISTRY ACTIVITIES OF OCM

At present there are two Chinese services (Mandarin translated into Cantonese) and one English service held each Sunday morning. A total of one thousand attend the Chinese services, and about four hundred attend the English service. Available for children during services are various activities, including nursery, Sunday school, praise singing, and children's church. In the morning and early afternoon there are several adult classes held in Mandarin, Cantonese, and English.

Among the twenty-seven distinct outreach ministries are those that serve children, youth, and the elderly. Reflecting the Asian culture's respect for the elderly, there are several ministries for senior citizens, offering free blood-pressure readings, refreshments, birthday parties, and occasional short outings for senior citizens. The senior citizens' center is an outreach specifically for nonbelieving elderly people in the community. Open every Monday and Thursday afternoon, the center lists "Chinese boxing" exercises as one of the activities.

An after-school program serves approximately eighty students from the community from 2:30 to 6:00 P.M. each school day. The children are given help with schoolwork and offered refreshment and recreational activities. The program is staffed by ten paid part-time workers and approximately seven volunteers.[17] The summer day camp is an eight-week ministry that attracts over three hundred children. English classes are a popular way Chinese churches use to make a concrete, valued, visible contribution to the community, and OCM offers several levels of instruction to meet the needs of those who desire to improve their English skills. Most of the students are new immigrants.

Besides the social service activities, OCM does not shy away from pure evangelistic activities. Since 1989 the Evangelism Explosion course, created by D. James Kennedy, has been offered for two semesters each year, training members in leading others to faith in Christ. Gospel teams conduct musical evangelistic meetings in the city.

MISSIONS

The centrality of missions to OCM is reflected in the very name of the church—Oversea Chinese Mission—and it is very much a "missions church." Mission efforts include providing scholarships to Chinese seminary students in the United States, Canada, and Singapore, both OCMers and non-OCMers. The 1996 budget for the nineteen seminary-student scholarships was $32,000, or 10 percent of the total missions budget of $320,000.[18] The church also sponsors short-term mission teams and also organized Gideon Troop, comprised mostly of youth and young adults who have expressed an interest in serving as missionaries. OCM hopes that the mutual nurturing and encouragement will yield full-time missionaries.

The most anticipated gathering of the year is the annual missions conference, held during the entire month of October. Each of the Sunday services is devoted to missions, as are the Sunday school classes. Faith promise pledges are collected, and the annual missions publication, the *Missions Journal,* is distributed. The *Missions Journal* is quite a substantial undertaking, being about one hundred pages long, with articles in Chinese and English giving reports on short-term missions and local evangelism endeavors as well as the vision and goals—including the budget—of the missions department for the coming year.

DISCIPLESHIP MINISTRY

The discipleship ministry of OCM is designed to foster growth in new believers through one-on-one mentoring. Those interested are put in contact with the appropriate Chinese-speaking or English-speaking discipleship coordinator who then matches the individual with a suitable discipler (all disciplers undergo a thirteen-week training course). The two individuals then establish mutually convenient times and locations to meet to do a systematic study of 1–2 Timothy. The program helps to build an infrastructure of laypeople equipped to disciple others.

FELLOWSHIP GROUPS

OCM's beginning sprang out of a small fellowship group of college students, and fellowship groups remain an essential part of its structure and ministry. Because OCM is a large church without official membership, its twenty to twenty-five fellowship groups meet several needs: fellowship, nurturing, discipleship, accountability, and recreation. According to Pastor DeCastro, the fellowship groups, with approximately one thousand regular members, also "serve as a side door to the church."[19] It is quite common for members to invite nonbelieving friends to a fellowship group, see them eventually come to faith, mature, and move on to active service in the church.

The fellowship groups are ordered according to language, age, and sometimes marital and family status. However, some people choose to stay in their fellowship groups after they have "aged out" or have gotten married. The generally homogenous groups facilitate mutual support and cause newcomers to feel more comfortable when they are surrounded by others facing the same life issues. Most fellowship groups meet at the church, though a few of them are home based.

The fellowship groups, however, are more than small groups; they are more like semiautonomous churches—as a profile of one will show. Cornerstone, an English-speaking fellowship group for those age twenty-eight and above, has approximately thirty-five to forty involved in its weekly Friday night meetings and is fairly typical of other groups in its range of activities. Cornerstone has compiled its own songbook, determines its own outreach efforts, selects and supports its own missionaries, collects and manages its own funds, conducts follow-up on its absentee members, and conducts its own small-group Bible studies.

According to Kelly Ng, the chairperson of Cornerstone, several of the attenders on a given Friday night are new believers and nonbelievers.[20] Some have come at the invitation of friends, and others have been attracted by some of Cornerstone's outreach activities. "Fun nights" have included bowling, crabbing, a rafting trip, a ski trip, and dinner at members' homes. "The idea," according to Ng, "is to bring non-Christians into a nonthreatening environment where they can be with people who love God and have fun." On alternate Fridays there is an activity, a presentation, or a message by a member of the pastoral staff or an outside speaker (occasionally, speakers are asked to give an evangelistic message). On the other fun-night weekends these activities are replaced by "growth groups," which are small-group Bible studies, each generally attended by nine to twelve people. The four studies being conducted by Cornerstone at the time of this writing are Wholeness, Lifestyle, the Book of James, and Stressed Out. Most of the spiritual nurturing takes place in these growth groups. In addition to the Bible studies, members share their concerns and problems, and non-Christians are able to express their honest doubts with people with whom they feel comfortable.

Cornerstone also has a caring committee, which seeks to meet the special needs of members. They try to contact, by phone or letter, anyone who has missed three consecutive meetings. A newsletter, published once every two months, keeps the fellowship members and alumni informed; it is also sent to missionaries. The six elected staff members who coordinate Cornerstone's ministry are all laypeople.

CHURCH PLANTING

Under Torrey Shih, OCM planted churches overseas and in other U.S. cities. His immediate successor, finding it difficult to supervise the distant churches, shifted the focus to planting branch churches in the local New York area. The first branch church, Boon Parish, was planted in the burgeoning Chinese community of Flushing, Queens, in 1985. The church's goal is to plant a branch church every five years, and they are ahead of schedule. By 1992 two other churches were planted, one in Aberdeen and another in Teaneck, New Jersey. During this period there has been a granddaughter church added, as Boon Parish successfully planted a church in Long Island.

The basic format that OCM has successfully employed is to start a monthly home fellowship in the targeted area, usually on Saturday nights. After sufficient growth and stability have been achieved, the group rents a church on Saturday nights and holds a full array of programs, including children's and youth programs and a fellowship dinner after the service. During this phase, home prayer meetings and Bible studies are held once a month on a weeknight at a home. After a year, the church is usually able to move to weekly services on Sunday morning, and after three years the church is expected to be self-supporting.

Grace Church in Teaneck, New Jersey, is an example. Grace Church, having gone from approximately seventy people to over two hundred in three years, is the fastest growing of the branch churches. DeCastro first led the seven lead couples through a ten-week discipleship program, formally covering basic Bible doctrine and informally covering relevant aspects of church administration, counseling, and so on. The group then held monthly home fellowships on a Saturday night for a few months. With sixty to eighty attenders, the leadership group departed from the usual procedure by immediately meeting on Sunday mornings.

For the first two years Pastor DeCastro preached once a month, and other staff helped with the preaching responsibility. OCM supported Grace Church in three ways: manpower, accountability, and finance. Not only did DeCastro and other pastoral staff assist in the preaching ministry, but some lay members of OCM made six-month to one-year commitments to help Grace, and one OCM staff person was committed to conducting visitation for Grace congregants on a part-time basis. However, the local leadership was responsible for most of the counseling, visitation, and follow-up aspects of the ministry. The local leadership was accountable to Pastor De-Castro and OCM staff, who were available to guide and mentor the new leaders. Branch churches can choose to remain in fellowship with OCM. If they do, the pastor is invited to join OCM's weekly pastors' prayer meeting.[21] By the end of 1995 OCM's branch churches had a total of more than thirteen hundred members.[22]

POSSIBLE DIRECTIONS FOR THE FUTURE

OCM is a church that has had a significant impact on its target population, yet its leaders feel that there is much more that they should do. OCM has had an administrator in the past, and now there is a need to reexamine its organizational structures to determine if one is still relevant. DeCastro is conducting an evaluation of OCM's administration for this purpose.

Given its size and location, OCM feels it needs to be more involved in the Chinatown community. Evangelism leaders are recruiting and training members who will spearhead a new grassroots ministry to reach more of the blue-collar and illegal immigrant population of Chinatown.

Rev. DeCastro also desires to strengthen the capability to follow up on members and keep them accountable. Approximately 35 percent of the congregants do not participate in a fellowship group and are likely to be lost. One possible method under consideration is to have Sunday service attenders sign a log or attendance cards as a way of getting an attendance baseline.

DeCastro also has a vision of establishing a seminary at OCM. Given OCM's central location and the dearth of evangelical seminaries in New York City relative to its population, it is possible that the proposed seminary will attract many non-Chinese as well.

EVALUATION AND DISCUSSION

Without a doubt, OCM's greatest strength (from a human point of view) is its "from the bottom up" style of leadership, with many initiatives originating from and/or carried out by the laity. As Pastor John Ng (who has a doctorate in church growth from Fuller Theological Seminary) states, "The genius of OCM is its dependence on the laity." This is how such a large church with ministries conducted in three languages can thrive with only an eight-member full-time ministerial staff.

Such a leadership model can work only when the pastoral

staff does not feel a need to control everything in the church and places a great deal of trust in the laity. Frankly, this is extremely difficult for many pastors and ministers to do, but following the example of the early church, OCM's founder and current leadership believe that freely trusting the laity demonstrates their trust in the Holy Spirit to do his work in the church. The fellowship-group structure, the one-on-one discipleship program, and the church-planting efforts, all result from, and thrive in, an ethos of lay leadership. For instance, despite the increasingly vital and active youth ministry of OCM, there is presently no youth pastor. The reason is revealing: "We are considering it, but it is going so well, we have to be sure we don't mess it up." Pastor Ng explained that sometimes adding formal structures can hinder what God is doing. The tendency to impose formal control and administrative structures only when needed, instead of habitually, stems from a deep trust in the laity (even youth!) and the Holy Spirit.

The pastoral staff expresses gratitude for an extremely talented and gifted laity ("We have the best laypeople in the world," says one), but *how* did the laity become so talented? Is it any wonder that OCM has been able to plant three churches in seven years when its members have been involved in discipling and being discipled and have been nurtured in fellowship groups led by laity? "The fellowship groups have been given a great deal of freedom by the pastors," states Kelly Ng of Cornerstone. The result is that the fellowship groups end up being even more than semiautonomous churches led by laity—they are little "factories" whose "products" are, not just evangelism, but a laity that is trained in discipling, caring for each other's needs, and managing the financial and administrative affairs of small groups of believers and seekers. In short, the fellowship groups produce trained potential church planters.

Another strength of OCM is a highly trained, experienced pastoral staff. All members of the ministerial staff have had formal seminary education, and some members have advanced theological degrees and have served on seminary faculties. While highly trained leadership is not essential for a church's growth, in OCM's case it insures that sufficient theological resources are within the church.

Yet another strength of OCM is discipline, for accountability is an important function of the church. Since there is no formal membership in OCM, church discipline is extremely difficult to carry out. It is "impossible," Pastor DeCastro bluntly stated, before quickly adding, "but discipline does take place." However, discipline takes place, not at the church leadership level, but in the context of relationships (which is an appropriate method for the relationship-oriented Chinese culture) within the fellowship groups. A growth-group leader may approach a member about an unsettling issue, and if it is not sufficiently addressed, the fellowship-group staff becomes involved and, if necessary, the designated counselor on the relationship committee. If successful resolution is not achieved, the pastoral staff becomes involved. Generally, because of the friendships within the group, and the nonthreatening nature of the fellowship groups, such discussions rarely go outside the group. OCM is probably ahead of most churches that practice formal church discipline, which tend to discipline either harshly or capriciously or go to the other extreme and never discipline at all. OCM has developed a biblical, culturally sensitive, and effective means of helping struggling brothers and sisters.

It is extremely common within Chinese churches for there to be tensions between the English-speaking American-born Chinese (ABC), the English-speaking American-raised Chinese (ARC), and the Chinese-speaking overseas-born Chinese (OBC). In fact, several churches have split over such cultural and generational strains. Gail Law reported in her 1984 study that approximately half of all new Chinese churches were splinters of previously existing churches. While some were the result of strategic church planting (as OCM carries out), perhaps for the majority the impetus involved personal and cultural problems within the previous church.[23] Even OCM has not been immune from this problem.

It is almost inevitable that tensions will arise. The OBC, who are generally older, place a high value on the Confucian ideals of filial loyalty and respect for one's elders. The ABC place a higher value on Western values of independence and self-determination. It usually takes a long time before the Chinese congregation (and leaders) can view the English-speaking congregation as equals. For the most part, the English-speaking congregation in OCM is thriving and feels comfortable there. The primary reason, according to DeCastro, is "the good relationship among the pastoral staff." Pastor DeCastro, being relatively young and having been educated in the Philippines and the United States, fully understands and empathizes with the ABC mentality. The fact that most of the pastoral staff is to some degree bicultural and bilingual aids in the largely separate English and Chinese ministries remaining united within OCM. For example, Pastor Ng was born and raised in Chinatown, yet he is said to retain a high degree of "Chinese-ness." Still, the continued growth of the English congregation, both in numbers and maturity, raises questions.

Ng's vision is to nurture and expand OCM's large ABC ministry, but there are many factors that have to be overcome. First, most of the adult ABC do not live in Chinatown. Second, the Chinese decor of the building and mostly Chinese-language bulletin boards may not be appealing to many ABCs. Third, the church was founded by an overseas Chinese for the purpose of reaching other overseas Chinese, and this is reflected in some of the church's organizational mechanisms. For instance, Mandarin is the official language of the church and is used in business meetings (with appropriate translation). Finally, the very name of the church, Oversea Chinese Mission, may present a hurdle for some ABCs because its nominal emphasis may not seem inclusive. Though OCM has successfully navigated these hurdles to date, the time may come when a spin-off church—all or part of the English ministry—to a location outside Chinatown (not necessarily outside New York City) may need to be considered. The deliberations would have to consider that separating would make it impossible for some families to worship together and would remove, not only the tensions that can arise from intergenerational and intercultural interaction, but also the strengths. In addition, some ABCs would still not be attracted to the ministry. "The ABC community is very diverse," says Pastor Ng, and no one type of church can serve all of them. "My associate Ben Kong and I were raised in Chinatown, and that affects our ministry. Some ABCs would never feel comfortable here. I thank God for the other churches, because we couldn't reach them."

Two somewhat-related aspects of OCM's ministry must also be evaluated: its level of social involvement and its mission. First, OCM is located in a community with many social needs, but its level of social involvement is not where Pastor DeCastro would like it to be. Rev. Stanley Kwong, an acting director of Alliance Theological Seminary's Chinese Pastoral Program and a former member of OCM, notes that under the present leadership OCM's involvement is increasing quickly, but "given its size, OCM is still about average among evangelical churches that are involved in the community."[24] Chinatown is not only a community with many social needs; it is a community with many social problems. There is a great deal of illegal and substandard housing, many illegal aliens, tremendous exploitation of workers in sweatshops and restaurants[25] (for example, only one of the five hundred restaurants in Chinatown is unionized),[26] and pervasive organized crime. Yet, one will not find OCM (or many other churches) addressing these systemic problems through social action. This is due, not only to the theological emphasis on evangelism, but also to an aspect of the Chinese culture. Churches are not involved in developing housing or conducting voter registration drives because "basically, Chinese do not get involved." Pastor Ng explains, "Chinese Christians don't vote, and Chinese non-Christians don't vote." For better and for worse, Chinese in general—and especially those in Chinatown—have an insular orientation. They have relatively little interaction with the larger society and its institutions.

Second, OCM's focus is narrower than making disciples—it is making disciples *among Chinese.* In this regard, OCM is typical of much of the body of Christ. This commitment to focus largely on Chinese people is both a strength and a potential weakness. It has given OCM a "zeal for evangelism of Chinese people," according to Ng, yet it can also limit their perspective on how God may want them to be involved in the building of the Kingdom. Their large missions budget, for example, is devoted almost exclusively to ministries targeted to Chinese people. This is typical of most churches, especially those comprised predominantly of an ethnic minority group. However, this does not necessarily have to be the case. For example, another church in Chinatown, a church whose missions budget is dwarfed by OCM's, has seen fit to support not only an African American family for its ministry to Chinese but also an African American for ministry in Kenya. As John Ng wrote, "To do missions among the Chinese . . . is important. But to do missions solely among them is negligent and disobedient." His words are relevant, not just to his congregation, but to all in the body of Christ.[27]

PART FIVE

Missions of Mercy

Ray Bakke writes that the early church "did not preach out of success but out of images of misery, transforming them into love and fellowship." In Alexandria, Christian women rounded up destitute babies and orphans and cared for them. In other Egyptian cities, Christians knocked on poor people's doors and offered to move in to nurse the sick, deliberately exposing themselves to illness. Wherever they went, Christians expressed themselves in care for widows and orphans, in visits to prisons, and in social action in times of famine, pestilence, and war. This "practical application of charity" is perhaps the single most potent cause of Christian success in the ancient world. "We do not need new technologies to work in the city," Bakke writes, "but a rediscovery of [the early church's] energy, vision, and compassion."[1]

Two New York City ministries that are meeting this challenge are the McAuley Rescue Mission and All Angels' Episcopal Church. By providing havens for people for whom there is no room in other social institutions, they are meeting some of the city's most critical social and spiritual needs. At a time when New York City churches categorized the poor as "worthy" or "unworthy" of charity, Jerry McAuley threw the doors of his mission open to the misfits of society, many of whom were trapped in cycles of addiction and antisocial behavior. For 125 years, the mission has operated a full-service ministry that provides "soup, soap, and salvation" for the city's destitute.

All Angels' Episcopal Church has developed a congregational life that is as diverse as the neighborhood in which it is located. Artists, musicians, investment bankers, university students, and homeless people worship together at the church's three services that incorporate soul, jazz, classical, and Caribbean music. A gospel choir, which includes several homeless people, leads Sunday-night worship. The inclusion of the neighborhood's poor in the worship life of the church has undercut the "we/they" mentality that plagues many parish outreach programs. The homeless congregants at All Angels' are valuable contributors to the life of the church, and they are part of what gives the congregation its distinctive flavor. As Robert Gross writes in chapter 16, "For the homeless, 'their feeding program' has become 'our church home.' For the parishioners, 'those people' have become 'our brothers and sisters.'"

16

Setting the Oppressed Free

New York City Rescue Mission

Jim Varnhagen

David Nasmith is recognized as the originator of the town and city missions that were established around the world in the early nineteenth century.[1] Although Nasmith had a deep interest in extending compassion to "worthy" and "unworthy poor" alike, his vision eroded as a more professional posture developed in charitable organizations. Eventually, only the "worthy poor" were treated with compassion.[2] In the year of Nasmith's death a man was born who would become the catalyst for the next wave of city missions where ministry to the "undeserving" or "unworthy poor" continued, though no direct connection existed between the work of the two men.

Jerry McAuley pioneered the "rescue mission movement" when he opened the doors of America's first rescue mission in October 1872. This ministry has continued uninterrupted for

---

Jim Varnhagen has been the executive director of the New York City Rescue since 1990. He has served in the U.S. Air Force, in a variety of engineering and management positions, and with the Detroit Rescue Mission.

over twelve decades. Central to the mission's work was, and still is, the biblical mandate to extend compassion to the poor and needy. This mandate is clear when Jesus quoted from the book of Isaiah, giving special attention to the poor: "The Spirit of the Lord is on me, because he has anointed me to preach good news to the poor" (Luke 4:18, NIV).

The uniqueness of McAuley's work was his emphasis on ministry to the "unworthy poor," those whom society had given up for lost. Once considered incorrigible themselves, Jerry and his wife, Maria, understood what was involved with helping children, widows, and men who often experience setbacks. But to treat drunks and tramps—no matter how foul or unkempt— as the best people in the world was unheard of, and the idea overwhelmed many of the early participants who attended services at the chapel known as Helping Hand for Men. McAuley's mission, located at 316 Water Street on Manhattan's Lower East Side, was never intended to help the "worthy" or "deserving" but was a haven for the misfits of society who were considered "undeserving." In contrast with other established charitable outreaches to the poor and needy, McAuley's work was unique.[3]

A HELPING HAND

The mission opened by McAuley was formally named the McAuley Water Street Mission but became generally known as the Jerry McAuley Mission. Recently the name New York City Rescue Mission has been adopted for general use. For nearly 125 years, salvation through Jesus Christ has been proclaimed to those who attend the gospel services at the mission.

With facilities now located at 90 Lafayette Street, the New York City Rescue Mission makes available a full-service minis-try to provide for both physical and spiritual needs. Staffed by committed and dedicated Christians who use the Bible as a foundation upon which men and women can build their lives, the mission's ministry remains dynamic and effective. Help is provided in many practical ways, but only God has the plan for establishing new order in people's lives, and healing from God is provided as mission staff introduce men and women to the Great Physician. These inner-city missionaries interact with hurting people from New York City just as Jesus did when he came to call upon sinners. The staff members of New York City Rescue Mission recognize their work, as Christ did, to be to the least attractive, a recognition they find rooted in the gospel of the Kingdom: "It is not the healthy who need a doctor, but the sick. I have not come to call the righteous, but sinners" (Mark 2:17, NIV). Many frequenting the mission do not need to be reminded that they are sinners. Indeed, they are often very open to receive Christ as Savior during a gospel service.

We may never know how many poor and destitute people the New York City Rescue Mission has helped or to what extent its work this has influenced others. Just such a case involving a parishioner of an uptown church came to light following a mission presentation at the church. The parishioner approached a mission staff member and said, "I stayed at the mission overnight on one occasion and was saved during the evening gospel service." He continued, "This occurred over twenty years ago." The parishioner was asked if he ever talked to anyone from the mission regarding his conversion. The answer was no. He then introduced his wife and daughter and then explained that he "lived in the neighborhood, became a member of the church, and worked nearby." By God's grace people like this regain meaningful employment and develop a self-sufficient place in life.

CURRENT MISSION PROGRAMS

Transformation does not come instantly to most who accept Christ while kneeling at the chapel rail at the mission. When a man or woman comes to the Lord, his or her sins are forgiven, but repentance itself rarely takes away addiction to alcohol and/or drugs or resolves family or social predicaments immediately. The person gains a new lease on life, but that person must then put the new power within to work. Consequently, a full range of services at the mission in addition to gospel services and Bible studies includes shelter, food, clothing, medical care, counseling, and educational programs. In the early days "soup, soap, and salvation" was the fond description given to rescue mission services. Today's mission client is often in greater need because of the more complex world in which we live.

A two-tiered program at the mission serves seventy transient guests direct from the street and thirty-five rehabilitation program residents selected from among the transient population. In addition to providing sleeping accommodations for 105 men, the mission offers other services to additional men and women from the street. Transient guests have night-to-night accommodations based on bed availability. New arrivals (men not having stayed at the mission previously) are shown preference by being placed ahead of the line and given a bed for three consecutive nights.

Program guidelines require that rehabilitation program residents stay at the mission for six months to one year. In special cases some have stayed for longer periods. (The rule of thumb is a one-month stay for each year of addiction.) During their stay these residents are required to attend scheduled Bible studies, participate in individual and group counseling sessions, and become involved in a job assignment. This arrangement insures discipline in Bible training, personal counseling, and job-skill development.

For many who find themselves at the mission, it has taken a long time for problems to develop. Likewise, for many, a lengthy process of recovery must occur before binding habits will be overcome. Addictions of every description threaten to prevail and erode progress as young believers experience the Holy Spirit's new control over their lives. Men having a wide variety of ailments have become well as their relationship with the Lord has deepened. They may remain at the mission for an extended period of time to establish their bearings.

The story of one man is typical. Two years after completing the rehabilitation program, Norman continues living a productive life. He had been at the mission for almost five years after arriving with such complex problems as drug abuse, divorce, epileptic seizures, educational setbacks, and a problematic employment record. Nevertheless, Norman was encouraged to complete his college degree over a three-year period of full-time studies while having minimal mission assignments. He was able to overcome the habit of cocaine and crack addiction, and through medical help his seizures were brought under control.

Upon graduation from college, Norman interviewed for several jobs, receiving guidance from mission staff. He was counseled to be honest and straightforward regarding his past, and an employer who admired his honesty and his victories hired him. Norman now works for a private agency in Brooklyn as a counselor visiting and checking up on mentally ill patients in group homes. Periodic contact with Norman's employer brings word that "he is hanging in there." Norman gives God the credit for all he achieved at the mission and beyond. And it all started at a gospel service when Norman gave his heart to the Lord.

Transitional housing is provided for men as they adjust to a work schedule and develop outside living arrangements. In Norman's case transitional shelter was provided during the period of college studies. Others who may need special extended living arrangements are those with disabilities. A few reserved beds are provided until more adequate housing is acquired. Those having the means are asked to make a contribution to the mission while using transitional housing.

Today, as in the past, the mission is not occupied with simply helping the "worthy" or "deserving poor" but is a haven for the misfits of society, the "unworthy" and "undeserving poor." In this way the work continues its unique role in contrast to other established shelters and outreaches to the poor and needy.

Members of the staff have agreed that the established purpose of the mission is to provide spiritual hope, food, clothing and shelter to the needy at its door. Providing food, clothing, and shelter is an immense task at times, but giving spiritual and emotional counseling along with general guidance is even more demanding. The expanded purpose statement of the mission includes the following goals: (1) to provide regular gospel services to minister to the spiritual needs of all those who enter the mission; (2) to provide food, clothing, and shelter for homeless and neglected individuals; (3) to provide Bible studies for the spiritual enrichment of those who have received Jesus Christ as their personal Savior; (4) to provide Christian counseling and guidance to those who have social, psychological, and spiritual problems; (5) to counsel individuals in acquiring help for personal medical problems; (6) to counsel individuals regarding personal employment and educational needs; (7) to provide individual and group counseling for those addicted to alcohol and illegal drugs; and (8) to provide adequate facilities and staff to accommodate a Christian rehabilitation program in the mission's current and future locations.

In order to accomplish a multifaceted program that fulfills the stated goals, adequate staffing is essential. Staff members and chaplains must have a strong background in the areas described. It is no easy task to bring all the necessary disciplines to bear upon the lives of hurting and destitute people, but with God's help it is being done 365 days a year.

CHURCH AND VOLUNTEER PARTICIPATION

Various church groups extend their ministry to include the New York Rescue Mission as part of their outreach program. Evening gospel meetings are conducted on a monthly or bimonthly basis by some forty churches that provide a variety of ministry opportunities for those in attendance.

Rescue missions have great latitude to be inclusive of people working together from a variety of denominations. Church groups and denominations have distinctions that often lead to separation between Christians of various stripes. But in the mission context barriers are removed when Christians of differing backgrounds work together. Board members, superintendents, and staff members representing various churches and denominations work together to provide the leadership for the New York City Rescue Mission.

Churches and individuals often support ministries that are more prominent and less offensive than the New York City Rescue Mission. Though the ministry of rescue missions may not be in the forefront of many churches' plans or priorities when it comes to financial commitment, individual Christians and some churches are committed to supporting this much-needed work. People from churches active in our mission work share our commitment to providing Christian outreach for meeting the physical and spiritual needs of hurting people in New York City.

Often those from pleasant circumstances must be reminded

that they are sinners just like the people they are serving. This was true of a young man named Jonathan from the Midwest, who had studied in New York and later returned to take up residence in the city. As a good member of the community, he attended Calvary Baptist Church and, because of his skills as a pianist, was asked to participate in a monthly gospel service sponsored by the church. It was during one of these meetings, after hearing testimonies from destitute men who were now full of joy, that Jonathan realized he himself did not possess that kind of happiness.

Jonathan thought, "This isn't fair. I have a good job, an apartment, savings, a college education . . . and yet I do not have joy like these who have nothing." Jonathan was under conviction that evening when he returned to his home. He knelt beside his bed, confessed he was a sinner, and received Christ as Savior. Thus we are reminded that the mission's ministry is directed not only to those in dire need of help but to others who may not realize that they also are indeed lost.

It is unfortunate when Christians do not have the desire to be involved in ministry directed to poor and destitute people. Those who work in the trenches day in and day out often speak of their rewarding experiences with joy. It appears that the Christian community at large needs to take the Scriptures more seriously with its many instructions to help the poor and needy. Indeed, Scripture provides an imperative for believers to be compassionate:

> Is not this the kind of fasting I have chosen:
> to loose the chains of injustice
>   and untie the cords of the yoke,
> to set the oppressed free
>   and break every yoke?
> Is it not to share your food with the hungry
>   and to provide the poor wanderer with shelter—
> when you see the naked, to clothe him,
>   and not to turn away from your own flesh and blood?
> —Isaiah 58:6-7 (NIV)

The Bible is replete with passages emphasizing the Christian's responsibility to provide for the needs of poor and hurting people. In fact, there are almost 250 references to the poor in the Scriptures.[4] We have a mandate to be interested and involved with the prisoner, the poor and needy, and those who need food, clothing, and shelter. We must pay attention to Isaiah's words "to provide the poor wanderer with shelter." The mission keeps this mandate alive and has encouraged responsibility on the part of Christian churches to provide for the social needs of poor and destitute people.

CURRENT ISSUES

Since much of the work of the New York City Rescue Mission relates to providing for the social and physical needs of hurting people, a certain visibility is raised at community and government levels. Often the mission is observed as another social service provider. How such an organization is viewed can help or hinder its overall ministry in the community and determine the extent of community support. New York City Rescue Mission is prominent for being viewed not only as a service providing social and physical help for homeless individuals but as a religious institution providing for their spiritual needs. Issues affecting mission operations that are dealt with regularly fall into the categories of welfare, education, health, and government funding.

Welfare

Often it is difficult to control the activity of men in the mission's rehabilitation program if they receive government funds, which include general assistance, disability payments, and food stamps. This money becomes divisive and is often used to propel the recipient back to his old habits. It is the policy of the mission to discourage residents from being dependent on government handouts. Marvin Olasky, in his book *The Tragedy of American Compassion,* argues that indiscriminate handouts of government aid harms individuals by fostering moral laxity and irresponsibility. He harkens back to principles of an earlier day by suggesting that individuals that are better off should help the poor and needy live out the biblical work ethic in their lives.[5]

When an individual is accepted as a rehabilitation program resident, he must agree to forego any government entitlement for the duration of the program. Normally upon program completion the resident acquires full-time employment. Under certain circumstances, such as disability, the mission may encourage the resident to acquire government support.

Education

Many people today are not trained for current job-market opportunities. This is especially true of those who frequent the mission. In addition they are not apt to discipline themselves with good study methods. The mission offers residents the opportunity to learn computer skills and expand their knowledge of computer programs currently used in business settings. For those who have literacy problems or who need to achieve high school equivalency, a GED program is available.

The mission's learning center, located next to the dining area, was developed through generous corporate support and contributions. For instance, the computers were a donation from IBM, and the learning center enclosures were a gift from Canadian National Railroad. Residents proceed in their educational goals at their own pace with occasional help from mission staff. Because progress is made at an individual rate, there is a great sense of accomplishment, and residents gain the self-worth that is often lacking in their lives.

Health

Each week a medical clinic is provided in mission facilities. The clinic, sponsored by an organization known as the Institute for Urban Family Health, has operated in the mission for several years and provides immediate and ongoing care for homeless people who would not otherwise get treatment for their ailments. Appointments are established for homeless men and women located in the general vicinity of the mission. Residents of the mission are encouraged to have physical examinations upon entrance to the rehabilitation program. In conjunction with the clinic, a podiatrist is available on a monthly basis, and a social worker is available two times each week.

Numerous medical problems confront homeless people. It is estimated that HIV infects approximately 10 to 15 percent of the mission population. Normal precautions are taken with this group as with all others. No restrictions are applied regarding mission program placement of those suffering with the HIV

infection. They are treated with the same love and care received
by other mission guests.

Government Funding

A minimal portion of the mission's budget is derived from
government funding. Less than 2 percent of mission income is
derived from United States Department of Agriculture (USDA)
donated food, Federal Emergency Management Administration
(FEMA) grants, and other local food-bank donations. No
"strings" that would restrict the mission's religious objectives
are attached to receiving these funds. Indeed, extreme care is
taken not to compromise the ministry's purpose by accepting
government funds that would conflict with restrictions imposed by the principle of the separation of church and state.
Government grants to be used in general operating funds would
normally have these restrictions, but food grants and donations
can be used without compromising mission programs.

CONCLUSION

To believers, Jerry McAuley's vision is simply God's providential work in the heart of a man chosen for a task, that is, giving
birth to an idea and ministry that was to spread to other
countries. Some of the men Jesus Christ found and touched
while they were sitting on the hard chapel benches of the New
York City rescue mission went on to establish similar havens
of rest for broken spirits across the United States and in Canada.
In the intervening years the rescue mission movement has
spread to many cities—from Aberdeen, Washington, to Yuma,
Arizona; from Boston, Massachusetts, to Butte, Montana.

Today, the membership of the movement's association, the
International Union of Gospel Missions (IUGM), numbers ap-
proximately 250; they form an association of rescue ministries.
IUGM missions currently functioning in New York City include
the Bowery Mission and St. Paul's House in addition to the New
York City Rescue Mission.

Opportunity for workers abound today more than ever before. People with skills in evangelism, counseling, management, business/accounting, fund-raising, maintenance, food
service, and so on are needed in existing ministries. Some

rescue mission positions have their counterpart in the local church setting. The position of executive director, for instance, can be compared to the position of senior pastor in the local church. Training for this position is quite lengthy and may require seminary or graduate studies. Other positions, if they are to be performed effectively, may require extensive training; these include program director, director of ministries, chaplain, case manager, and counselor.

The ministry of rescue as a vocation is a hard and difficult task. Individuals with a vision to plant a rescue mission have many needy cities to consider in North America alone. Often the beginning work of a rescue mission is undertaken by a husband/wife team. Without this type of mutual commitment many rescue missions would never have begun. Above all, individuals contemplating rescue as a vocation must have the definite call of God upon their lives. With the confirmation of God's direction and blessing in ministry, the work will have a strong and meaningful emphasis. People of vision, exercising faith in God while depending on answered prayer, will accomplish lasting results in the work of rescue mission ministry.

17

Entertaining Angels Unawares

All Angels' Church

Robert E. Gross

> Let mutual love continue. Do not neglect to show hospitality to strangers, for by doing that some have entertained angels without knowing it.
>
> —Hebrews 13:1-2 (NRSV)

In the American wing of the Metropolitan Museum of Art, amid an array of stunning sculpture, stand the pulpit and choir screen of All Angels' (Episcopal) Church. The pulpit's sound board is crowned with the exquisite form of a carved angel, trumpet raised, and the choir screen is a stone frieze of angelic musicians in joyful procession. Thousands view these pieces of craftsmanship every week. But at the corner of West End Avenue and Eighty-first Street stands, not the grand twelve-hundred-seat church facility from which the pulpit came, but a twenty-two-story apartment building. In 1979, after 120 years

Robert E. Gross lives in New York City with his wife Charlene and son Evan. He serves as Regional Director for InterVarsity Christian Fellowship in New York/New Jersey. He attends All Angels' Church.

on this corner (having been incorporated in 1859), the church was torn down.

During the 1970s the parish had faced dwindling membership and strained finances in a time of changing neighborhood demographics and volatile economic conditions. The small congregation deconsecrated the building, auctioned its contents, and sold the property. They then moved to the narrow, five-story parish house around the corner on West Eightieth Street. One parishioner, Paul Johnson, remembers the final months as the old building was dismantled. Certain legal factors necessitated that a group meet on site at least weekly. "So a half dozen of us would gather early on Wednesdays for morning prayer—with the walls literally coming down around us," explains Johnson. As the demolition progressed, this saddened handful would pray. "We were part of a tiny determined remnant," reflects Johnson. "Our faith was largely uninformed, but it must have been at least a mustard seed's worth." It was enough.

Now, over sixteen years later, on a given Sunday morning you will spot on the corner of Broadway and Eightieth Street on the bustling Upper West Side a colorful banner marking All Angels' Church. You will be warmly greeted and directed upstairs to a simple chapel, paneled in natural oak and filled with morning sunlight from tall, clear windows. An unadorned cross hangs above the altar, and a plain lectern stands at floor level. Neither is museum quality. But the worship is rich, and the experience of sacrament and Word are powerful.

More than one hundred worshipers, mostly young families, gather at 9:00 A.M. for the celebration of the Holy Eucharist. Special attention is given to children during this service. Those ages three to eight are dismissed for a period of children's worship with its own liturgical character. At the heart of this time, the children sit on mats in a rapt semicircle, listening and watching as the teacher, in a quietly engaging manner, presents the gospel lesson in a story form using small props and people figures. Afterward, the children rejoin their parents upstairs for Communion and concluding worship. At 10:30 the service ends with a pastoral dismissal, "Go in peace to love and serve the Lord, Alleluia," and a rousing reply, "Thanks be to God.

Alleluia!" Children head for Sunday school, and on this Sunday adults choose between a course on Genesis (Creation, Covenant, and Calling) and one on developing a Christian world-view (Eyes of Faith in a Secular Society).

At 11:30 the chapel fills again with some 150 worshipers, mostly young adults. They are brokers, physicians, artists, lawyers, teachers, homemakers, and students, as well as some who are unemployed. Worship is vibrant, with energetic singing accompanied by instrumentalists. The Episcopal liturgy (Rite II in the *Book of Common Prayer*) is complemented by congregational prayer huddles, liturgical dance, and original drama sketches. Afterward, the hospitality time is abuzz with conversation and laughter.

The final and largest worship gathering begins at 5:00 P.M. It is a striking contrast to the morning services. Attendance ranges between 150 and 200, perhaps 80 percent African American and 20 percent white or other ethnicity (just the reverse of the racial mix in the morning). A large number of these parishioners are homeless, unemployed, or drug addicted. The worship form is still the Episcopal liturgy, but the style is black, urban gospel! The preaching tends toward the evangelistic, and the racially mixed All Angels' Gospel Singers are backed by piano, electric bass, and percussion. This Eucharistic service is the evening centerpiece, but what happens before and after is also crucial.

The gospel choir, open each week to anyone willing to come to rehearsal at 3:20 P.M., enjoys a significant degree of camaraderie. Then at 4:00 P.M., sixty to seventy people meet for Bible study. The focus is basic—such as the life of Christ or daily Christian living—and the application is practical, that is, it must fit life on the street. Most of the hour is spent in small discussion groups. Then, during the worship service, teams of people prepare meals so that afterward they can distribute one hundred or more take-out dinners and serve eighty sit-down dinners, with choir members and Bible-study participants having priority for the sit-down meal. Thus, by the end of the evening, All Angels' has met, in some measure, the spiritual, physical, and relational needs of its parishioners.

The preamble of the church's vision statement, developed

during 1994, captures both the current ethos and future aspiration of the parish: "All Angels' is a diverse community of the Episcopal Church under the Lordship of Jesus Christ. We are gathered and unified by the Holy Spirit. We affirm the authority of scripture. We are a vibrant Christian community in an urban setting. We are gathered for engaging and inspiring worship, committed to prayer, active in service, and called to be Christ's transforming presence in the world." The statement then expresses vision in six areas: worship, community, education, evangelism, service, and parish involvement. Of these six areas, education and evangelism are the least developed. The adult education program is in its infancy, and while many have experienced conversion through the ministry of All Angels', the church lacks a coherent strategy for its evangelistic mission. In the other four areas, however, the church shows distinctive strengths: liturgy infused with life, community amid diversity, holistic service, and lay involvement.

Paul and Mary Johnson became involved at All Angels' in 1972. Paul, a musician, hoped to join the paid choir. Eventually, he not only sang but played drums in a jazz band as part of the experimental folk mass. When the church was sold, the Johnsons were part of the handful that hung on. The building sold for $1.1 million. Threats of lawsuits overshadowed the church's finances for several years, but they spent a considerable amount on badly needed renovation of the parish house and placed the rest in endowment. Having little to lose, this remnant was willing to risk new things.

In 1979 the tiny church called the Reverend Carol Anderson to be the new rector (pastor). She became the first female rector in the Diocese of New York. Mary Johnson recalls Anderson's first sermon, a call to trust in God and rebuild on the foundation of biblical faith. "Every sermon that first year was on the same theme: Trust God," remembers Mary, "and in year two she preached 'Know Jesus' and then 'Go deeper' (in relationship with Christ)."

Anderson started a Bible study on Wednesdays where Paul, for the first time, was confronted with the uniqueness of Jesus. "Becoming convinced intellectually," Paul explains, "I ventured to live as if Jesus was real. Carol warned me I'd never be the same, and she was right. I was converted!" Anderson provided encouragement through evangelical preaching. She taught people to pray aloud in their own words and introduced "renewal music." She explored and developed a ministry of healing prayer. "She evangelized the church!" says Paul with a smile, "and slowly we began to be a genuine spiritual community."

Under Anderson, the church formed a mission statement that remains the touchstone today: "To Know Christ. To Worship Christ. To Proclaim and Serve Christ." Indeed, an opportunity to serve Christ sat right on the church doorstep. Gentrification took hold on the Upper West Side in the 1980s, and the homeless population soared. The church's nearest neighbor, for example, turned people out of their tiny hotel, which had provided housing for some of the neighborhood's poor, in order to expand their delicatessen catering to the upwardly mobile. After much debate, the church cautiously initiated a Sunday afternoon feeding program.

Quickly word spread and people came. A hot meal was served family style. One scene still sticks in Paul Johnson's mind: "Sir, would you like some more coffee?" one parishioner asked a bearded man. "Moi?" he replied in a loud voice. "Yes, you, sir." He then turned suddenly in his seat and said to the whole table, "She called me sir!" It was said of the program that the atmosphere was the best and the food the worst of all the city's soup kitchens!

In time, additional volunteers developed a "drop-in" time and served a hot meal to over two hundred on Tuesdays and Thursdays. Later, other volunteers offered shelter for about twenty on Saturday and Sunday nights. The programs caused contention in the church. Many were uncomfortable among so many poor, mentally ill, and drug-addicted persons and all the problems that "those people" caused. These programs served social needs but had little if any spiritual dimension.

Carol Anderson left in June 1986 after six years of pastoral leadership. The ensuing two-year interim was difficult, but the church maintained its core life and ministry until a new rector arrived in June 1988. Martyn Minns, having worked in corporate management before pursuing the priesthood, brought a decisive leadership style and a more overt evangelical emphasis. A large number of members were uneasy with him and left the church in his first year, but even more newcomers arrived. Minns and his wife, Angela, exhibited a team approach to ministry. For example, Angela initiated a children's program, and this opened the door to many young families. Under Minns, utilizing liberal withdrawals from the endowment, staff and programs were expanded dramatically and facilities improved significantly (for example, central air-conditioning and computers). He came with an engaging personality, an effective teaching gift, and a strong vision. His impact might best be summed up in the word *integration*. Two examples are striking.

When Minns came, the three worship services varied greatly in tone and musical style: early morning was folk, with guitars and praise book; later morning was classical, with organ and hymnals; and evening was a Taize-style prayer and praise. Martyn expanded the role of Ron Melrose from part-time director for the classical service to full-time director of music overseeing all services. Paul Johnson was named director of worship arts. The two made a strong complementary team. Melrose, with a background in Broadway music, brought an extraordinary level of talent and a vision for greater integration of music, message, and worship. During this time, Melrose experienced conversion from an intellectual and aesthetic faith to a more personal relationship with God.

Minns, Melrose, and Johnson greatly expanded the place of the arts in the life and worship of the parish. Melrose and Johnson between them have written at least six service music settings or masses, setting key parts of the Episcopal liturgy to music. Each of these is musically distinctive and adds a rich originality to All Angels' services. Many artists have made All Angels' their home and have contributed their gifts, including ballet dancers, actors, writers, visual artists, calligraphers, musicians, soloists, and designers.

The second major "integration" took place between the small Sunday-evening worship group and the large crowd at the Sunday feeding program. Minns's custom was to stand on the church steps and greet people as they arrived. He became increasingly disturbed by the upstairs/downstairs dichotomy:

whites going up to worship and blacks going down for supper. One Sunday, Gloria Goodman, a black woman from the feeding program, asked Minns if he would baptize her six-month-old baby. Minns instinctively said yes and suggested she participate in the worship service for the next few weeks as preparation. Goodman then asked, "Will I be welcome?" For several weeks, she and a few friends visited. Meanwhile, Minns announced that all of the downstairs crowd were invited to join in worship and witness the baptism and that afterward all would be invited downstairs for the meal.

The night of the baptism arrived. A fierce storm thinned the white group but expanded the ranks of homeless. All gathered for worship, but Minns quickly realized that the simple praise songs were falling flat with this group. "This was a stupid idea," he thought. He turned to Melrose and pleaded, "Do something." Melrose remembers the evening vividly: "I only knew two songs that might work, 'His Eye Is on the Sparrow' and 'Amazing Grace.'" As Melrose sang the first, a tall black man slipped to the piano bench beside him and joined in. On "Amazing Grace" everyone enthusiastically sang. They had connected!

People saw Minns's and Melrose's heart intent and responded. Within three weeks seventy people from "downstairs" were coming to worship! Both Minns and Melrose worked hard to contextualize the service for this new group of worshipers. Melrose, who is white, admits to being scared and unsure of how to relate. His first step was to contact black directors he knew from Broadway, "Who should I listen to? Where do I go to learn?" He visited churches in Harlem and spent hours listening to recorded gospel music. Soon, he announced the start of a choir, open to anyone who came an hour early to rehearse. Eight came the first night, and the All Angels' Gospel Singers was born. Lucas Brisbane was one of those eight: "I was living in the park—I had been through some major disasters with my marriage and job—and coming to All Angels' for the chicken dinners. I wasn't so surprised at the feeding program, but I was shocked to see them reaching out across the racial lines. This wasn't uptown, afterall."

"Our great challenge," reflects Minns, "was overcoming the deep-seated prejudices that cause factions between black and white, rich and poor, men and women, traditionalists and 'renewal-ists.' This is always a very slow and painful process." The transformation of the evening service was a breakthrough that fundamentally undercut the "we/they" mentality. For the homeless, "their feeding program" became "our church home." For the parishioners, "those people" became "our brothers and sisters."

Meanwhile, under the leadership of Jim Barnes, the newly appointed director of community ministries, the separate feeding, drop-in, and shelter ministries were being integrated. Spiritual components were added: Bible study after meals, prayer time before bedding down in shelter, and discipleship group on Sunday afternoons. "I remember one angry black man named Ron," says Barnes. "At first he was just using us, but after a while he began to change, and eventually, he was leading Bible studies for fellow street people." Slowly, some were moving from alienation to belonging, as they experienced the tangible love of Christ. "Still," laments Barnes, "many regular members had difficulty with what was happening." For example, there was discomfort when homeless people came on Sunday morning, concerns about rugs and furniture, questions about the insurance for volunteer doctors.

A growing number of members, however, risked extending themselves in service and relationship. There was a new policy that everyone would wait in line outside prior to the worship service, not just folks waiting to receive a meal ticket. "You shouldn't have to wait in line outside," a street person protested to Angela Minns one Sunday evening. "But I'm going to church . . . with you," she humbly replied. Brent Elliott was one of a group of young adults who invested in this ministry and found himself stretched and changed as a result. "I started with a white-knight mentality," admits Brent, "but I was quickly humbled." He goes on, "I was blown away that those whose circumstances were so much worse than mine had so much to share spiritually. They had an integrity, an openness, an honesty about their struggles, whereas I had learned to disguise mine. I sought to serve, but then I learned to be served."

In March 1991, after less than three years as pastor, Martyn Minns left All Angels' to become rector of a large parish near Washington, D.C. Suddenly, after a high-energy, staff-intensive period of growth, the church faced what proved to be a stressful two-year interim, during which the Reverend Jonathan King, as part-time interim rector, provided a steadying presence.

Like a pair of stark bookends, two tragic deaths bracketed this period. The Reverend Herman Heade, a newly ordained African American priest, had served part-time under Minns, with a primary focus on the Sunday-evening ministry. His journey from prison to priesthood resonated with many of the participants. After Minns left, Heade became the full-time assistant rector. No one realized how deeply he was troubled in his personal life. His suicide three months later shocked the church and left everyone deeply shaken.

Despite this tragedy and the accumulating strain because of declining attendance and a prolonged pastoral search, the church actually grew in strength. "There's no question that lay leaders stepped up to the plate," affirms Pano Anthos, senior warden (top lay position) during that time. "The ownership of vision increased; our sense of community deepened; the number of house churches [small groups] expanded; even financial giving went up." Community ministries continued under a new director, Rob Buckley. Buckley and other volunteers wrestled with the logistical demands of running an extensive program with limited funds and facilities. They struggled to create community, which is difficult when food is often the main "carrot" for many. Buckley, although only twenty-five, gained great respect and appreciation from those he served. He was both compassionate and tough. Finally, in November 1992, a new rector, the Reverend Colin Goode, was called, and the weary church breathed a collective sigh of relief as they awaited his arrival in February.

Then suddenly, in January 1993, Rob Buckley was hospitalized with cancer. He deteriorated rapidly and then died. It seemed to many that Satan, who had injured the church at the outset of the interim, was now striking a cruel blow to undermine the community at the point of resurgent hope. Buckley died on the first Monday of February, the new rector arrived on Thursday, and the funeral took place on Friday. The chapel overflowed, rich and poor, black and white, as Martyn Minns, Jonathan King, and Colin Goode, symbolizing continuity of leadership, combined to pastor the grieving flock in a poignant memorial service.

Colin Goode, although British born, lived most of his life in South Africa, where he married Moira, a white South African. In his earlier years of ministry during the era of brutal apartheid, Goode as well as Moira grappled with racism and injustice. Their efforts to resist apartheid and promote reconciliation brought them under increasing scrutiny and pressure. In 1983 they made the agonizing decision to move with their two young daughters to North America, where Goode pastored churches in both Canada and the United States. He has brought a quiet strength, a generous spirit, and a humble spirituality to his pastoral role at All Angels'. During their initial year, Colin and Moira adjusted to the rigors of urban life, and the church slowly healed from its painful blows. The church moved forward, building on its key strengths: the articulation of biblical foundations; dynamic, heartfelt worship, within the Anglican tradition; "house churches" for spiritual community and discipleship; concern for the poor and homeless; the practice of healing prayer; and affirmation of the gifts within the body of Christ.

During Goode's second year, two accomplishments especially stand out: the forging of the vision statement (mentioned earlier) and the reversal of an ominous financial trajectory. The leadership of the church set in motion a five-year plan to reduce expenditures and increase congregational giving. The end goal was a balanced budget that would free the endowment for, in Colin's words, "God's work outside this parish." In the first phase, the vestry sought to reduce and restructure staff without undermining the fundamental character and ministries of All Angels'. At the same time, key leaders challenged the church to a far greater stewardship of time, talent, and treasure. In 1994 and 1995 giving increased dramatically; many began tithing for the first time. In addition to clear teaching and compelling testimonies about biblical stewardship, a new sense of vision and momentum fueled this remarkable progress.

Maturing in the area of stewardship fits with the vision of training and empowering the laity. Goode and the others on staff, in keeping with Ephesians 4:11-13, see themselves as called to "equip the saints" for the work of service within the church and witness in the community. In addition to a strong and active leadership body (the vestry), lay leaders and volunteers facilitate worship, prayer ministry, children's programs, adult education, and community ministries. Perhaps most strategic are those who "pastor" house churches. These small groups of twelve to eighteen people meet weekly or biweekly in homes and provide opportunities for spiritual friendship, study of Scripture, and Christian growth.

A powerful example of All Angels' advocacy of vocational stewardship is its affirmation of artists. As many as one-fourth of the members are involved in some aspect of the arts, whether performing, visual, or literary. Many are accomplished professionals. This reflects both the church's context—many artists reside on the Upper West Side—and the church's conviction that all of life holds redemptive potential under the lordship of Christ, including the creative arts. "In other churches I've attended, I've felt slapped on the wrist for having creative thoughts," says John Bjerklie, an artist who makes mixed-media sculpture and paintings. "At these churches, people are guided to think in certain restrictive, legalistic ways about what a Christian artist should do. It would leave me angry." He continues, "At All Angels' it's just the opposite! Here, I'm affirmed that God has given me these gifts and wants me to use them fully. At All Angels' art can happen!"

Not only are creativity and artistic expression integral to the church's worship, but the church encourages artists in other ways. For several years, parishioner Madeleine L'Engle, the acclaimed author of *A Wrinkle in Time* and over forty-five other books, has offered a writer's workshop for All Angels' members seeking to develop their creative writing. Another unusual endeavor is the All Angels' Artists Assistance Network or Angels' Net. In support of Christians who are making their living in the professional arts, a marketplace often hostile to the gospel, the church has established a fund to help underwrite artists who integrate quality work with committed faith.

All Angels' dramatically demonstrated its commitment to art and artists in the first Hosanna! Festival in May 1995. The theme for this month-long celebration was "the intersection of art and faith, with a special focus on the ability of artists to minister and evangelize," in the words of Ron Melrose, producer. The festival included three major elements: a series of four Friday-night performances by All Angels' musicians and dramatists, the installation in the chapel of more than a dozen works of painting or sculpture by four parishioners, and the publication of *Doorways,* a literary magazine featuring the poetry and prose of ten members of the congregation.

John Bjerklie, one of the artists exhibited, and his wife, Poogy, worship primarily at the Sunday evening service. John sees an artistic dimension to the free and expressive worship. "Art usually happens in places where people are downtrodden, where there is a great need to express something very deep and often painful," he muses. "At the evening service—in the music, the praying, the voicing of needs, however unpleasant—there is a freedom for creative expression, an atmosphere that works for me as an artist."

Indeed, this place of belonging, this time for honest struggle, this opportunity for healing celebration, is a distinctive strength of All Angels'. Hundreds come each week, including many who are poor. The physically hungry receive a hot meal, the spiritually empty are filled in worship, and the socially outcast are given dignity, especially those using their gifts in the gospel choir. While there is much to applaud here, the community ministries remain All Angels' most daunting challenge, an area in which problems defy easy solutions and failures still outweigh successes.

Currently, church leaders are wrestling with three substantial issues: (1) bridging the barriers between morning and evening congregations, (2) helping persons experience more complete transformation, and (3) raising up leaders from within the evening group. Goode takes pains to emphasize the brokenness and sinfulness that all share: "We are all addicted in some way, including those addicted to work, power, and status; only, some manifestations seem more obvious or destructive." Such perceptions, with their accompanying prejudices, comprise part of the continuing barrier between "morning folks" and "evening folks." A handful of the homeless worship in the morning, and a number of the middle class worship in the evening. Some do both. By and large, however, a gulf remains. A number of people report feeling unwelcome, uncomfortable, and even "looked down on," when they have attended on Sunday morning. There is rarely open or overt discussion of racial dynamics in the church. Goode, however, discerns a deepening commitment by a growing core of parishioners to build a more integrated community. "But I don't want people to cross over out of a sense of guilt or duty," states the rector, "rather out of a heart of genuine love, a heart like that of God's as revealed in Isaiah 58."

Debbie Starks's story illustrates the potential for significant transformation and the impediments to such change. Stark became involved at All Angels' in 1988 when she was doing drugs and struggling to care for her two-year-old daughter. Over the next two years, Stark went through a suicide attempt, a crack binge, the loss of custody of her child, two drug rehabilitation programs, and the incarceration of her boyfriend. "All during this time, Rob and Brent and Pam gave me the support I needed without judging me," she says of the community ministries leaders.

By 1991 Debbie had married her husband, Eddie, and regained her daughter. Both stayed drug free and became more involved at All Angels'. Debbie even did periodic work for the church. Ironically, they found it increasingly difficult to participate in the Sunday-evening community. "We tried to be helpful to others," explains Debbie, "but many of them would doubt that we had changed and would not accept the persons we were trying to be. Being around them became negative for us, so we felt we needed to drop out." At present, they are struggling to raise their four children on Eddie's limited income. They are housed, drug free, and employed, but they continue to have mixed feelings about All Angels'.

Like Debbie and Eddie, a handful have experienced a measure of transformation through All Angels', but for many, positive changes are limited and come about slowly. All Angels' is not equipped to offer housing assistance, employment counseling, or drug and alcohol rehabilitation. In fact, the church is not yet in a position to consistently refer people to and support them through programs existing elsewhere. "We are now in a process of shifting our emphasis from meeting the needs of the many to investing in more comprehensive development of the core of committed members of the Sunday-night congregation," indicates Goode. "We want to fulfill both parts of the Great Commission (Matthew 28:18-20): Go make disciples and teach them to obey everything, both evangelism and transformation of life."

Perhaps this shift in emphasis will lead to the development of leaders from within the evening congregation. The current staff and vestry are predominantly white, as are the key leaders of the Sunday-afternoon Bible study. They recognize this imbalance as a problem but so far have failed to identify and develop candidates to fill the vacuum. "We have found it very difficult to find those who can maintain a level of stability that would allow a significant contribution at the leadership level," says the rector. "So many are in a survival mode, facing enormous temptations that tend to undermine stability," he observes.

In light of this vacuum, the leaders of the church took one step that has proven effective. In 1991 the church asked the Reverend Bill Paige, an African American Pentecostal minister, to serve as a regular guest preacher (twice a month) on Sunday evenings. Paige worked for many years in law enforcement and, upon retirement, began serving as chaplain for a residential treatment center for emotionally disturbed children. His tough-love, evangelistic sermons are much appreciated by the congregation. "I speak their language and share honestly out of my own life," explains Paige. "I'm not dogging or shaming them; I challenge them to take the gospel seriously, to accept Christ as the solace for their pain."

Paradoxically, then, the weaknesses of All Angels' community ministries parallel the strengths. The church offers a genuine worshiping community but one that does not always reinforce transformation or fully extend across the racial and economic barriers. The church sees people as individuals who share both human dignity and brokenness, but then fosters too few relationships of mutual commitment and accountability, the kind that can bring about change. The church practices cultural contextualization but still lacks lay leaders who have arisen from that context.

All Angels' reached a milestone in its journey at the annual parish retreat in September 1995. Nearly two hundred attended the weekend gathering at a Connecticut conference site, and all three services were well represented. It was titled "Pictures of the Kingdom, Acts of Faith." Many threads of the church's vision converged into a single tapestry. The major sessions explored three themes: conversion, community, and culture. Each session was a collage of twelve presentations: musical portraits, enacted passages from the Book of Acts, personal snapshots (testimonies), dramatic sketches, and short teachings. For the first time, the gospel choir played an integral part in a retreat, moving all to joyful dance. Artists used their gifts to teach and encourage. The youth group presented a powerful drama that directly addressed the issue of racism. A lawyer and an educator each spoke of how faith shaped their work. On Saturday, the community gathered at lakeside to share in the moving baptism of Hiro Yokose, a Japanese painter from the evening congregation who spoke eloquently of his conversion and its effect on his art. On Sunday, the community assembled in the rustic chapel for Holy Eucharist; it was an outpouring of prayer and song, of tears and testimonies, of affirmations and words of forgiveness. One older black man stood and told of arriving with an unpleasant skin ailment and feeling "untouchable," especially among so many he did not know. Then, tearfully, he described how one of the parishioners, a white man, had embraced and cared for him, filling him with an extraordinary sense of love and acceptance. An act of faith. A picture of the Kingdom. A church entertaining angels unawares.

18

Epilogue

Robert D. Carle

We live in cities badly; we have built them in culpable innocence and now fret helplessly in a synthetic wilderness of our own construction. We need . . . to comprehend the nature of citizenship, to make a serious, imaginative, assessment of that special relationship between the self and the city; its unique plasticity, its privacy and its freedom.

—Jonathan Raban, *Soft City*

New York City is a dramatic example of how we do, indeed, live in cities badly. Eugene Linden wrote that to call New York a Third World city is "an insult to the Third World."[1] A recent *New York Times* editorial argued that the poorest neighborhoods in Calcutta have less crime and more community spirit than New York. A man in Bangladesh can expect to live longer than a man in Harlem. Parts of the South Bronx, Bradhurst, and Bushwick fulfill every criteria of urban blight, with cracked facades, abandoned tenements, and rubble-strewn lots where drug dealers and prostitutes congregate. Epidemics of AIDS, tuberculosis, and hepatitis have pushed New York's health-care system to the breaking point. A generation ago, New York had the best public schools in the world; today less than a third of New York's public school children read at or above grade level, and one-third of the city's local school boards are under investigation for corruption. After billions of dollars of social spending, New Yorkers are, by many key indices, worse off today than they were in 1940.

And yet this is not the whole story. The city continues to be a magnet for the most talented people from all over the United States and from around the world. With a flood of new arrivals from Europe, Latin America, the Caribbean, the former Soviet Union, and Asia, New York's population is once again growing. Despite the rise of European and Asian markets, the New York Stock Exchange remains the world's most prestigious financial market, on which stocks worth trillions of dollars are traded. In culture, too, New York is a pacesetter. Few cities have even one world-class performing arts troupe. New York has dozens. As showcases for theater and for the visual arts, Broadway, the Metropolitan Museum of Art, and the Museum of Modern Art have few rivals.

"The price of a city's greatness," writes Eugene Linden, "is an uneasy balance between vitality and chaos, health and disease, enterprise and corruption, art and iniquity."[2] In New York, this balance has always threatened to tip in the direction of anarchy, but until recently, there was in New York a civic culture, nurtured by religious institutions, that kept the forces of disintegration at bay. This civic culture has been fraying for years, and a return to religious sensibilities is perhaps the only way to salvage the social fabric. As economist Glenn Loury said in a recent interview, "I don't think that tinkering with economic incentives can get us to where we need to go. Indeed, people are recognizing that the only way to respond effectively to the difficult[ies] is through revivalism and evangelism." John DiIulio reminds us that "despite living in desperate economic poverty, under the heavy weight of Jim Crow, and with plenty of free access to guns, the church-going, two-parent black families of the South never experienced anything remotely like the tragic levels of homicidal youth and gang violence that plagues some (not all!) of today's black inner-city neighborhoods."[3]

This book dramatizes the ways in which churches in America's largest and perhaps most secular city are transforming nearly every aspect of urban life. The churches and church-based coalitions described in this book are making neighborhoods more livable by building houses, rehabilitating vacant buildings, opening charter and parochial schools, and applying pressure on public officials to improve police responsiveness, repair the city's infrastructure, and curb corruption. Perhaps most importantly, churches are transforming lives by bringing the gospel of Christ to New Yorkers who are defeated by their own bad choices or by the cruelty of others.

Lying behind these stories is an argument that when it comes to community development, churches are New York's greatest resource. Whereas government agencies and nongovernmental organizations are outsiders in neighborhoods where they seek to effect change, churches bring to the task of development community roots, hard-earned legitimacy, a solid organizational base, and congregations of members for whom service is not only a duty of citizenship but a responsibility of faith.[4] Furthermore, churches proclaim a gospel that enables people to make moral sense of life. As the Reverend Eugene Rivers says,

> The missing element in secular-policy-oriented strategies is the transcendent sacredness of life. Faith makes all the difference in how humans respond to adversity. With faith we can see beyond discrimination to a future that has meaning. Without faith there are no rules, no restraint . . . [no] moral difference between spitting on the ground and killing another black person.[5]

Rivers's message is that "religious institutions are better equipped to deal with the problems of the poor than the government is, and that they should receive public support to do everything from crime prevention to welfare reform."[6]

After decades of hampering church-based community development efforts by rigid interpretations of the doctrine of the separation of church and state, leaders on all sides of the political spectrum are encouraging churches to assume greater responsibility for community development. Republican and

Democratic lawmakers are forging a new framework for America's assistance to the poor that will make government a support, rather than a substitute, for religious charity. The most significant legislation in this regard is the Ashcroft (or Charitable Choice) Amendment. This initiative encourages states to team up with churches and faith-based agencies, and it promises to those organizations a range of protections to enable them to retain their religious character despite receiving public funds. Whereas in the past legislation encouraged religious charities to dispense government-style welfare services, public monies are now able to support faith-directed antipoverty work.[7]

Senator Dan Coates has proposed a dozen bills to promote the renewal of civil society by putting government influence and resources on the side of "private and religious institutions that shape, direct, and reclaim individual lives." The centerpiece of this legislation is a dollar-for-dollar reduction in federal income taxes of up to $500 ($1,000 for joint filers) to match donations to qualified charities. Eligible charities must demonstrate that their "predominant activity" is the provision of anti-poverty services to poor persons and families and that they devote at least 70 percent of their expenditures to direct anti-poverty services. In particular, Coates seeks to undergird religious charities, for they "not only feed the body but touch the soul." Coates argues that religious charities are more effective than government because they make demands as well as offer help, interact with the needy personally rather than bureaucratically, and "provide an element of moral challenge and spiritual renewal that government programs cannot duplicate."[8]

Democrats in the Senate echo Coates's enthusiasm. Minnesota's Paul Wellstone voted for charitable choice but against the final welfare reform bill. "Some of the best anti-poverty work I've seen," he said, "has come from faith-based agencies." Senator Bob Kerrey expressed agreement: "If I were running a public school system, I'd contract with the parochial schools—as Mayor Giuliani wanted to do in new York—and have them educate some of the poorest kids. I don't see the First Amendment as so rigid that it prevents us from contracting with people who are getting the job done right."[9]

What shape new public-religious collaborations will take in

the process of welfare reform remains to be seen. Critics on the religious right see these collaborations as a cynical attempt on the part of government to limit religious expression. "Government money comes with strings, or rather ropes," runs this argument, "and a chief target of government rules is the overt expression of religion by service agencies." The religious left, on the other hand, argues that the evil of dismantling the New Deal/Great Society approach to fighting poverty outweighs any possible positive outcomes of proposals to increase collaboration between government and religious charities. After reviewing the critics on both the right and the left, Stanley Carlson-Thies offers a more positive perspective:

> In concept, at least, these new policy ideas should hold significant attraction for the churches, despite their polarized reactions. The charity tax credit is explicitly designed to enhance service to the needy, not to replace the government safety net, and to do so without harming the religious character of faith-based charities. "Charitable choice" is meant to guarantee the religious integrity of ministries that collaborate with public welfare, while protecting the religious rights of beneficiaries, and in principle it involves a change, not diminution, of the government commitment to the poor.
>
> These proposals represent genuinely new concepts for social policy; they represent practical mechanisms to overcome past dilemmas of statist welfare versus private charity, secularized public assistance versus religiously robust government aid. In principle, they should resonate strongly with Christians who believe that the call to love our needy neighbors is addressed not only to individuals but also to the church and the political community.[10]

The Chinese word for "crisis" is composed of the character for danger followed by the character for opportunity. Danger and opportunity are what characterize contemporary struggles of urban life and ministry. The reforms of the past year threaten to fray the fragile safety net supporting America's poor, but the reforms also open up unprecedented opportunities for religious-public collaboration in working for the common good. Designing and working out the details of this collaboration will take all the talent Christian ministries can muster. Prayer, good analysis, and involvement in the details of policy making are skills churches must hone as they approach this new playing field. And as religious institutions take a more active role in fighting poverty as we know it, they well have to manifest the creativity, the passion for serving the needy, the integrity, and the tenacity demonstrated by the churches in this volume.

But as New Yorkers approach the twenty-first century, the churches of our city will perhaps be called upon to fulfill a function even more vital than that of fighting poverty. Rev. Andrew Greely writes: "No one has yet phrased in cogent enough terms for modern man the argument that love and civility are the only way to prevent the metropolis from destroying both the vision that brought it into being and [those] who have created it. . . . Unless there is an emergence of a new urbanity, disaster is inescapable." Religious institutions make life in the city possible. They serve culture by doing two vital things: they set forth a web of moral demands and provide the means through which people can find respite from the tensions created by those demands. From churches, we learn moral laws, but we also hear the gracious good news of the gospel, "with its own joyful motivations to do the work of building the earthly city." That is why Andrew Greely concludes that "modern man will probably turn at least once more to his churches as the only institutions capable of creating a new urbanity, of providing a vision of the possibility of metropolitan community."[11]

Notes

Chapter 1: Introduction

1. New York City Department of Planning, *Demographic Profile*, August 1992.

2. "New York Ascendant: The Report of the Commission on the Year 2000" (June 1987): 56. Robert F. Wagner, chair.

3. Op. cit., "Demographic Profile."

4. John DiIulio, "Building Spiritual Capital: How Religious Congregations Cut Crime and Enhance Community Well-Being" (briefing on "Religion in American Life," New York, N.Y., 5 October 1995), 9.

5. Ibid., 11.

6. Quoted in Robert Carle, "Church-Based Community Development and the Transformation of New York," *Trinity News* 44, no. 1 (1997): 14.

7. Op. cit., DiIulio, 2.

8. John Mollenkopf and Manuel Castells, eds., *Dual City* (New York: Russell Sage Foundation, 1991), 323.

9. Joe Klein, "In God They Trust," *The New Yorker* (16 June 1997): 42.

10. Lyle Schaller, introduction to *Center City Churches* (Nashville: Abingdon, 1993), 11-20.

11. See Ray Bakke, *The Urban Christian* (Downers Grove, Ill.: InterVarsity Press, 1987), chap. 4.

12. Ibid., 80.

13. See Ronald Sider, "Religious Faith and Public Policy: Can They Be Partners?" *ESA Advocate* (April 1992): 1-4; LeRoy Gruner, "Heroin, Hashish, and Hallelujah: The Search for Meaning," *Review of Religious Research* 26, no. 2 (December 1984): 176-84.

14. DiIulio, "Building Spiritual Capital," 12-13.

15. Quoted in Diane Wilson, "Black Church Expands Communitarian Tradition," *Progressions* 5, no. 1 (February 1995): 17.

16. Carol Steinbach, "Program Helps Restore Health to Ailing Community," *Progressions* 5, no. 1 (February 1995): 21.

17. Quoted in Wilson, "Black Church Expands Communitarian Tradition," 16.

Chapter 2: Seeking the Shalom of the City

1. Quoted in Kenneth Miller and Ethel Miller, *The People Are the City* (New York: Macmillan, 1962), 6.

2. Quoted in John Goodbody, *One Peppercorne* (New York: Trinity Episcopal Church, 1982), 30.

3. Charles Foster, *An Errand of Mercy* (Chapel Hill: University of North Carolina Press, 1960), 137.

4. Carroll Smith Rosenberg, *Religion and the Rise of the American City* (Ithaca, N.Y.: Cornell University Press, 1971), 45-46.

5. Clifford Morehouse, *Trinity: Mother of Churches* (New York: Seabury, 1973), 28.

6. Ibid., 27.

7. See Foster, *An Errand of Mercy.*

8. Later renamed the New York City Missions Society.

9. Rosenberg, *Religion and the Rise,* 73.

10. New York City Tract Society, *Ninth Annual Report,* 1836, 15.

11. New York City Tract Society, *Forty-First Annual Report,* 1867, 18.

12. Rosenberg, *Religion and the Rise,* 190-91.

13. Ibid., 252-53.

14. Ibid., 270.

15. "Salvation Work on Cherry Hill," *The Conqueror* 4 (October 1895): 470.

16. Aaron Ignatius Abell, *The Urban Impact on American Protestantism 1865–1900* (Cambridge: Harvard University Press, 1943), 127.

17. Ibid., 40.

18. J. G. Holland, "A New System in City Churches," *Scribner's Monthly* 8 (June 1874): 241-42.

19. Abell, *Urban Impact,* 7.

20. James Parton, "Our Roman Catholic Brethren," *Atlantic Monthly* 21 (April–May 1868): 432-51; 556-74.

21. Abell, *Urban Impact,* 28-29.

22. Miller and Miller, *The People Are the City,* 69.

23. Ibid., 70.

24. Ibid.

25. Ibid.

26. George Manson, "Progressive Methods in Church Work," *Christian Union,* 28 November 1891, 1946.

27. Abell, *Urban Impact,* 151.

28. Quoted by Harry Fosdick in the introduction to *A Rauschenbusch Reader* (New York: Harper Brothers, 1957), xv-xvi.

29. Ibid., xv.

30. "Rauschenbusch," in *The Encyclopedia of Religion,* ed. Marcus Eliade (New York: Macmillan, 1987), 12:218.

31. Quoted by Fosdick in *A Rauschenbusch Reader,* xvi.

32. Jay P. Dolan, *The American Catholic Experience* (Garden City, N.Y.: Image Books, 1985), 408.

33. Quoted in Mark Noll, *A History of Christianity in the United States and Canada* (Grand Rapids: Eerdmans, 1992), 514.

34. Quoted in Joseph Chinmichi, *Living Stones* (New York: Macmillan, 1989), 186.

35. James Kenneally, *History of American Catholic Women* (New York: Crossroads, 1990), 169.

36. Dolan, *The American Catholic Experience*, 408.

37. Ibid., 411.

38. Ibid., 413.

39. Kenneally, *History of American Catholic Women,* 171.

40. Tim Keller, "An Evangelical Mission in a Secular City," in *Center City Churches,* ed. Lyle Schaller (Nashville: Abingdon, 1993), 36.

41. Redeemer is a member of the Presbyterian Church in America, which is smaller and more theologically conservative than the Presbyterian Church (U.S.A.).

42. Keller, "An Evangelical Mission," 40-41.

43. Trinity Church on Wall Street, for example, invests up to $1 million per year to support church-based coalitions that are committed to the renewal of New York's poorer neighborhoods.

44. Martin Marty, *Protestantism in the United States* (New York: Scribner, 1986), 261.

45. Ibid.

Chapter 3: Shelter in the Time of Storm

1. Robert Franklin, "The Safest Place on Earth: The Culture of Black Congregations," in *American Congregations,* ed. James Wind and James Lewis (Chicago: University of Chicago Press, 1994), 2:257.

2. Roi Ottley and William Weatherby, *The Negro in New York* (New York: New York Public Library, 1967), 56.

3. Franklin, "The Safest Place on Earth," 2:257.

4. Ottley and Weatherby, *The Negro in New York,* 55.

5. Edward Smith, *Climbing Jacob's Ladder* (Washington, D.C.: Smithsonian Institution, 1988), 39, 47.

6. Ibid., 12-13.

7. Gilbert Osofsky, *Harlem: The Making of a Ghetto* (New York: Harper and Row, 1966).

8. "Million Dollar Deal," *The New Age,* 30 March 1911. See also *The Crisis 2* (May 1911): 5.

9. Seth Scheiner, *Negro Mecca* (New York: New York University Press, 1965), 91-92.

10. Clarence Taylor, *The Black Churches of Brooklyn* (New York: Columbia University Press, 1994), 28.

11. Scheiner, *Negro Mecca,* 101.

12. Quoted in Michael Eric Dyson, *Between God and Gangsta Rap* (New York: Oxford University Press, 1996), 43.

13. Ibid., 44-45.

14. Ibid., 40.

15. Taylor, *The Black Churches of Brooklyn,* 124-49. For a history of black activists-pastors in Brooklyn, see chapters 4-5.

16. Eric Lincoln and Laurence Mamiya, *The Black Church in the African American Experience* (Durham, N.C.: Duke University Press, 1990), 210-11.

17. Quoted in Dyson, *Between God and Gangsta Rap,* 44.

18. Ibid., 211-12.

19. Allen Spear, *Black Chicago: The Making of a Negro Ghetto, 1890–1920* (Chicago: University of Chicago Press, 1967), 175.

20. Taylor, *The Black Churches of Brooklyn,* 53-55.

21. Melvin D. Williams, *Community in a Black Pentecostal Church: An Anthropological Study* (Prospect Heights, Ill.: Waveland Press, 1974).

22. Taylor, *The Black Churches of Brooklyn,* 63.

23. Ibid., 101.

24. Lawrence Mamiya, "A Social History of Bethel African Methodist Episcopal Church in Baltimore," in *American Congregations,* ed. James Wind and James Lewis (Chicago: University of Chicago Press, 1994), 265.

25. Quoted in Mamiya, "A Social History," 266. Bryant is currently pastor of Bethel A.M.E. Church in Baltimore.

26. Franklin, "The Safest Place on Earth," 2:260.

27. Ibid., 2:265.

28. Williams, *Community in a Black Pentecostal Church,* 157.

Chapter 4: Booming Churches in Burned-out Districts

1. Quoted by William Martin, *Billy Graham* (New York: Free Press, 1993), 225. Reinhold Niebuhr repeatedly attacked Graham and in a sour symbolic gesture refused even to meet the evangelist.

2. U.S. Census press release, 1 July 1995.

3. "Hispanic Voting Patterns," Hispanic Research Center, Fordham University, 1995.

4. Celia W. Dugger, "A Cultural Reluctance to Spare the Rod," *New York Times,* 26 February 1996, B1, B7.

5. "Ethnic Identification Among Evangelicals in New York City," International Research Institute on Values Changes, February 1997.

6. The results of the NSRI are in Barry A. Kosmin and Seymour P. Lachman, *One Nation Under God* (New York: Crown Trade Paperbacks, 1993), 110.

7. Quoted in John T. McGreevy, *Parish Boundaries: The Catholic Encounter with Race in the Twentieth-Century Urban North* (Chicago: University of Chicago Press, 1996).

8. Allan Figueroa Deck, "The Challenge of Evangelical/Pentecostal Christianity to Hispanic Catholicism," in J. P. Dolan and A. F. Deck, eds., *Hispanic Catholic Culture in the U.S.* (South Bend, Ind.: University of Notre Dame Press, 1994), 409-39.

9. Kosmin and Lachman, *One Nation,* 138-39.

10. Robert Gonzalez and Michael LaVelle, *The Hispanic Catholic in the U.S.* (New York: Northeastern Pastoral Center, 1988), 10. Protestant seminaries and schools of theology have three times the number of Hispanic students as do Catholic seminaries. Kosmin and Lachman, *One Nation,* 138. Bishop Edwin O'Brien of St. Joseph's Seminary in Yonkers says that only about a dozen new priests are ordained each year by the whole archdiocese of New York.

11. David Martin, *Tongues of Fire: The Explosion of Protestantism in Latin America* (Oxford: Blackwell, 1990).

12. James Guth and Corwin Smidt, "The Mismeasure of Evangelicals and an Attempt at a Correction," *Books and Culture Review* (January 1996). Internet source. Based on this definition, this section lumps evangelicals, fundamentalists, Pentecostals, and charismatics together as "evangelicals."

13. Since the 1990 National Survey of Religious Identifications says about 26 percent of the U.S. population is Roman Catholic, and, according to James Guth's and Corwin Smidt's 1992 American Evangelicalism survey, about 4 percent of the U.S. population are evangelical Roman Catholics, this may mean that about 15 percent of the U.S. Roman Catholic population is evangelical. In New York City this would suggest that 6 to 7 percent of New Yorkers may be evangelical Roman Catholics.

14. Christian Smith, *American Evangelicalism: Embattled and Thriving* (Chicago: University of Chicago Press, 1998), 245. We have conservatively estimated that 60 percent of African American Protestants hold evangelical beliefs.

15. Using 1996 U.S. Census figures for ethnicity in New York City. Cf. Mitchell Moss, "Analysis of U.S. Census Survey of Housing in NYC, 1996," Taub Urban Research Center, New York University, 1 December 1997. About 40 percent of U.S. Protestants may be classified as evangelicals. See Smith, *American Evangelicalism,* 236. In 1987 a Princeton Religion Research Center's national survey of Americans found that 44 percent identified themselves as "born again" or "evangelical" Christians. *Emerging Trends* (Vol. 9, No. 2., February 1987), 2. We have conservatively estimated that 60 percent of African American Protestants hold evangelical beliefs. The International Research Institute on Values Changes estimates that about 80 percent of New York City Hispanic Protestants are evangelical. An estimated 80 percent of Korean immigrants identify themselves as Protestant, as do 10 percent of Chinese immigrants. Various estimates say that 70 to 80 percent of Korean-American Protestants are evangelical and 90 percent of Chinese-American Protestants are evangelical.

16. Interview, 5 May 1998.

17. These and other figures for the general population of New York City evangelicals come from "The Market for Higher Education among the Evangelicals of New York City," a report of The King's College in New York City Steering Committee, New York: International Research Institute on Values Changes, 1995. A survey of 2,484 leaders and members of 49 churches drawn as a random sample, stratified by ethnicity, borough, and class, from 4,025 evangelical churches in New York City between March and December 1995.

18. Ibid., 17-18.

19. Mark J. Penn and Douglas E. Shoen, "A Tale of Four Cities. The 1995 *New York* New York Poll," *New York Magazine* (21 August 1995): 25-31.

20. Francis Fukuyama, *Trust* (New York: Free Press, 1995), 303.

21. Cf. Benjamin Mays and Joseph Nicholson, *The Negro Church* (New York: Russell and Russell, 1934/1969), 54-55.

22. Cf. Richard Lewis, *Black Cop: The Real Deal* (Shippensburg, Pa.: Destiny Image Publishers, 1996), back cover.

23. Hart M. Nelsen, "Unchurched Black Americans: Patterns of Religiosity and Affiliation," *Review of Religious Research* (June 1988), 398-412.

24. Wade Clark Roof and William McKinney, *American Mainline Religion* (New Brunswick, N.J.: Rutgers University Press, 1987), 91. At a minimum "churched" means church membership and church attendance within the last six months. Also, see *Emerging Trends,* Princeton Religion Research Center (Vol. 9, No. 5, May 1987), 5. In 1989 the center reported a 64 percent churched rate for African Americans. *The Unchurched American . . . 10 Years Later* (Princeton: Princeton Religion Research Center, 1989), 37.

25. Quoted in Andres Tapia, "Soul Searching: How Is the Black Church Responding to the Urban Crisis?" *Christianity Today* (March 1996). Internet source.

26. Edward D. Smith, *Climbing Jacob's Ladder: The Rise of Black Churches in Eastern American Cities* (Washington, D.C.: Smithsonian Institution for the Anacostia Museum, n.d.), 26.

27. For classical studies of the African American church, see John Dollard, *Caste and Class in a Southern Town* (New York: Harper and Bros., 1937); W. E. B. DuBois, ed., *The Negro Church* (Atlanta: Atlanta University Publications, 1903); Arthur Huff Fausset, *Black Gods of the Metropolis* (Philadelphia: University of Pennsylvania, 1944); Benjamin Mays, *The Negro's God as Reflected in His Literature* (New York: Atheneum, 1968); Benjamin E. Mays and Joseph Nicholson, *The Negro's Church* (New York: The Institute of Social and Religious Research, 1933); Carter G. Woodson, *The History of the Negro Church* (Washington, D.C.: The Associated Publishers, 1945).

28. Kelly Miller, *Radicals and Conservatives and Other Essays on the Negro in America* (New York: Schocken, 1968), 152.

29. Beverly Hall Lawrence, *Reviving the Spirit* (New York: Grove Press, 1996), 6.

30. Ibid., 9.

31. *The 1997 Theological Certificate Program Survey.* New York: International Research Institute on Values Changes for New York Theological Seminary/Ford Foundation project. "A Study of the Social Service Dimension of Theological Education," directed by H. Dean Trulear, 1997. Two hundred seventy-one New York City African American church leaders were interviewed.

32. Asher Arian et al., *Changing New York City Politics* (New York: Routledge, 1990), 180.

33. James W. Wood, *100 Years of the African Methodist Episcopal Zion Church; or, The Centennial of African Methodism* (New York: AME Zion Book Concern, 1895), 6-7.

34. Henry Mitchell, *Black Preaching* (Philadelphia: Lippincott, 1970), 36.

35. *The 1997 Theological Certificate Program Survey.* New York: International Research Institute on Values Changes for New York Theological Seminary/Ford Foundation project. "A Study of the Social Service Dimension of Theological Education," directed by H. Dean Trulear, 1997. Two hundred seventy-one New York City African American church leaders were interviewed.

36. Fukuyama, *Trust*, 7.

37. Mitchell Moss, "Analysis of U.S. Census Survey of Housing in NYC, 1996," 1 December 1997. For 1990 U.S. Census figures for Hispanics in New York City, see *U.S. Census 1990 Report* (28 February 1992): 16.10.6.5.

38. U.S. Bureau of the Census, *Hispanic Population in the U.S.* (March 1990), Current Population Reports, ser. P-20, No. 443, Washington, D.C., GPO, 1990.

39. Richard Alba, "Interethnic Marriage in the 1980 Census," in Stanley Lieberson and Mary C. Walters, eds., *From Many Strands: Ethnic and Racial Groups in Contemporary America* (New York: Russell Sage, 1988), 199.

40. George Barna, *The Second Coming of the Church* (Nashville: Thomas Nelson Publishing, 1998), 63.

41. Nathan Glazer and Daniel P. Moynihan, *Beyond the Melting Pot*, 2d ed., 118. Also, cf. "Hispanic AFDC recipients in NYC: Prospects for Employment and Self-Sufficiency," Office of Program Planning, Analysis and Development, New York State Department of Social Services, July 1990, 18.

42. L. H. Gann and Peter J. Duignan, *The Hispanics in the U.S.: A History* (Boulder, Colo.: Westview Press, 1986), 80.

New York City Mission in the African American Context

1. Diane Winston, "Black Church Expands Communitarian Tradition," *Progressions* 5, no. 1 (February 1995): 15.

Chapter 5: Concord Baptist Church

1. This quotation and all others from Gary V. Simpson are from an interview with him conducted by the author.

2. Tom Skinner, *Campus Crusade for Christ Training* (1971), audiotape.

3. This and all historic information on Concord Baptist Church of Christ is from Clarence Taylor, *The Black Churches of Brooklyn* (New York: Columbia University Press, 1994), and from interviews conducted by the author.

4. Taylor, *The Black Churches of Brooklyn*, 131.

5. Both references are from "The Pulpit King," *Christianity Today*, 11 December 1995, 25-26.

6. Ibid., 26.

7. Taylor, *The Black Churches of Brooklyn*, 147.

8. All quotations and information in this section are from an interview with Vicki McMillan conducted by the author.

9. All information and quotations in this section are from interviews with Aleathia V. Boddie and Pastor Gary V. Simpson conducted by the author.

Chapter 6: This Far by Faith

1. Steve Klots, *Richard Allen* (New York: Chelsea House, 1991), 45.

2. Unless otherwise indicated, quotations are from interviews conducted by the author with the persons indicated.

3. Taken from "The Pastor's Word," *The Allen Spirit*, September–October 1995.

4. Allen A.M.E. Church, *Annual Report 1995.*

5. Julius D. Eastman, *History of Allen A.M.E. Church* (Jamaica, N.Y., 1981), 92.

6. Allen A.M.E. Church, *Annual Report 1995.*

7. Eastman, *History of Allen A.M.E. Church,* 92.

8. "A Step Forward in Black Congressional Power," *Ebony,* February 1987, 87.

9. "Flake Carves," *New York Daily News,* 15 October 1995, 22.

10. Quoted from "This Congressman Preaches in Church Every Sunday," *Christianity Today,* 20 March 1987, 59.

11. Taken from "Milestones," *Time Magazine,* 13 August 1990, 73.

12. "Congressman and Wife Freed after Federal Government Drops Charges," *Jet Magazine,* 22 April 1991, 33.

13. Initial only is used to preserve anonymity.

Chapter 7: Bethel Gospel Assembly

1. I have refrained from calling Bethel an "evangelical" church since the term tends to force black Christians onto the procrustean bed of white evangelicalism—negating the uniqueness of the African American Bible-believing tradition. See Ron Potter, "Thinking for Ourselves," *The Other Side,* July–August 1975, 2-3, 56-63.

2. Interview with Ezra N. Williams by author, spring 1995, Bethel Gospel Assembly.

3. "The History of Bethel Gospel Assembly," *Bethel's Voice,* 6 November 1994, 4.

4. Interview with Walter Wilson by author, fall 1996, Bethel Gospel Assembly.

5. Interview with Joyce M. Ford by author, fall 1996, Bethel Gospel Assembly.

Chapter 8: Redeeming Babylon

1. Bruised Reed Ministries is located at the Latino Pastoral Action Center and receives technical assistance from LPAC, but it has its own board of directors and its own nonprofit (501c3) status.

Chapter 9: A Reformation in Brooklyn

1. Thomas Exter, "The Largest Minority," *American Demographics* (February 1993): 59.

2. Manuel Ortiz, *The Hispanic Challenge* (Downers Grove, Ill.: InterVarsity Press, 1993), 50.

3. Samuel Diaz, *Estudio Integral Sobre La Organizacion Del Centro Cristiano De Bay Ridge* (Consultor Eclesiastico, 1993), 13-16, 51.

4. Ortiz, *The Hispanic Challenge,* 50.

5. Ibid.

6. Pastor Valle, Padilla's predecessor, served as the overseer of the daughter churches until his death in 1974.

7. Luciano Padilla Jr., interview by McKenzie Pier, 8 August 1996.

8. Source unknown.

9. Ortiz, *The Hispanic Challenge* (Washington, D.C.: ASPIRA Association, 1987), 171.

10. Carlos Jimenez, interview by McKenzie Pier, 17 September 1996.

Chapter 10: A Gospel of Power

1. From Ralph Foster Weld, *Brooklyn Is America* (p. 99), as quoted in Toby Sanchez, *The Bushwick Neighborhood Profile* (Brooklyn, N.Y.: Brooklyn In Touch Information Center, 1988), 1.

2. Sanchez, *The Bushwick Neighborhood Profile*, 1.

3. Clifford Krauss, "Police Hit Drug Suppliers; Serious Crime Falls, Too," *New York Times*, 26 August 1996, 1.

Chapter 11: "Come, Let Us Rebuild the Walls of Jerusalem"

1. The conviction of former Congressman Robert Garcia was overturned on technicalities. Former Congressman Mario Biaggi's sentence was commuted because of illness, but this did not stop him from running again for public office once he was freed from prison. Stanley Friedman, the chair of the Bronx Democratic Party, and Stanley Simon, the Bronx borough president, both served time in prison.

2. "Planned shrinkage" was the term given by the Regional Plan Association to describe the municipal policy that reduced city services, such as fire protection and ambulances, in low-income areas.

3. Bob Kappstatter, "Award Brings Cheer to Bronx," *New York Daily News* (9 June 1997), 3.

4. The Industrial Areas Foundation (IAF) is the largest and oldest institution for community organizing in the United States. Founded by Saul Alinsky, and now directed by Ed Chambers, the IAF's mission for over fifty years has been to train people to organize to take responsibility for solving the problems in their own communities and to renew the interest of citizens in public life.

5. The history of the founding of SBC is given in James Rooney, *Organizing the South Bronx* (Albany, N.Y.: State University of New York Press, 1995).

6. Nehemiah single-family homes are built twenty-two to the acre. While this would be considered extremely high density for most of the United States, it is considered low in New York City.

7. The "density versus affordability" issue is a central concern in the redevelopment of the Bronx and a prime case of public resources being selectively used to favor private developers and relatively better-off home buyers. Single-family homes are less expensive to the city and to the individual home buyer than are multiple-family homes. The per-unit subsidy from the city to private developers is twice to three times that given to Nehemiah homeowners. Nehemiah is more affordable: most private developers require a minimum income of $35,000, instead of the $20,000 required to purchase a Nehemiah home. Twice as many people in the South Bronx make $20,000 as those who make $35,000 annually.

Chapter 12: Redefining the Public Sphere

1. The Public Education Association is the oldest advocacy group for public education in New York City. Formed over one hundred years ago, it is a dominant voice in school reform efforts and has worked closely with South Bronx Churches to formulate and implement strategies to improve the performance of local school districts.

2. As of November 1, 1995, there were ninety-eight schools in New York State "under registration review," meaning that their performance is so low that the State Education Department is considering revoking their licenses to teach. Of these ninety-eight, ninety are in New York City. Forty are in, or next to, districts where South Bronx Churches is organizing.

3. *New York Daily News,* 4 December 1995.

4. The IAF affiliate in Baltimore, BUILD, won an increase in wages paid to city contract workers from $4.25 to over $7 per hour, with the increase taking place over several years. The metropolitan New York IAF affiliates proposed a living-wage standard for N.Y.C. contract workers of approximately $18,000 in salary and full family health benefits. The living-wage legislation will help reverse the negative effects of privatization (lower wages for private employees doing city work than for city workers) and the trend of an increasing number of people working full time while remaining in poverty. The living-wage legislation (Local Law 648) required prevailing wages to be paid to custodians, office workers, food-service workers, and security guards working on city contracts. The law was passed over mayoral veto. *New York Times,* 8 April 1996.

Chapter 13: Raising Lazarus

1. For additional insight on the history of Harlem, the following texts provide a comprehensive look at the social, cultural, political, and economic phenomena that have helped shape the reality of this community considered as a "cultural mecca" and the "capital of black America": Jervis Anderson, *This Was Harlem: 1900–1950* (New York: Noonday, 1981); James Weldon Johnson, *Black Manhattan* (New York: Da Capo, 1930); David Levering Lewis, *When Harlem Was in Vogue* (New York: Oxford University Press, 1981); Gilbert Osofsky, *Harlem: The Making of a Ghetto, Negro New York 1890–1930* (New York: Harper and Row, 1971).

2. *United Methodist City Society* 3, no. 2 (winter 1993).

3. Nemora Carr's 1991 study "Housing Impact on Infant Mortality" found that streets were filthy as a result of "accumulations of garbage and infrequent trash collections." In addition she states, "Some families have to share inadequate kitchen and toilet facilities." Her study detailed how Harlem's deplorable housing helped to inflate the community's infant mortality rate to 29.6 percent in 1986. This rate was the highest in country—three times that of the national infant mortality rate.

4. Carr, "Housing Impact on Infant Mortality," 31.

5. *HUDC Reports* (spring 1987): 1.

6. The daily management of HCCI's community development efforts are carried out by paid staff.

7. *HUDC Reports* (spring 1987): 1.

8. Bradhurst (also referred to as Area III in HUDC planning documents) was selected as a result of a study that determined that the area was most suited for continued study considering time, resources, complexity of issues, and its spatial composition that made it more manageable as a project. Bradhurst's boundaries are 139th to 155th Streets, Adam Clayton Powell Jr. Boulevard to Bradhurst/Edgecombe Avenues (after West 110th Street, Central Park West becomes Frederick Douglass Boulevard and Seventh Avenue becomes Adam Clayton Powell Jr. Boulevard).

9. Mayor Giuliani's former housing commissioner Deborah Wright is responsible for overseeing the Empowerment Zone (its boundaries are Harlem, Washington Heights, and parts of the South Bronx). Her goal, as reported in the *New York Daily News,* is to create 55,000 jobs—to "rebuild the poorest parts of Harlem and Washington Heights." The Empowerment Zone's budget commands $300 million in government funds over ten years. To be successful, Wright must navigate "through a political and racial minefield," made no easier by recent federal cuts to programs that helped what little economic activity already existed. Some have referred to the Empowerment Zone as "mission impossible."

10. Clipping file, Harlem Congregations for Community Inprovement, *New York Times* article.

11. *Bradhurst Revitalization Planning Document,* 10.

12. The 1990 census figures were disputed by community leaders. A decline in population would have many ramifications, i.e., jeopardization of federal funding, jobs, and political representation. In the 1992 report "An Analysis of Unequal Opportunity in Central Harlem and Recommendations for an Opportunity Zone," Leith Mullings of the City University of New York implies that the undercounting could be attributed to societal disregard for the poor and the lack of consideration for communities such as Harlem.

13. *New York Newsday,* 12 May 1991.

14. Since the 1990 census HCCI has housed approximately four thousand persons who did not formally reside in Bradhurst, a large number of whom were formerly homeless (one thousand) and are low-income residents.

15. The educational demographics of Bradhurst residents, as cited by HUDC's *Bradhurst Revitalization Plan,* illustrate the educational gap that needs to be addressed. Education levels for Bradhurst are recorded for persons over twenty-five years of age and the number of years of school completed. For persons in this age group, more than half (55.3 percent) completed less than three years of high school. Approximately 29 percent of the population completed high school. Slightly less than 10 percent obtained up to three years of college, and 5.8 percent completed four or more years of college education.

16. *City Limits,* February 1996, 15.

17. HCCI sponsored construction training workshops for community members and advocated for their employment at the various construction sites.

18. HCCI, *Housing Report, Area III,* 37-38.

19. Of the 248 commercial units in the area 49 percent were vacant, and approximately 22 percent were unclassifiable or used for purposes other than retail activity. Only 43 percent were occupied *and* used for commercial purposes. These business were predominately eating and drinking establishments and clothing and beauty services.

20. The term *redlining* applies to the discriminatory lending practices of many banks who draw red lines around districts where poverty and crime hurt profits and refuse to lend money there.

21. HCCI, *Housing Report, Area III*, 3.

22. The six buildings proposed by Biderman were six out of a four-hundred-building housing stock in Central and West Harlem. Bradhurst had eighty-five abandoned buildings (approximately 8,150 residential units) and vacant lots in a concentrated fourteen-block area.

23. Initially, the Koch administration agreed to let the group develop fifty-eight apartments, a gesture that Rev. Dr. Wyatt Tee Walker, a member of the consortium, considered an insult.

24. In 1986 HPD initiated a ten-year, $5.1 billion capital plan to revitalize devastated neighborhoods (the plan was on the drawing board since the late 1970s). The HPD capital plan was supposed to create, rehabilitate, or preserve 252,000 units of housing by 1996. The figure has not been realized.

25. *New York Daily News*, 2 November 1988, Metro section.

26. *New York Newsday*, 8 April 1991.

27. *City Limits*, April 1992, 20.

28. The city of New York purportedly owned 90 percent of the area housing stock.

29. In 1994 HCCI solicited funding from various sources and developed a business plan with the assistance of independent outside consultants and graduate students from Columbia University's School of Architecture and Urban Planning and Columbia's Business School. The start-up program in housing management and maintenance is sponsored through a three-year grant and no-interest loan through Banker's Trust.

30. This section provides an overview of programs, as outlined in the *Bradhurst Social Service Delivery Plan* and HCCI's *Organizational Profile,* that were instituted by HCCI through 1995.

31. To Mayor Giuliani's credit, his capital plan allocated $60 million of the budget for the expressed purpose of rehabilitating thousands of deteriorating city-owned, tax-foreclosed buildings. The administration planned to renovate the properties and sell them, as quickly as possible, to not-for-profits and private, for-profit landlords. Housing commissioner Deborah Wright launched the program, which created twenty thousand new housing units throughout New York City.

32. *City Limits*, March 1994, 10.

33. *City Limits*, February 1996, 19.

34. Ibid.

35. Ibid.

36. Ibid.

37. For further insight on how churches can participate in community redevelopment efforts, Alice Shabecoff's *Rebuilding Our Communities* (Monrovia, Calif.: World Vision, 1992) provides insight on financing quality housing for low-income families. Additionally, please see Michael E. Porter, "The Competitive Advantage of the Inner City," *Harvard Business Review* (May–June 1995). The article discusses the competing ideologies in inner-city economic development and offers insightful recommendations.

Chapter 14: The Seoul of New York

1. Bureau of the Census, *Asian and Pacific Islander Population* (Washington, D.C., 1980).

2. Bureau of the Census, *Asians in America by Ancestry Group Population by Selected Ancestry Group and Region, 1990* (Washington, D.C., 1990).

3. Brian Lahrer, *The Korean Americans* (New York: Chelsea House, 1986), 69.

4. Seth Mydans, "Koreans Rethink Life in Los Angeles," *New York Times,* 21 September 1992, sec. 1.

5. Lahrer, *The Korean Americans,* 69.

6. Ibid.

7. Bureau of the Census, *Social Characteristics of Selected Asian and Pacific Islander Groups by Nativity, Citizenship, and Year of Entry* (Washington, D.C., 1990), 85, table 3.

8. Lahrer, *The Korean Americans,* 69.

9. Ibid.

10. Ibid.

11. Ibid.

12. Ibid.

Chapter 15: Equipping the Saints for the Work of the Ministry

1. John Ng, "Doing Pastoral Work in the Big Apple," in *1994 Missions Journal: Heart for the World* (New York: Oversea Chinese Mission, 1994), 7.

2. J. Doyle and M. Khandelwal, "Asians and Pacific Islanders Enumerated in the 1990 Census" (Asian/American Center of Queens College of the City University of New York, n.d).

3. Bureau of the Census, *We the Americans . . . Asians* (Washington, D.C., 1993).

4. Ibid.

5. Ibid.

6. Jane Fritsch, "One Failed Voyage Illustrates Flow of Chinese Immigration," *New York Times,* 7 June 1993.

7. Seth Mydans, "Chinese Smugglers' Lucrative Cargo: Humans," *New York Times,* 21 March 1992; "A Third Smuggling Group," *Wall Street Journal,* 19 July 1993; Merle Wolin, "From China to America via Moscow," *New York Times,* 25 August 1993; Seth Faison, "After Crackdown, Smugglers Find New Routes," *New York Times,* 1 November 1994.

8. Donateth Lorch, "Immigrants from China Pay Dearly to Be Slaves," *New York Times,* 3 January 1991.

9. As someone who grew up in a predominantly Hispanic and African American ghetto in Brooklyn, and who has been active in a Harlem church for six years, the author has observed during his time of living in and being associated with Chinatown, that Chinatown shares many of the characteristics common to the "inner city": there are many people who do not speak English as their first language; there are many who are poorer than the average New Yorker; those who succeed generally move out of the community; there is a large underground

economy with many people working "off the books" in legitimate activities; and there is the presence of a very influential criminal element.

10. There are no hard figures on Chinatown's population, though one hundred thousand is a commonly quoted estimate.

11. Evelyn Shih, *Torrey Shih: The Lord's Servant* (Edmonton, Alberta, Canada: Shih EE Foundation, 1994), 136-37.

12. Ibid., 139.

13. Fred Pei, "Outreach Ministry—Progress and Future Prospect," in *1995 Missions Journal: Toward A.D. 2000* (New York: Oversea Chinese Mission, 1995), 43.

14. Shih, *Torrey Shih,* 165.

15. *1995 Missions Journal: Toward A.D. 2000* (New York: Oversea Chinese Mission, 1995).

16. Oversea Chinese Mission Constitution, Article IV.10.

17. Tina Lui, interview by author, 27 October 1995.

18. *1995 Missions Journal.*

19. Rev. Dean DeCastro, interview by author, 27 October 1995.

20. Kelly Ng, interviews by author, November 1995.

21. DeCastro, interview.

22. Wang Corneille, Girgis Raouf, and Timothy Chang, "Church Development Project" (paper on OCM was done by seminary students at Alliance Theological Seminary, Nyack, N.Y., in 1995, as part of their coursework), 1.

23. Gail Law, "A Model for the American Ethnic Chinese Churches," *Theology, News and Notes* (December 1984): 21-26.

24. Stanley Kwong, interview by author, 15 November 1995.

25. Monte Williams, "Labor Department Hears Tales of Sweatshops, Restaurants, and Fear," *New York Times,* 6 August 1995.

26. Jane Li, "Why Is This Bowl of Noodles So Cheap?" *New York Times,* 13 April 1995.

27. Ng, "Doing Pastoral Work," 10.

Missions of Mercy

1. Ray Bakke, *The Urban Christian* (Downers Grove, Ill.: InterVarsity Press, 1987), 83.

Chapter 16: Setting the Oppressed Free

1. *Dictionary of National Biography* (London: Oxford University Press, 1968), 111-12.

2. Carroll Smith Rosenberg, *Religion and the Rise of the American City: The New York City Mission Movement 1812–1870* (Ithaca, N.Y.: Cornell University Press, 1971), 193.

3. Arthur Bonner, *Jerry McAuley and His Mission* (Neptune, N.J.: Loizeaux Brothers, 1990), 11.

4. Martha Hollowell, "Evangelizing the Homeless," *Urban Mission* 7, no. 3 (January 1990): 36-37.

5. Marvin Olasky, *The Tragedy of American Compassion* (Wheaton, Ill.: Crossway Books, 1992), 37-42.

Chapter 18: Epilogue

1. Eugene Linden, "Megacities," *Time Magazine*, 11 January 1993, 33. See also Joel Attinger, "The Decline of New York," *Time* (17 September 1990), 36-44.

2. Ibid.

3. John DiIulio, "Building Spiritual Capital: How Religious Congregations Cut Crime and Enhance Community Well-Being" (briefing on "Religion in American Life," New York, N.Y., 5 October 1995), 10.

4. See Lynn Huntley, "Why We [the Ford Foundation] Fund Church-Based Ministries," *Foundation News and Commentary* (May–June 1995).

5. Wendy Zoba,"Separate and Equal," *Christianity Today,* 5 February 1996, 22. See also articles by Eugene Rivers in *Policy Review* (Fall 1994); *Globe Magazine,* 17 July 1994; and *Christianity Today,* 4 March 1996.

6. Joe Klein, "In God They Trust," *The New Yorker* (16 June 1997): 40.

7. Stanley Carlson-Thies, *Capital Commentary,* 2 September 1996.

8. Stanley Carlson-Thies, "Churches in Partnership with Public Welfare Programs" (speech delivered at the annual meeting of the American Political Science Association, San Francisco, 1996).

9. Klein, "In God They Trust," 46.

10. Carlson-Thies, speech.

11. Quoted in Gaylord Noyce, *Survival and Mission for the City Church* (Philadelphia: Westminster, 1975), 153-56.